CAMBRIDGESHIRE

THE
CAMBRIDGESHIRE DOMESDAY

ALECTO HISTORICAL EDITIONS
LONDON
1990

ISBN for Cambridgeshire volumes: 0 948459 23 9
ISBN for this volume: 0 948459 87 5

Printed in England

ALECTO HISTORICAL EDITIONS
46 Kelso Place, London W8 5QG, England

CONTENTS

PREFACE

THIS is the thirteenth volume of the Alecto County Edition of Domesday Book to be published. Although Cambridgeshire comes eighteenth in the order of counties in Great Domesday Book, the spacing and style of the main scribe's writing show that its folios were written early on in the programme in which the thirty counties were inscribed.

In the manuscript, two gatherings of eight and six folios respectively constitute the section for Cambridgeshire, and taken overall the columns present an attractive, well-ordered uniformity typical of those shires which were enrolled at the beginning of the enterprise. Only folio 200 is much affected by the need to add in the margins matter that arrived late or had to be altered. Because this bears the first entries of the very large fief of Picot, the rapacious sheriff of Cambridge, one may speculate that these additions are testimony to the ever-acquisitive activities of that official in the county under his control.

Normally each part of this series contains a large-scale map limited to the county in question, but in this case Cambridgeshire is mapped with Huntingdonshire since the two shires are most conveniently combined in this way both at Domesday and today.

Throughout this edition the names and extent of the counties are those which obtained prior to the restructuring of the counties in 1974. Since their traditional boundaries had remained virtually unchanged since the time of the Domesday survey, there seemed little purpose in following recent, arbitrary innovations which have neither historical justification nor useful function in this context. In that year Cambridgeshire was fortunate in escaping much alteration so far as its boundaries on the east and south are concerned, though the ancient identity of the county was lost altogether on being merged with Huntingdonshire on the west. In this volume and on the associated county map the two shires are regarded as separate and the boundary between them is restored, as was the situation for a thousand years or more.

The three volumes that constitute each part of the County Edition are designed to be mutually supportive and are separated in this way for the reader's convenience. For instance, it is desirable for the facsimile folios to be present in one book and the parallel translations in another so that both can be consulted side by side. For the same reason the key to the symbols employed in the translations for Great Domesday's marginal notes and signs (Appendix I), and the list of abbreviations found in the manuscript (Appendix II) are best incorporated in the third volume, *Domesday Book Studies*, so that they, too, can be used in conjunction with the folios of translations and facsimile to which they refer. A fourth separate element is the large-scale county map which is provided as a loose-leaf folded sheet in order to be spread out near at hand if required.

Besides the book containing the facsimile folios and the maps, the division of text into two further self-contained volumes reflects the character and scope of their contents. *Domesday Book Studies* (which is common to the entire County Edition) is a book of essays on topics concerning Domesday Book in general, while this volume contains all matter specific to the locality in question. The translations are put at the end, unusually after the indices, where they are easiest to find and where their pages can be matched with the facsimile of the manuscript by the same folio numbers without disrupting the pagination of the rest of this book.

In a project so closely bound up with local history, place-name identification will constitute a salient feature affecting all its aspects, especially in the translations, indices and maps where their occurrences must always be consistent. By chance, the present publication was first set in motion towards the end of a period when the place-names recorded in Domesday Book had come under particular scrutiny, but not always with unanimously accepted results. The only recourse was to log every mention of a name on to a card index and enter into it all dissident opinion. This organized body of raw material was then submitted to F. R. Thorn, appointed for his special knowledge of the Domesday hundreds and place-names, and who has also established their position on the map. Dr Thorn in turn wishes to acknowledge the help of his wife Caroline at every stage of indexing, mapping and writing the material for this county.

Those responsible for the making of the facsimile and for the production of the edition are noticed in the acknowledgements printed in the accompanying *Domesday Book Studies,* other than W. S. Cowell Ltd. of Ipswich who have typeset this particular volume. Special mention should also be made of Westerham Press for the complex task of setting the translations to match the Latin text of the manuscript with such success. The database for the manipulation of the place- and personal names for the Indices has been developed by James Brennan. The design and typography for this, as for the rest of the work, is by Ian Mortimer, I. M. Imprimit, London.

Our thanks are due especially to Elaine Shaughnessy who has controlled the editing of this volume overall, to Basil Harley for guiding the diverse elements through the press, to Brian Martin for overseeing production of the translation at Westerham Press, to Terry Concannon of W. S. Cowell Ltd., and also to the following for their diligence in the accomplishment of its various parts:

Bibliography: Dr David Bates, for rearranging his *Domesday Bibliography* already published; editing, Patricia Gibson.

Indices: Jenny Page for keying-in the material for the database from which both Indices are derived; Douglas Matthews for the compilation of the Index of Persons; Jenny Page, Cyril Simsa and Elizabeth Mostyn-Owen for editing.

Translation: initial standardization, Eric Hemming, Paul Francis and Stephen Wilson; copy-preparation at Oxford University Press, George Tulloch; editing, J. D. Foy, Christine Shaw, Caroline Thorn; initial typesetting at Westerham Press, Clive Logsdon.

Map: assistance with the design, Tom Phillips; compilation and editing, Frank Thorn, Des Seal, Cyril Simsa; drafting, Sheila Hodson; overseeing production at Cook Hammond and Kell Ltd., Jackie Hoy.

Maps in the text: initial compilation, Michael Young; final drafting, John Laing.

Finally, at Alecto, for the myriad incidental activities that such a project requires, we must thank Sarah Burton, Maggie Innes and Henrietta Pearson.

Ann Williams, *Editor-in-Chief*

R. W. H. Erskine, *General Editor*

The following is a list of abbreviations which are used throughout this edition. References to other publications are given in their abbreviated form if they occur in the county bibliography. The county volumes in this series which have already been published are cited in full at the end of the bibliography, as references to them are also abbreviated.

AntJ	*Antiquaries Journal*
ArchJ	*Archaeological Journal*
ASE	*Anglo-Saxon England*
BAR	British Archaeological Reports
BL	British Library
CA	*Current Archaeology*
DB	Domesday Book
EconHR	*Economic History Review*
EETS	Early English Text Society
EHR	*English Historical Review*
EPNS	English Place-Name Society
Exon	Exeter Domesday Book
GDB	Great Domesday Book
HMSO	Her Majesty's Stationery Office
JBAA	*Journal of the British Archaeological Association*
JMH	*Journal of Medieval History*
LDB	Little Domesday Book
MA	*Medieval Archaeology*
MS, MSS	Manuscript(s)
MS	*Mediaeval Studies*
NGR	National Grid Reference
N&Q	*Notes and Queries*
PBA	*Proceedings of the British Academy*
PRO	Public Record Office
TRHS	*Transactions of the Royal Historical Society*
VCH	*The Victoria Histories of the Counties of England*

INTRODUCTION

AN INTRODUCTION TO THE CAMBRIDGESHIRE DOMESDAY

R. E. GLASSCOCK

CAMBRIDGESHIRE (*Grentebr'scire* in 1086) is particularly fortunate in that it has been remarkably well served both by the scribes of late eleventh-century England and by recent historians of Domesday Book. Given that a major university is located there, modern historical interest in the county is hardly surprising but there is a more fundamental reason for, as R. Welldon Finn has remarked, 'With the exception of the south-western counties, where we have the material of the Liber Exoniensis available, we can evaluate Domesday Book nowhere better than in Cambridgeshire . . .'.[1]

He made this observation because the shire is unique in having three surviving versions of the Domesday survey, for in addition to that in Great (or Exchequer) Domesday Book there are others in the Inquisitio Eliensis and the Inquisitio Comitatus Cantabrigiensis, although unfortunately both are incomplete. These two 'satellite' documents will be discussed below (pp.3–5): suffice to say here by way of introduction that the comparative study of the three versions has been important not only in unravelling Domesday Cambridgeshire but in throwing additional light upon the collection of the information, its collation and final presentation for the country as a whole. For this reason the shire has been central to Domesday studies, especially since 1897 when F. W. Maitland (Fellow of Downing College) published his *Domesday Book and Beyond*, now widely recognized as one of the great works of early Domesday scholarship. More recently interest has been continued by several other Cambridge scholars, most notable among them being R. Welldon Finn, sometime Scholar of Peterhouse, and H. C. Darby, Fellow of King's.

THE DOCUMENTS OF THE SURVEY

Editions of the Domesday Text

While awareness of the historical importance of Domesday Book dates back at least to the seventeenth century, the serious study of the texts dates only from the late eighteenth century when Great and Little Domesday Books were edited by Abraham Farley and printed at Government expense. In two volumes, they were set in a specially designed type which, unfortunately, was destroyed by fire in 1808. In 1816, however, Sir Henry Ellis, rightly believing that 'Domesday Book is a mine of information which has not yet been sufficiently wrought', edited the texts of four Domesday satellites (including the Inquisitio Eliensis) and added indices to Farley's texts in two further volumes for the Record Commissioners.[2] Later, in the 1860s, the Cambridgeshire folios, along with those of other counties, were photozincographed by the Ordnance Survey and produced in facsimile for the first time.[3] These publications made possible more detailed analysis of the text. The first twentieth-century translation of the Cambridgeshire folios was that by the Revd C. H. and H. G. Evelyn-White which first appeared in instalments in the *East Anglian* (1905–8) and which was subsequently published in 1910.[4] This translation was based upon an earlier and unpublished mid-nineteenth-century translation by the Revd William Bawdwen now to be found in the manuscript collection of the British Library.[5] When the editors

[1] Welldon Finn, 'Some Reflections', 29.

[2] *Domesday Book*, 4 vols. (Record Commission, London, 1783–1816); the Cambs. folios are in vol. i. 189–202.

[3] James (director), *Domesday Book*.

[4] Evelyn-White and Evelyn-White, *Cambridgeshire Portion of the Great Survey*.

[5] BL Additional MS 27, f.769.

of the *Victoria County History* began work upon Domesday Cambridgeshire, the Evelyn-White translation was found to be not wholly reliable and a new and more scholarly translation was made from the Ordnance Survey facsimile by Miss Jocelyn Otway-Ruthven. Her version was published in 1938 in the first volume of the *VCH* for the county and it remains a standard work.[1] Notwithstanding this version, it was of great interest when, just a few years ago, the Farley text was photographed and used as the basis for a series of county Domesday texts under the general editorship of John Morris; Cambridgeshire, eighteenth in the series, appeared in 1981 with a new translation edited by Alexander Rumble from a draft prepared by Jennifer Fellows and Simon Keynes.[2] In this version the 'nearest ordinary modern English' was used wherever possible. As a result the terminology is rather different from that of the versions of 1910 and 1938. A sample entry for the king's holding in Chesterton on folio 189v will serve to illustrate the differences and the problems involved in translation.

Evelyn-White and Evelyn-White (1910), p.11:

> Cestretone (Chesterton) a demesne village of the King's answered for thirty hides. There is land to sixteen ploughs. In the demesne there are three, and nine might still be made. There are two villanes and sixteen bordars and six cottagers with four ploughs. A priest has one virgate of land. Meadow for eight ploughs. From the marsh a thousand eels. It pays fifteen pounds burnt and weighed; and thirteen pounds eight shillings and four pence of white money for honey, wheat, and malt, and other customs. T.R.E. it paid fifteen pounds by tale; and so much as ought to be paid for the custom.

Otway-Ruthven (1938), *VCH Cambridgeshire*, p.361:

> CESTRETONE (Chesterton), a demesne vill of the King, is assessed at 30 *h*. There is land for 16 ploughs. There are 3 on the demesne, and 9 might be added thereto. Here (are) 2 villeins and 16 bordars and 6 cottars with 4 ploughs. The priest has 1 *v*. of land. (There is) meadow for 8 ploughs. From the fen (*maresch'*) (come) 1,000 eels. It pays 15 *li*. assayed and weighed and 13 *li*. and 8*s*. and 4*d*. in white money for honey, corn, and malt and other customary dues. T.R.E. it paid 15 *li*. by tale and as much as was necessary for the customary dues.

Rumble (1981), *Domesday Book: Cambridgeshire*, p.189d:

> CHESTERTON is a lordship village of the King's. It answers for 30 hides. Land for 16 ploughs. In lordship 3; a further 9 possible. 2 villagers, 16 smallholders and 6 cottagers with 4 ploughs. A priest has 1 virgate of land. Meadow for 8 ploughs; from the marsh 1,000 eels. It pays £15 assayed and weighed, and £13. 8*s*. 4*d*. in white coin for honey, corn, malt and other customary dues; before 1066 it paid £15 at face value and, in proportion to this, as much customary dues as was needed.

Yet a fourth version of this passage will be found in the new translation (based on Otway-Ruthven) at the end of this volume on f.189v, right column, at the third • from the top.

Commentary and Analysis

Just over a century ago the Revd Bryan Walker, Rector of Landbeach, published a commentary on, and an analysis of, the Cambridgeshire Domesday.[3] The details that he included are, in fact, more numerous than the 'measurements and valuations' of his title suggest; his tabulations,

[1] *VCH Cambridgeshire*, i (1938), 358–99.
[2] Rumble (ed.), *Domesday Book: Cambridgeshire*.
[3] Walker, 'Measurements and Valuations of the Domesday of Cambridgeshire'.

published as a supplement to his paper, include place-name identifications, holders of land (Saxon and Norman) and other miscellanea. His supplement, which remains the only published breakdown of the Cambridgeshire Domesday in tabular form, is still an essential aid to detailed work on the county. Moreover his paper was one of many which contributed to the great advances in the study of Domesday in the last quarter of the nineteenth century, a period which was to culminate in J. H. Round's *Feudal England* (1895), generally recognized as the foundation upon which all subsequent Domesday scholarship has been built.

After Walker, the *Communications* (and later the *Proceedings*) *of the Cambridge Antiquarian Society* continued to be an outlet for publication concerning the Domesday survey for the county. In 1884–5, O. C. Pell communicated two papers[1] to the Society but his rather curious interpretations of some aspects of Domesday were short-lived and were largely discredited by Round in 1895. It was not until forty years later that there was another flurry of Domesday activity in the pages of the Society's journal; this time the contributions were longer-lasting. In 1933 Helen Cam used the Domesday evidence for Cambridge in her critique of Professor Carl Stephenson's theories on urban origins,[2] and a year later H. C. Darby published a paper on the geography of the county as reconstructed from the Domesday record,[3] one of a number of studies which led ultimately to his overall scheme for the study of the geography of Domesday England. His later work on Cambridgeshire appeared in 1952 in the first of five regional volumes designed to cover England as a whole.[4] By that time the second volume of the *Victoria County History of Cambridgeshire and the Isle of Ely* had appeared (1948) to which Darby had contributed a section on Domesday Cambridgeshire which added to the very valuable introduction which L. F. Salzman had written ten years earlier to the new translation of Domesday published in the first volume.

In 1960 R. Welldon Finn maintained the tradition of Domesday publications in the *Proceedings of the Cambridge Antiquarian Society* with a paper that combined his thoughts on the evidence of the Exchequer Domesday and of the Inquisitio Eliensis.[5] Darby's chapter in the *Domesday Geography of Eastern England* had meanwhile been slightly revised for the second edition (1957) and there was further slight revision for the third in 1971.

With all this work in print, and with increasing critical awareness of the importance of the evidence, it is not surprising that Domesday has been increasingly used in studies of particular aspects of the county's history. E. Miller used it in his research on the Ely estates,[6] Darby in his studies of the Fenland and of medieval Cambridgeshire,[7] and C. Taylor in his work on the evolution of the landscape of the county.[8] On the development of the medieval town, the Royal Commission[9] and the *VCH* have built upon the earlier work of Maitland, A. Gray and Cam,[10] among others.

The Inquisitio Comitatus Cantabrigiensis and the Inquisitio Eliensis

While the principal record of Cambridgeshire in 1086 is contained within Great, or Exchequer, Domesday Book the shire is unique in having two other versions of the survey, although both are unfortunately incomplete. While the Inquisitio Comitatus Cantabrigiensis (ICC) covers the greater part of the shire, the Inquisitio Eliensis (IE) includes only the holdings of the Abbot of Ely. Both versions have been the subject of detailed studies elsewhere[11] but brief

[1] O. C. Pell, 'Upon Libere Tenentes, Virgatae and Carucae in Domesday . . .', *Communications of the Cambridge Ant. Soc.* 6 (1891), 17–40; O. C. Pell, 'On the Domesday Geldable Hide . . .', ibid. 65–176.

[2] Cam, 'Origin of the Borough of Cambridge'.

[3] Darby, 'Domesday Geography of Cambridgeshire'.

[4] Darby, *Domesday Geography*.

[5] Welldon Finn, 'Some Reflections'.

[6] Miller, *Abbey and Bishopric of Ely*.

[7] Darby, *Medieval Fenland*; H. C. Darby, *The Changing Fenland* (Cambridge, 1983), Ch. 1; *idem*, *Medieval Cambridgeshire*.

[8] Taylor, *Cambridgeshire Landscape*.

[9] Royal Commission on Historical Monuments, England, *City of Cambridge*, 2 vols. (HMSO, London, 1959).

[10] F. W. Maitland, *Township and Borough* (Cambridge, 1898); A. Gray, 'The Dual Origin of the Town of Cambridge', *Cambridge Ant. Soc. Quarto Publ.* ns 1 (Cambridge, 1908); Cam, 'Origin of the Borough of Cambridge'; H. M. Cam, 'The City of Cambridge', *VCH Cambridgeshire*, iii (1959), 1–149.

[11] J. H. Round, *Feudal England* (London, 1895), esp. pp.6–27 and pp.123–42; V. H. Galbraith, *The Making of Domesday Book* (Oxford, 1961), 123–45; R. Welldon Finn, 'The *Inquisitio Eliensis* Re-considered', *EHR* 75 (1960), 385–409; R. Welldon Finn, *Domesday Studies: The Eastern Counties* (London, 1967), 81–95.

mention must be made of them in any introduction to Domesday Cambridgeshire.

The ICC, which survives as a single manuscript in the British Library, is thought to be a twelfth-century copy of an early draft of the Domesday returns from the shire. It was first brought to notice in a paper to the Society of Antiquaries of London by P. C. Webb as long ago as 1756 but was not published until over a century later.[1] Unfortunately the manuscript is incomplete; there are no records for the hundred of Chesterton, for the two hundreds of Ely and for some places in the hundreds of Papworth, Longstowe and 'Northstowe'. Notwithstanding these omissions, the returns for the remaining hundreds are detailed and they are of great interest for the differences they show from Great Domesday Book. V. H. Galbraith may have got a little carried away when he said that the publication of the ICC in 1876 'took the learned world by storm'[2] but there can be no doubt that it has influenced all subsequent Domesday inquiry and scholarship. J. H. Round was the first to appreciate its fundamental importance; writing in 1895 he opened Part I of his book on *Feudal England* with the words, 'The true key to the Domesday Survey, and to the system of land assessment it records, is found in the Inquisitio Comitatus Cantabrigiensis.'[3]

Wherein lies its importance? First and foremost it is because the information within the ICC is arranged geographically by hundreds, and within them by vills, in marked contrast to the arrangement by fiefs in Great and Little Domesday Books. There has been considerable and inconclusive debate over whether this represents the preliminary way in which the detail was assembled; the ICC therefore figures prominently in any discussion on the making of Domesday Book.[4] On matters of detail the ICC includes the names of the jurors in each hundred and the numbers of livestock on many demesne lands; it also mentions the occasional small estate not recorded in Great Domesday, as for example that of Guy de Raimbeaucourt at Haslingfield. On the other hand it omits the details of some royal estates; S. P. J. Harvey has suggested that this was because surveys of these already existed and it was not necessary to include them.[5]

For the Cambridgeshire estates held or claimed by the Abbot of Ely there is a separate version of the Domesday survey in the Inquisitio Eliensis, a survey which also includes the Ely holdings in five other shires—Norfolk, Suffolk, Essex, Hertfordshire, and Huntingdonshire. The IE survives in three manuscripts; two are in the library of Trinity College, Cambridge and one in the British Library. It was first printed by Sir Henry Ellis in 1816[6] and later, together with the ICC, by Hamilton.[7] It is from within this document that we have a remarkable glimpse of the so-called 'terms of reference' for the Domesday survey.[8] The holdings of Ely are arranged as a fief in the IE; as A. B. Clarke has recently pointed out, the monks of Ely probably valued having two detailed surveys, one arranged feudally, the other (the ICC) geographically. He reminds us that this administrative dualism is a feature both of the Domesday satellites and of their post-Domesday successors.[9]

The IE sometimes gives the extent and value of individual holdings which Domesday Book itself does not. Additionally, like the ICC, it includes livestock numbers on demesnes although there are sometimes slight differences in detail.[10] Where there are variations it is impossible to know in most cases which of the three versions of the survey is the more reliable. In one instance, that of a holding at Great Shelford, Round concluded that the IE was the best of the three.[11]

There has been much debate about the origins of the IE and ICC and especially over whether they are copies of the actual returns made by the Domesday jurors, as originally suggested by

[1] Hamilton (ed.), *Inquisitio Comitatus Cantabrigiensis . . . Subjicitur Inquisitio Eliensis* (abbr. *ICC* and *IE*). There is a translation by J. Otway-Ruthven, *VCH Cambridgeshire*, i. 400–27.

[2] Galbraith, *Making of Domesday Book*, 123.

[3] Round, *Feudal England*, 3.

[4] See, for example, H. B. Clarke, 'The Domesday Satellites', *Domesday Book: A Reassessment*, ed. P. H. Sawyer (London, 1985), 50–70.

[5] S. P. J. Harvey, 'Domesday Book and its Predecessors', *EHR* 86 (1971), 770–1.

[6] Ellis (ed.), *Libri Censualis, vocati Domesday Book*, iv. 497–528. A sample of the IE is translated in D. C. Douglas and G. W. Greenaway (eds.), *English Historical Documents 1042–1189*, ii (2nd edn., London, 1981), 946–50.

[7] Hamilton (ed.), *IE*, 97–183.

[8] H. R. Loyn, 'A General Introduction to Domesday Book', *Domesday Book Studies*, eds. A. Williams and R. W. H. Erskine (London, 1987), 4–5; Douglas and Greenaway (eds.), *English Historical Documents*, ii. 946.

[9] Clarke, 'Domesday Satellites', 53.

[10] For an example of the comparative entries for the same Cambs. vill in GDB, ICC and IE, see the entries for Hauxton reproduced in Darby, *Domesday Geography*, 278–9 (references cited here are to the 3rd edn.).

[11] Round, *Feudal England*, 18.

Round.[1] Their importance has never been doubted not only because they give some extra information that does not appear in Great Domesday but, more especially, because the ICC suggests that the material was probably assembled, as it was gathered, on a geographical basis. Only at a later stage was the detail recast on a tenurial basis, thereby imposing a seigneurial pattern upon a territorial one. In so doing the scribes omitted some information and made occasional mistakes, especially when copying numerals.

Cambridgeshire in Domesday Book

Unlike some parts of the north of England where the process of shiring had not yet been completed, the shires of the East Midlands and East Anglia were already established by 1086. Only in the Fenland and around its margins did the boundaries of Cambridgeshire remain uncertain. The survey shows that the Domesday shire had substantially the same outline as the modern county, at least as it was until 1974 when Huntingdonshire was incorporated into a new Cambridgeshire. Even so, there were differences in only a few places.

In the south, Heydon, as well as Great and Little Chishill were only added to Cambridgeshire in 1895; their entries are therefore to be found in the Essex folios of Little Domesday Book. Some Essex manors had holdings in Cambridgeshire in 1086; they were Great Chesterford which had holdings in Hinxton and Babraham, and Newport which had a holding in Great Shelford. On the western edge, part of Papworth St Agnes was returned in the Huntingdonshire survey and on the east, Exning, in the Cambridgeshire folios in 1086, was soon to be transferred to Suffolk. It was from here that the new town of Newmarket was created on the boundary between Cambridgeshire and Suffolk in the early thirteenth century.

In the Fenland, where boundaries may have continued to be uncertain throughout the early Middle Ages, Stanground was returned in the Huntingdonshire folios in 1086 while Upwell and Outwell are to be found in the Norfolk folios of Little Domesday Book. While parish boundaries had probably been determined by 1086 some uncertainties may have continued at the borders with other shires especially in the Fenland. Elsewhere there were probably many minor differences between Domesday parishes and those of later medieval times when some were either split up or joined together in times of changing social and economic conditions.

At the outset of the Domesday survey, in order to expedite the procedure of investigation, the kingdom was divided into a number of 'circuits', each consisting of a group of contiguous counties. R. W. Eyton, writing in 1878, thought that Cambridgeshire and Bedfordshire formed one of the nine circuits which he had estimated as the likely number.[2] When the question was re-examined by A. Ballard in 1906[3] he reduced the proposed number of circuits to seven and grouped Cambridgeshire and Bedfordshire with Middlesex, Hertfordshire and Buckinghamshire (Loyn's Circuit III), an interpretation which has been generally accepted by more recent scholars.[4] Harvey notes that a characteristic of this five-shire circuit is that the assessment in hides is given only for 1086, in contrast to some other shires which give only the figures for the time of King Edward (e.g. Wiltshire and Dorset) and the south-eastern circuit which includes the assessments for both.[5] Whatever the exact extent of the circuits it seems certain that the shires and their internal divisions were the basic units of the survey. In Cambridgeshire these divisions were the sixteen hundreds, whose irregularity in size and shape (see Map 1 overleaf) raises interesting and unanswered questions about their pre-Conquest origins.

[1] The IE was exhaustively discussed by Round in Part 1 of *Feudal England*. See also the discussions in V. H. Galbraith, 'The Making of Domesday Book', *EHR* 57 (1942), 161–77; *idem*, *Making of Domesday Book*; Welldon Finn, '*Inquisitio Eliensis* Re-considered'.

[2] R. W. Eyton, 'Notes on Domesday', *Trans. of the Shropshire Archaeol. and Nat. Hist. Soc.* 1 (1878), 107–8.

[3] A. Ballard, *The Domesday Inquest* (London, 1906), 12–13.

[4] R. Welldon Finn, *An Introduction to Domesday Book* (London, 1961), 38–40; H. C. Darby, *Domesday England* (Cambridge, 1977), 5–7 (discussion and map). This is the division accepted in this edition; see Loyn, 'General Introduction', 3–4 and map.

[5] Harvey, 'Domesday Book and its Predecessors', 768.

Cambridgeshire is among those English shires where holdings were assessed in hides (about 120 acres) and virgates (about 30 acres), another characteristic of Circuit III. Only occasionally are acres mentioned; sometimes they are given as detail for large holdings (e.g. the Abbot of Ramsey holds nine hides, one virgate and five acres in Elsworth) and sometimes to specify the size of holdings below a virgate (e.g. Robert the Bald holds nine acres from Hardwin in Kingston).[1]

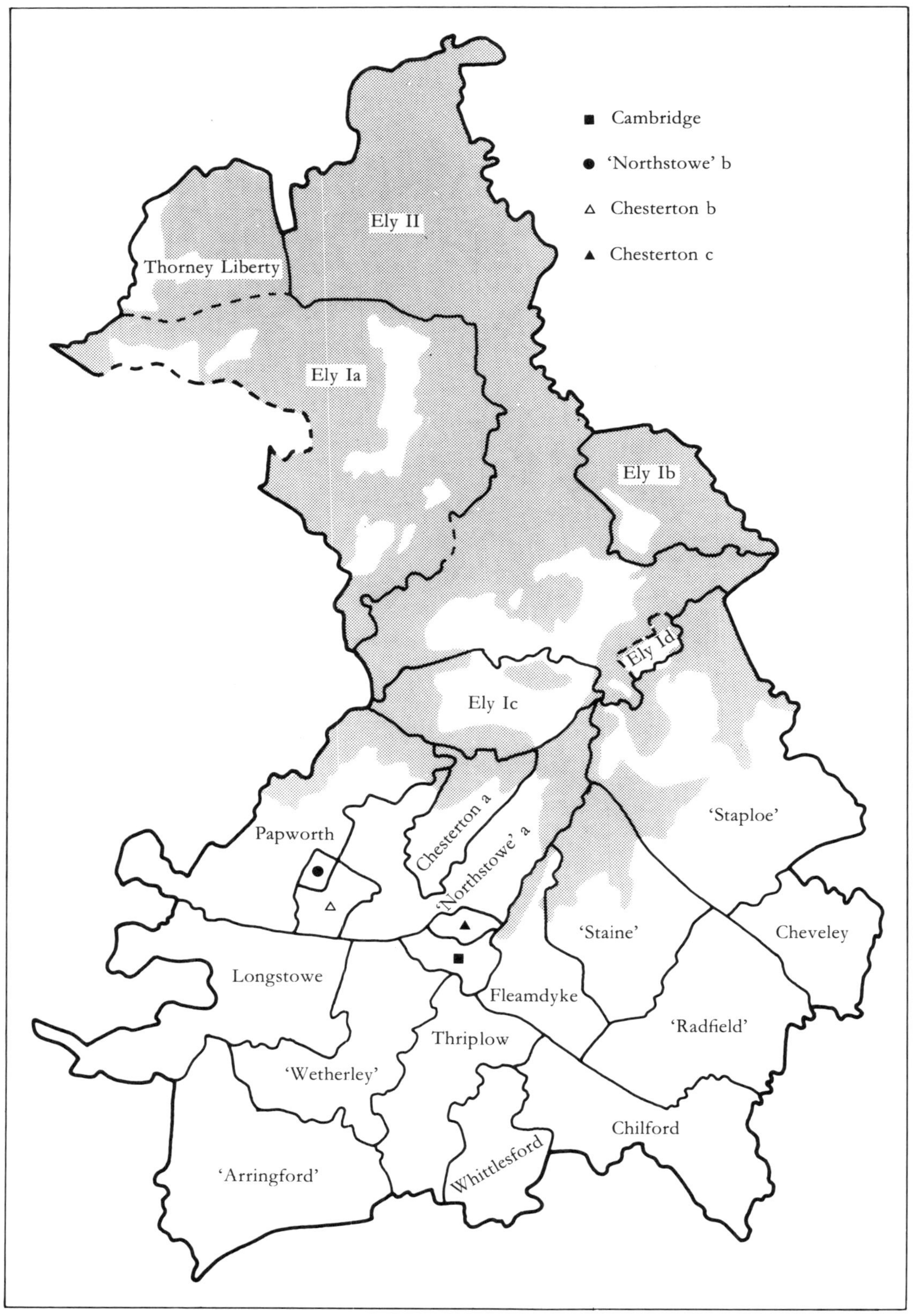

Map 1: The hundreds and county boundary in 1086 of Cambridgeshire

The system of hidage was inherited from late Saxon systems of fiscal assessment in which each hundred in a shire was given a valuation of a certain number of hides and this figure was then divided among its component vills. How far these values were conventional and what relationship they bore to reality, especially by the eve of the Norman Conquest, are matters of debate. From the Cambridgeshire evidence, and especially that of the ICC where the hidage of each vill is stated at the beginning of each entry, it was clear to Round that the Domesday assessment in the shire was based upon a conventional unit of five hides and its multiples. Thus, for example, at the most

[1] GDB 192v (Elsworth), 198v (Kingston).

straightforward level the ICC tells us that Stapleford was assessed at ten hides, all held by the Abbot of Ely. In a number of vills the holdings add up to multiples of five; at Croydon, for example, the seven recorded holdings total ten hides and at Fulbourn five holdings made up of $4 + 4\frac{1}{2} + 8 + 2\frac{1}{2} + 6$ hides add up to twenty-five hides. There are other vills where the five-hide unit is less immediately apparent but in some instances the multiple emerges again as Round demonstrated so effectively in the hundred of 'Wetherley' where, for example, the five four-hide vills of Orwell, 'Ratford', 'Witewell', Wimpole and Arrington add up to twenty hides. The figures do not always work out so convincingly. Sometimes this is due to inaccuracies in the record; for example in Domesday Book the holdings in Barrington total ten hides and one virgate, a figure which hints at an inaccuracy of an extra virgate somewhere in the record. This is confirmed by the ICC where the holding of Robert Gernon, given as seven hides, two and a half virgates in Domesday Book,[1] is apparently correctly given as seven hides, one and a half virgates. This is an instance where one Domesday record can be corrected by another and where Cambridgeshire has an advantage over other shires in having more than one surviving version of the survey. Even so, the additional records cannot always overcome the inconsistencies and complications. An added problem is that the assessments of six hundreds—'Staploe', Cheveley and 'Northstowe' to the east and Papworth, Longstowe and 'Arringford' to the west—were reduced between 1066 and 1086 and unevenly recorded, thereby giving rise to anomalies. Notwithstanding these problems, the Exchequer version of Domesday emerges remarkably well from comparisons with the two other versions and certainly well enough for it to be used as the main basis for an evaluation of the landscape and social structure of the shire in 1086.

THE LANDSCAPE OF CAMBRIDGESHIRE IN 1086

The geography of the shire in 1086 was dominated, even more so then than it is now, by the fundamental contrasts between the fenland in the north and the so-called 'upland' in the south (a relative term as the maximum height above sea-level is only just over 400 feet). Within fenland and upland there are other geographical differences which have affected the history of settlement and the evolution of the landscape both before and after 1086. In the fenland there are the sharp contrasts between the silt, the peat and the islands; in the upland the main difference is between the areas of chalk and boulder clay.

Prehistoric, Roman and Anglo-Saxon settlers were all greatly influenced in their choice of settlement sites and their use of land by differences in soil type, drainage, and, in the north of the county, by changing sea-levels. The landscape of 1086 was already a palimpsest of a long history of settlement; what the Domesday commissioners recorded in 1086 was just a stage in the continuous evolution of the physical and cultural landscape. Without their record, however, we would know very much less about what had gone before, or indeed, of the impact of what was to happen afterwards, for Domesday may be considered to be not only a summary of the period which links late Saxon and early Norman times but an important baseline against which to measure later medieval change.

Population

In the context of eastern England as a whole Cambridgeshire was not a particularly populous shire in 1086.[2] Only within about a ten-mile radius of Cambridge, where the average number of persons recorded in Domesday was between ten and fourteen per square mile,[3] did densities compare with those of Norfolk and Suffolk outside the Breckland. Elsewhere in upland

[1] GDB 196v.
[2] See maps in Darby, *Domesday England*, 90–1, figs. 34 and 35.
[3] Darby, *Domesday Geography*, 289, fig. 80.

Cambridgeshire lower densities of between five and ten per square mile were comparable to recorded levels of population over much of the East Midlands. The fenland was thinly settled except on the islands[1] but this does not mean that its resources were not fully exploited by those living around its margins.

As there are some defective entries as well as minor discrepancies between the Exchequer, ICC and IE versions of the Domesday survey it is not possible to arrive at a definitive figure of the recorded population of the shire. Making due allowance for these difficulties Darby arrived at a recorded Domesday rural population (within the outline of the pre-1974 county) of 4,849.[2] We must presume that almost all of these were heads of households. To gain an approximate idea of the total population this number must therefore be multiplied by an estimated figure for family size. There has been much debate on what this multiplier should be, but taking Maitland's original suggestion of five we arrive at a total of 24,245. A. E. Nash, in a recent analysis of the Domesday population of Wiltshire, argues that the size of households might have varied with status;[3] he therefore proposes that the recorded number of villans and 'miscellaneous' persons be multiplied by six, bordars by four and the remaining population, including slaves, by three. If sokemen, of whom there are few in Cambridgeshire by 1086, are included at the multiplier of six, a calculation for Cambridgeshire on these lines gives a total of 22,367 (see Table below).

TABLE: Population estimate for Cambridgeshire in 1086

Categories	Recorded population × multiplier	Total
Sokemen	177 × 6	1,062
Villans	1,929 × 6	11,574
Bordars	1,400 × 4	5,600
Cottars	770 × 3	2,310
Staves	539 × 3	1,617
Miscellaneous (including 28 fishermen)	34 × 3	204
	4,849	22,367

This total is therefore of much the same order as that based on a uniform multiplier of five, but J. F. R. Walmsley[4] and Sawyer[5] have both argued that Domesday omitted rent-paying tenants and, like M. M. Postan, who suggested that perhaps 50 per cent of all households were omitted,[6] they would no doubt argue for a much higher total population, maybe in the range of 35–45,000. Thus, while the arguments continue on this issue, we can estimate that the rural population of Cambridgeshire in 1086 was somewhere between 22,367 (probably an absolute minimum) and, say, 45,000. To this figure must be added an estimate of about 2,000 for the population of Cambridge itself. To put these figures in perspective the population of Cambridgeshire in 1851 was 185,405, and in 1971 303,044. By modern standards Domesday Cambridgeshire was still very thinly settled.

SETTLEMENTS

Whatever the exact numbers, where did these people live? Whatever its merits Domesday is seldom as precise as we would wish it to be: for its time, however, the survey was remarkably comprehensive. For the shire approximately 140 places are named;[7] the majority, especially

[1] H. C. Darby, 'The Geography of Domesday England', *Domesday Book Studies*, eds. Williams and Erskine, 27, fig. 1.

[2] Darby, *Domesday Geography*, 292.

[3] A. E. Nash, 'The Population of Southern England in 1066: a New Look at the Evidence of Domesday Book', *Southern Hist.*, 10 (1988), 1–28.

[4] J. F. R. Walmsley, 'The "*Censarii*" of Burton Abbey and the Domesday Population', *North Staffordshire Jnl of Field Stud.* 7 (1968), 73–80.

[5] P. H. Sawyer, 'The Wealth of England in the Eleventh Century', *TRHS* 5th ser., 15 (1965), 154.

[6] M. M. Postan, 'Medieval Agrarian Society in its Prime: England', *The Cambridge Economic History of Europe*, ed. M. M. Postan, i (2nd edn., Cambridge, 1966), 561–3.

[7] The exact number depends on how they are counted. For a comprehensive list, see H. C. Darby and G. R. Versey, *Domesday Gazetteer* (Cambridge, 1975), 25–31 and map 5.

those in the south-west of the county, are recorded for the first time. This alone serves to underline the fundamental importance of the Domesday survey to the study of English place-names and their origins. We do not of course know how far these names differed from their original forms or when they first came into use. Place-names had been handed down orally; not until the late Anglo-Saxon period were they written down and relatively few manuscripts of the period survive. It is to be expected that the exact forms of names would change over time—a process hastened maybe when Norman clerks wrote down vernacular names—although this begs the question as to whether or not they copied them from existing records.

In upland Cambridgeshire all but eight of the places which subsequently gave their names to parishes are named in the survey. Of these eight some are known from other documents to have already been in existence, for example Landwade, Fen Ditton and Newton (near Little Shelford). Others were dependencies of other places and were probably subsumed within them in the record; for example, Lode in Bottisham and Coton in Grantchester. Bartlow, Brinkley and Kneesworth are not recorded in documents until the late twelfth or thirteenth centuries and may or may not have been in existence by 1086. More names are missing from the Fenland, especially north of Ely: there is no mention, for example, of Manea, Mepal, Wimblington, Leverington, Coveney and Elm but some of these places were already in existence. Elm is recorded in monastic sources as early as 973.[1]

On the other hand some places named in Domesday did not subsequently become parishes and the settlements are still comparatively small, for example, Badlingham in Chippenham, Barham in Linton and Saxon Street in Woodditton. *Warateworde* ('Ratford') has gone entirely.[2]

Other Domesday vills which gave their names to parishes have either been deserted or are now very small. Such are Shingay, and villages deserted either in the later Middle Ages (for example, 'Clopton' with its impressive earthworks), or finally through later emparking (e.g. the sites at Childerley, Wimpole and Croxton).[3]

In Cambridgeshire there is difficulty in knowing whether Domesday place-names refer to manors or to vills. The clerks might have been careless in this respect for whereas some holdings are described in the text as a manor (e.g. Soham, *Saham manerium regis*, f.189) or are denoted as such by a marginal M (e.g. Elsworth, *Elesworde*, f.192v) other holdings are not. In all, ninety-one manors are specified but as Welldon Finn suggests many other holdings may in fact have been manors.[4] He cites the example of Hardwin who, according to the summary in the IE, had thirty manors in demesne (and others beside) yet only one of these, Caxton, is denoted as a manor in the Exchequer text (f.198v). Notwithstanding this difficulty, Welldon Finn concluded that whereas in other parts of the country, including nearby Norfolk and Suffolk, the unit of the survey was undoubtedly the manor, in Cambridgeshire and probably elsewhere on the same circuit, the unit seems to have been the 'village'. Further work is needed on this complex question; moreover the term vill, which implies a township including its settlement(s) and agricultural land, is to be preferred to 'village', which in modern usage implies a specific type of nucleated settlement which did not necessarily exist in 1086.

Whether the place-names refer to manors or to vills we are still left with the difficulty of not knowing what was actually there on the ground. It is perhaps as well to remind ourselves that Domesday is primarily a historical record of landholdings and their worth; it is not a geographical description and it therefore cannot be expected to supply the answers to some questions of a geographical nature. It is silent, for example, on the nature of settlements and upon the dwellings of both lords and tenants; even churches, the only buildings apart from castles that were likely to have been of stone, are mentioned for Cambridgeshire in only three places. There were

[1] For a discussion of the early settlement and landscape of the silt fens, see D. Hall, 'The Changing Landscape of the Cambridgeshire Silt Fens', *Landscape Hist.* 3 (1981), 37–49.

[2] The site of the last is thought to be in Wimpole parish, NGR TL *c.*346518, Royal Commission on Historical Monuments, England, *West Cambridgeshire* (HMSO, London, 1958), 210.

[3] For a list of the deserted medieval villages of Cambs., with grid references, see M. W. Beresford and J. G. Hurst (eds.), *Deserted Medieval Villages* (London, 1971), 184.

[4] Welldon Finn, 'Some Reflections', 36–7.

undoubtedly many more. There were probably very few manor houses as, at this stage, Norman manorialization was still comparatively recent and few vills would have had a resident lord or chief subtenant. Unfortunately Domesday tells us nothing about the distribution of the recorded population within each place nor of the size and shape of the settlements in which they lived.

In the past there has been a tendency to assume that the Domesday place-names of Cambridgeshire represent early forms for the nucleated villages that are known today. For some places this assumption may be correct but for others false; the whole question of when the nucleation of villages took place from one part of England to another is currently a matter of debate. The problem is exemplified by Christopher Taylor's study of Bottisham.[1] In Domesday, Bottisham, mentioned only once on f.196, is a valuable ten-hide holding of Walter Giffard; twenty-five villans, twelve bordars and fourteen slaves are mentioned in the entry. Was Bottisham already nucleated and the only settlement in the vill? By the thirteenth century there is documentary and/or field evidence for at least five other settlements in this fen-edge parish; did they already exist in 1086, subsumed under the heading of Bottisham or were they all post-Domesday settlements? Taylor argues from place-name and archaeological evidence that at least three (Anglesey, Lode and Long Meadow) were already in existence by 1086; moreover he suggests from historical evidence (including maps) that the village of Bottisham, now nucleated and of a 'street-village' type, consisted of two or maybe three distinct parts 'in the early medieval period'. We are left with the unresolved question of when these parts coalesced to form the present village, and in particular whether this was before or after 1086.

Taylor has asked similar questions about many an English village including some others in Cambridgeshire such as Sawston and Whittlesford.[2] In each case he argues that there was not only a dispersed pattern of settlement in 1086 but that the place which gave its name to the parish was not the single nucleated settlement that we know today. Domesday does in fact hint at this as three holdings are named for each place. Detailed local studies which combine historical and archaeological evidence may be expected to throw light on this question. Whatever the answers we are left with the unmistakable impression that first, the settlement pattern was more complex than the Domesday record would, at first sight, suggest, and secondly, that even those places which had already emerged as the most important by 1086 may have had very different forms from those that they have today. The place-names in Domesday were the main headings under which information was recorded. In much the same way as we might speak today of living in Cambridge without specifying whether this means in Newnham, Chesterton or Arbury, so the Domesday names were convenient generalizations and disguised a more complex settlement pattern.

We are unfortunate in that Cambridgeshire was apparently within a circuit in which the commissioners took little note of churches. In Bedfordshire and Buckinghamshire only four are mentioned: in Hertfordshire and Middlesex only three.[3] Cambridgeshire fared no better: only three are named, at Meldreth (f.198v), one of the Shelfords (f.191) and Teversham (f.201v); all three were on holdings formerly in the possession of the Abbot of Ely. Two priests are mentioned as landholders, one at Pampisford (f.202), the other at Oakington (f.191v); in neither place is there mention of a church. By 1086 it is certain that there were many more churches in Cambridgeshire which cannot have been so different from neighbouring Huntingdonshire where fifty-three are recorded or from Norfolk and Suffolk with 219 and 352 churches respectively. In any case, more than three are known from architectural evidence. H. M. Taylor identifies six churches in Cambridgeshire with surviving late Saxon fabric[4] and we must presume that, as elsewhere, many later medieval churches overlie their Saxon predecessors, as indeed they probably do at Meldreth, the Shelfords and Teversham.

[1] Taylor, *Cambridgeshire Landscape*, 56–9.

[2] Ibid. 60–1. For a general discussion, see C. Taylor, *Village and Farmstead: A History of Rural Settlement in England* (London, 1983), Chs. 8 and 9.

[3] See discussion and map for England as a whole in Darby, *Domesday England*, 52–6.

[4] H. M. and J. Taylor, *Anglo-Saxon Architecture*, ii (Cambridge, 1965), 726 (St Benet and St Giles in Cambridge, Little Abington, Ickleton, Little Shelford and Swavesey).

Land Use

By 1086 almost all the ancient woodland of the shire had been cleared; what remained amounted to no more than an estimated 3.3 per cent,[1] and was to be found on the heavier soils of the south-east.[2] Some small patches remained on the fen islands but they amounted in all to probably less than 2,000 acres; the last of these, at Doddington on the Isle of Ely, emparked by the bishops of Ely in the thirteenth century, survived until 1942.[3]

In the south-east of the county woodland (*silva* or *nemus* in Domesday) is recorded in terms of the number of swine that could be supported, as for example at Saxon Street where there was enough for forty (*silva xl porcis*, f.199v); in west Cambridgeshire the presence of woodland is indicated in terms of its potential use in other ways, e.g. for making fences, as at Childerley (*nemus ad sepes*, f.190v), and for houses, as at Bourn (*nemus ad domos et sepes*, f.195). This difference in the method of recording within the same shire suggests that the woodlands in the west of the county (calculated by O. Rackham at only 1,900 acres compared to 8,600 in the south-east) were much smaller in extent and were coppiced for fuel and fences rather than used for pasture. Remnants of a number of these Domesday woodlands still survive, as for example at Knapwell and Hardwick. That the amount of woodland in the shire had been slightly more extensive in mid-Saxon times is suggested by the presence of several place-names indicative of wood clearance especially those with the suffix *-leah* (ley).[4]

With the widespread clearance of woodland, we may presume that post-Conquest Cambridgeshire had already begun to take on its modern appearance as a predominantly arable shire. For upland Cambridgeshire, but not of course for the yet undrained Fenland, this is borne out in the Domesday record.

The survey usually recorded arable land not in acreages but in terms of the number of ploughs that were needed to till the land. The usual phrasing is *terra est* x *carucis* and the entries frequently specify how many ploughs were on the lord's demesne and how many on the lands of the peasantry. The same distinction is usually made in the other measure of agricultural activity, namely the number of plough-teams actually at work. Both sets of figures have their problems and this is an aspect where the ICC and the IE are useful in making good some of the omissions and/or minor inaccuracies in the Exchequer version. For example the Exchequer entry for Snailwell (f.199), while giving the total number of ploughs as ten, omits the number of peasant ploughs; both the other versions say there were eight. On the other hand, it is the Exchequer version which appears to be the more reliable in some entries and it is the ICC and the IE which are guilty of omission.[5] Notwithstanding these difficulties the figures may be used to build up a general picture of the extent and distribution of agricultural land.

When the totals of ploughs and plough-teams are compared, the total of ploughs in the area covered by the pre-1974 county (1,693) exceeds, as we might expect, the number of teams at work (1,494⅛).[6] The difference is in part explained in about half the individual entries for the shire which suggest, in a variety of ways, that the land could support more teams than were at work. Thus for Bassingbourn (f.190) we read:

> There is land for 3 ploughs. In demesne (is) one hide, and there is 1 plough. There is 1 villan and 4 bordars with 1 plough, and there might be another (*et altera potest fieri*).

In other instances the difference between the two figures is more problematic. It may be that the figure for ploughs refers to the extent of arable at the time of the Conquest and that the teams

[1] O. Rackham, *Ancient Woodland: Its History, Vegetation and Uses in England* (London, 1980), 123.

[2] See map and discussion in Darby, *Domesday Geography*, 297–300; for England as a whole, Rackham, *Ancient Woodland*, 113 and 116; Darby, *Domesday England*, 181–5.

[3] Rackham, *Ancient Woodland*, 196.

[4] See map in pocket at end of Reaney, *Place-Names of Cambridgeshire*.

[5] These inconsistencies are dealt with in some detail by Darby, *Domesday Geography*, 279–87.

[6] Ibid. 279.

are a measure of the situation as it existed in 1086. If this is so, then there has been some contraction over the intervening years as a consequence perhaps of the unsettled conditions resulting from the Norman take-over of Anglo-Saxon holdings. Only rarely does the number of teams exceed the number of ploughs; whether these very occasional entries reflect errors in the statistics or actual extension of arable remains unknown.

In overall terms the figures for ploughs and teams confirm that, as might be expected, the main areas of cultivated land were in the upland part of the county and, in particular, on the relatively well-drained slopes along the Cam valley and its tributaries. There were fewer teams per square mile on the heavier soils of the west and south-east where, as we have already seen, more woodland remained.[1] In general the intensity of cultivation in upland Cambridgeshire, as measured by the average number of teams per square mile, was comparable to that in the surrounding areas of south-west Suffolk, north-west Essex, north Hertfordshire and Bedfordshire.[2] In the north there were fewer teams except around the fen-edge and on the islands. There was, as yet, no sign of the great drainage activities of the later medieval period and of the seventeenth century that were to transform the Fenland into the arable landscape as we know it today.

Although the emphasis of the Domesday record of land use is on arable land there is, unfortunately, no mention of the crops which were grown; in all probability they included wheat, barley, rye, oats and legumes. Nor is there any mention of the field arrangements within which cultivation took place. The existence of plough-teams suggests that there was already a great deal of co-operation between cultivators and that common field-systems based on long plough strips were already in use.

Domesday gives information not only on arable land but on meadow (*pratum*) and pasture (*pastura*). In Cambridgeshire, as for other counties in the same circuit, meadow was usually recorded in terms of the number of plough-teams that could be fed from it. It has been suggested that three acres of meadow were needed to support one ox; a team of eight would therefore need twenty-four acres, but that can only be an approximation.[3] There are only five entries, all in the south-east, where acreages of meadow, a common form of return in all other circuits, are given, as for example at Ashley and Silverley (f.199v) where an acre is recorded at both places. At Westley Waterless meadow for two oxen is recorded (f.190v) but the ICC and IE entries read two acres, another example of puzzling small differences which probably arise from scribal errors. When all the figures are plotted for the shire they show that the largest amounts of meadow were recorded for the fen islands, along the fen margins, and in the south and south-west along the valleys of the Cam, Rhee, Bourn and other small streams.[4] The Domesday record again bears out what we might expect. Riverside meadow was a precious resource in medieval communities and it is not surprising that the commissioners took care to record the amounts, however small, for almost every place.

For the country as a whole the record of pasture is puzzlingly irregular and presents difficulties of interpretation.[5] Cambridgeshire is no exception although it does have a higher percentage of entries than all its neighbouring counties except Hertfordshire.[6] Entries are less numerous than for meadow; there is mention, usually in the form of 'pasture for the cattle of the vill' (*pastura ad pecuniam villae*), for just over half the places. It is hard to believe that all the remaining vills were without pasture; Salzman has suggested that it was not recorded when there was only enough for the stock and where it did not represent a possible source of income.[7] It is doubtful, however, that this argument could account for the almost total lack of information on pasture for so many counties of England.

An even more puzzling omission is that of livestock. In Cambridgeshire there is only one reference and only then to a flock of sheep at Abington which had been stolen; to make the point

[1] Darby, *Domesday Geography*, 284–5, figs. 77 and 78.

[2] Darby, *Domesday England*, 127, fig. 41.

[3] G. H. Fowler, *Bedfordshire in 1086: An Analysis and Synthesis of Domesday Book*, Quarto Memoirs of the Bedfordshire Hist. Record Soc. (Aspley Guise, 1922), 61–2, 106–7.

[4] Mapped by Darby, *Domesday Geography*, 302, fig. 83.

[5] Darby, *Domesday England*, 149–54.

[6] Ibid. fig. 51.

[7] *VCH Cambridgeshire*, i. 344.

Domesday records this twice (ff.190, 199v)! Yet entries in the ICC and IE, as well as those for Norfolk and Suffolk in Little Domesday Book, leave us in no doubt that livestock numbers were recorded in the survey, at least for the demesnes.[1] Why they were omitted, seemingly deliberately, from the final record remains in doubt.

It would seem, at least for the Domesday scribes at work on Cambridgeshire, that eels were considered more important than livestock, for entries on fisheries are surprisingly detailed. This is presumably because eels were rendered to lords, sometimes with an additional money payment, and that they represented important sources of income for landholders. The Abbot of Ely had large fisheries at Doddington, Stuntney and Littleport yielding 27,150, 24,000 and 17,000 eels respectively. He also had the largest render from Wisbech where others, including the Abbots of Ramsey and Crowland, shared in the enormous catch of 33,260 eels recorded in six separate entries. These numbers leave us in no doubt that eels, then as now, were a prized resource of Fenland rivers.

Water-mills, which also yielded income, are another feature of the late eleventh-century economy which seem to have been carefully recorded. Over a hundred are mentioned in the shire. Sometimes fractions of mills are recorded as for example the sixth part of a mill at Shepreth (f.194v); presumably this means that the mill was held jointly by several landholders. Most mills were located either on the south-eastern margin of the Fenland (they are curiously absent from the south-western edge) and in the Granta and Cam valleys.[2] Cambridge itself had five. There appear to be none in the Fenland.

The Borough of Cambridge

The Domesday record begins with a description of Cambridge (*Grentebrige*, f.189, also spelled *Grantebrige*, f.190). The town was divided into ten wards (*custodiae*) but for some reason the list omits the sixth. Possibly this was due to carelessness on the part of the scribe but it seems more likely to reflect the rearrangement of wards after 1066 (referred to in the description of the first ward) and after twenty-seven houses had been destroyed for the building of the castle in 1068. Including these houses it would seem from the wording that the town in 1066 must have had a total of 400 *masurae*. This word has been variously translated as burgage, dwelling and messuage:[3] tenement may be as good in that it implies not just a house (*domus*) nor necessarily a burgage, but certainly something more than just a building. Each ward had between twenty-nine and fifty-four tenements; Carl Stephenson's view that these were packed into the area of the fortified Roman enclosure on the north side of the river was firmly rejected by Helen Cam in 1935[4] and her views have been supported by later historians of Cambridge. There is now no doubt that Domesday Cambridge was situated on both sides of the river and that the boundaries of the medieval town on the south side had been established well before the Conquest.[5]

Cambridge was the only borough (*burgum*) in the shire and although Domesday is disappointingly silent on its economic activities it must already have emerged as the main commercial and administrative town, in contrast to Ely which was to remain the principal religious centre. There is mention of lawmen but except for some twenty-nine burgesses hardly any other persons are listed, yet, to judge from the number of *masurae*, Cambridge may have had a population of about 2,000. Forty-nine tenements are described as 'waste' (*wastae*), a detail

[1] Darby, *Domesday Geography*, 311–12, discusses this problem and includes a sample of the ICC entries of demesne livestock for the hundred of Whittlesford. See also his map of demesne sheep in 1086: 'Geography of Domesday England', 30, fig. 7.

[2] See map in Darby, *Domesday Geography*, 308, fig. 85.

[3] Burgage, *VCH Cambridgeshire*, i. 359; dwelling, Rumble (ed.), *Domesday Book: Cambridgeshire*, 189a; messuage, Darby, *Domesday Geography*, 310, and also the translations in this edition.

[4] Cam, 'Origin of the Borough of Cambridge'.

[5] For a recent discussion and bibliography, see J. Haslam, 'The Development and Topography of Saxon Cambridge', *Proc. of the Cambridge Ant. Soc.* 81 (1982–3), 13–29.

which was probably included to indicate that geld payment could not be expected from them. Except for the mention of five mills Domesday says nothing of other buildings or of the economic activity of the town; churches are not mentioned (although there is one in the IE version), nor is a market. There is no mention of a mint which is known to have existed in the late Saxon period. We are told that Picot demanded that the burgesses lend their ploughs to the sheriff nine times a year instead of three, as in 1066—an entry which, among others, led Salzman to say that 'Everything points to Cambridge being an agricultural community, as primitive as any county borough well could be.'[1] This may be regarded as an overstatement as all medieval towns were intimately connected to the agricultural land and rural life which surrounded them. While Domesday Cambridge did not look anything like the town we see today, the pre-Conquest evidence and its special treatment in Domesday show that, as the only borough in the shire, it was already very different in form, function and probably size from any other place and that it had already emerged as a central place in the administration and economy of the region. We know from additional entries in the IE that the Abbot of Ely held several properties in the town, an involvement which was later to be of considerable importance in the emergence of Cambridge as a centre of learning.

THE HOLDERS OF LAND

The form of the Domesday record for Cambridgeshire is much the same as that for other shires; it begins with an account of the main town and then lists the holdings of King William and the tenants-in-chief, ecclesiastical and lay, in order of rank. Apart from the king there were forty-three tenants-in-chief in the shire; they are numbered and listed in Domesday Book on folio 189, but the scribe was not always accurate with his numerals and the numbers given to the tenants in the left margin of the text are seldom the same. Thus, for example, Count Eustace is XV in the first list and XXV in the text; Picot is XXXIII to begin with but XXX in the text. The chief tenants range in importance from great men such as the Bishop of Winchester and the Count of Mortain to the wife of Boselin de Dives and Erchenger the baker at the other end of the scale. Their holdings are listed under the headings of the hundreds in which they are located; within each hundred, holdings are described under a place-name. While a few places were held by one person and therefore named only once (such as Graveley, held by the Abbot of Ramsey), other places in which a number of tenants held land are mentioned several times. Orwell, for example, is mentioned no less than eight times. In such cases the place-names, while recognizably of the same place, may have variant forms; for example Eversden, mentioned four times, appears as *Averesdone*, *Avresdone* and *Evresdone* (twice). In the ICC it is *Everesdona*. In 1086, as indeed throughout the Middle Ages, place-name spellings had not become standardized nor had some settlements emerged as distinct administrative units; it is over a century before there is specific record of Great and Little Eversden. Nor is a distinction made in Domesday between the Papworths, the Shelfords and the Camps. The Wilbrahams and the Swaffhams are not separated either but references in the ICC and the IE respectively make clear that in these two cases separate units were already in existence.[2]

Twenty years after the Conquest and following the reallocation of Anglo-Saxon estates to Normans there were still claims and counter-claims to land and property; this was almost certainly one of the reasons why William wanted a detailed survey of the position. Whether the resulting record was as important to contemporary society as it has been to historians of feudal England is a matter of continuing debate. Certainly Domesday affords us the only opportunity to see how the far-reaching changes in land holding and social structure were worked out in the landscape of late eleventh-century England.

[1] *VCH Cambridgeshire*, i. 357.

[2] In this edition the distinction between later known subdivision of DB holdings is made wherever possible.

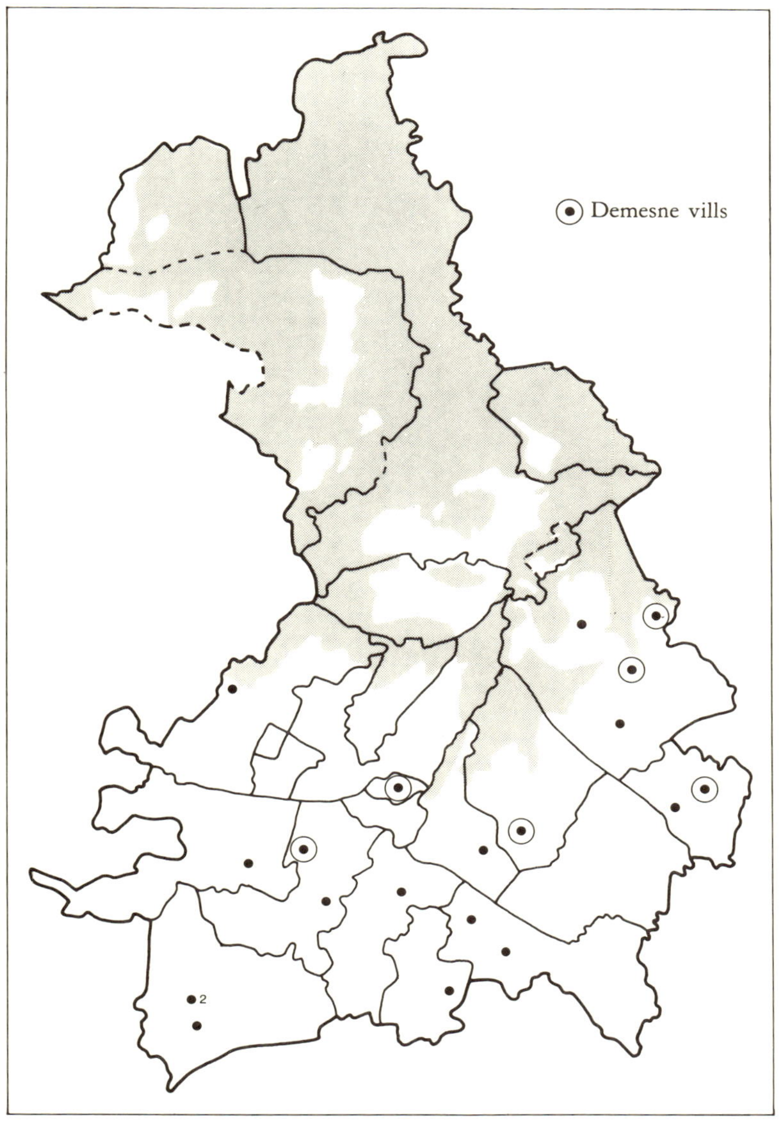

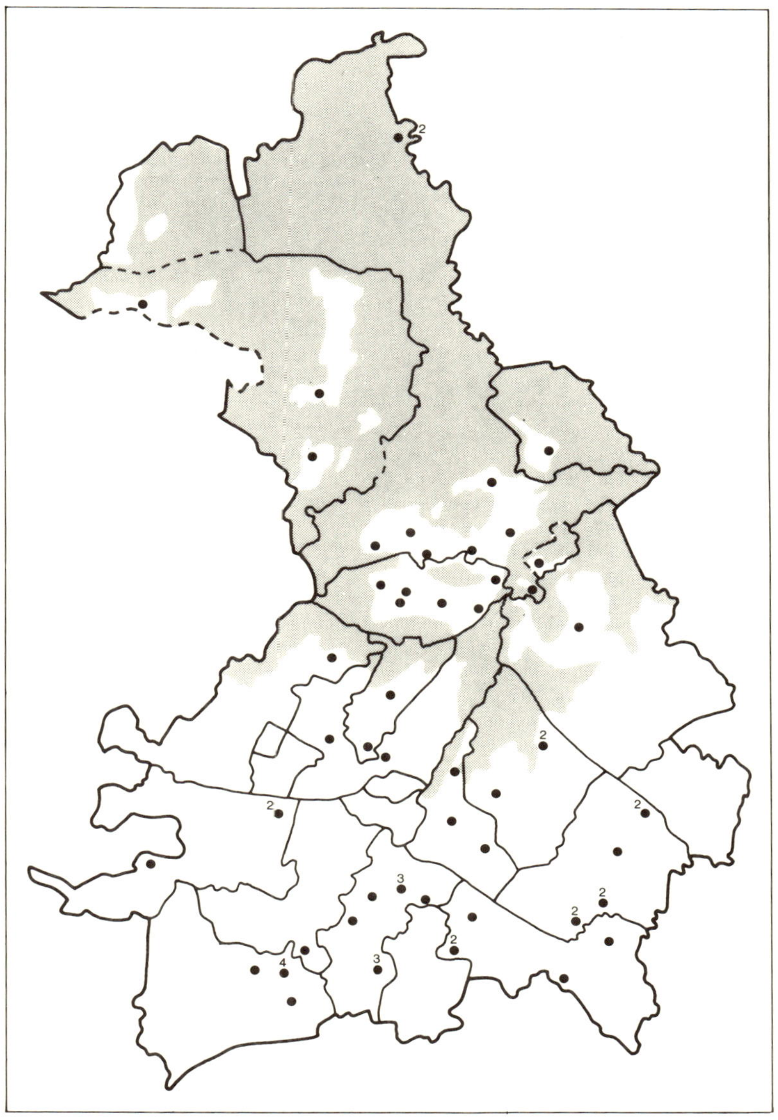

MAP 2: The holdings of King William in 1086

MAP 3: The holdings of the Abbot of Ely in 1086

The figures indicate the number of holdings in a vill, if more than one.

In Cambridgeshire the king's holdings included seven demesnes, three of them grouped together at Soham, Fordham and Isleham, the others scattered, at Cheveley, Great Wilbraham, Comberton and Chesterton (see Map 2 above). Whereas Soham is described as a manor in the text the others are described as demesne vills, but, except for Chesterton, they are denoted as manors by a capital M (for *manerium*) against their entries in the left margin. This sign appears sparingly throughout the record of Cambridgeshire and it is difficult to see why some places and not others are so described.[1] Some other royal holdings are denoted as manors in this way, for example, Woodditton, farmed to William de Noyers (f.189v), whereas others are not; an example is the larger and much more valuable estate at Exning, now in Suffolk (f.189v).

The holdings of the ecclesiastical tenants-in-chief are listed in order of seniority but the order bears no relation to the amount of land that they held in the shire. The senior bishop, Winchester, had only four small estates, all in 'Arringford' Hundred in the south-west. The Bishop of Lincoln had only six holdings, three of them in Histon, and the Bishop of Rochester held just one small piece of land in Isleham and that under Archbishop Lanfranc (f.190v).

Not surprisingly the largest ecclesiastical landholder, especially in the Fenland, was the Abbot of Ely whose possessions (see Map 3 above) still amounted to over 200 hides. This considerable holding had survived despite the fact that much Ely property had been appropriated by others in the years following the Conquest, not least because of the implication of the monastery in the resistance by Hereward. Whereas some properties had been restored to Ely as a result of an inquiry into their grievances, others remained in the king's hands.[2]

[1] The complexities of this problem have recently been explored by J. J. Palmer, 'The Domesday Manor', *Domesday Studies*, ed. J. C. Holt (Woodbridge, 1987), 139–53.

[2] For a detailed discussion of the matter, see *VCH Cambridgeshire*, i. 350–3. Miller, *Abbey and Bishopric of Ely*, Ch. 3, discusses at length the Ely estate and the Norman Conquest.

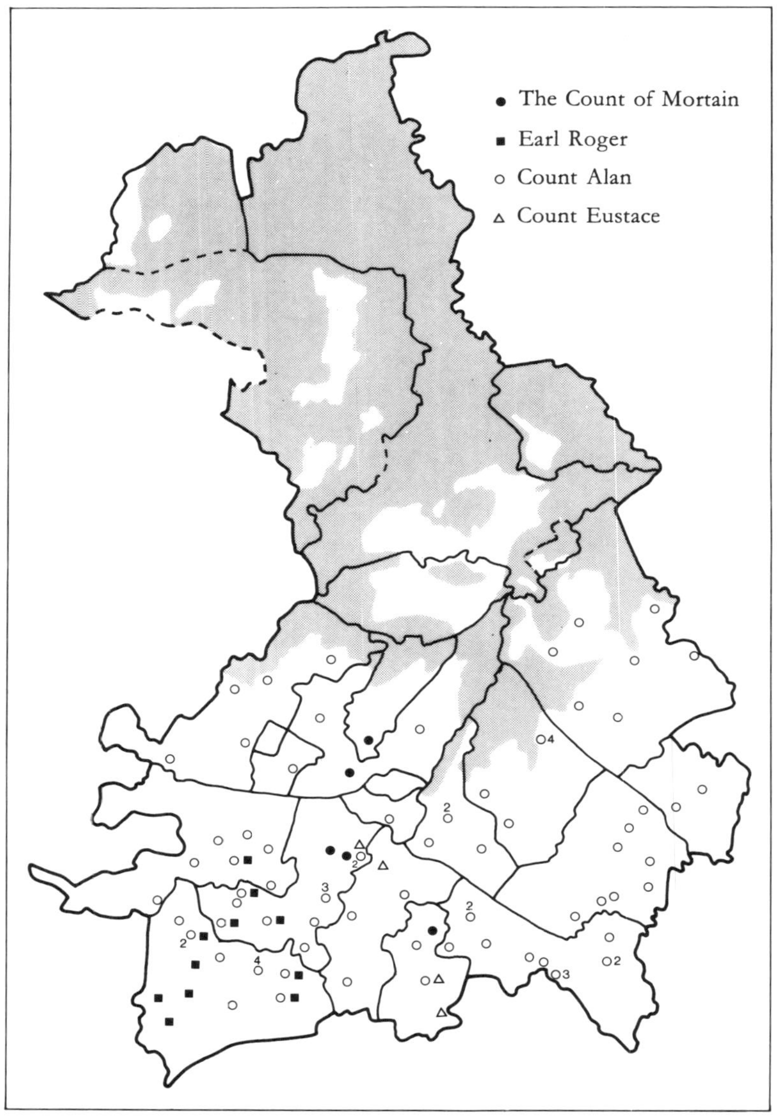

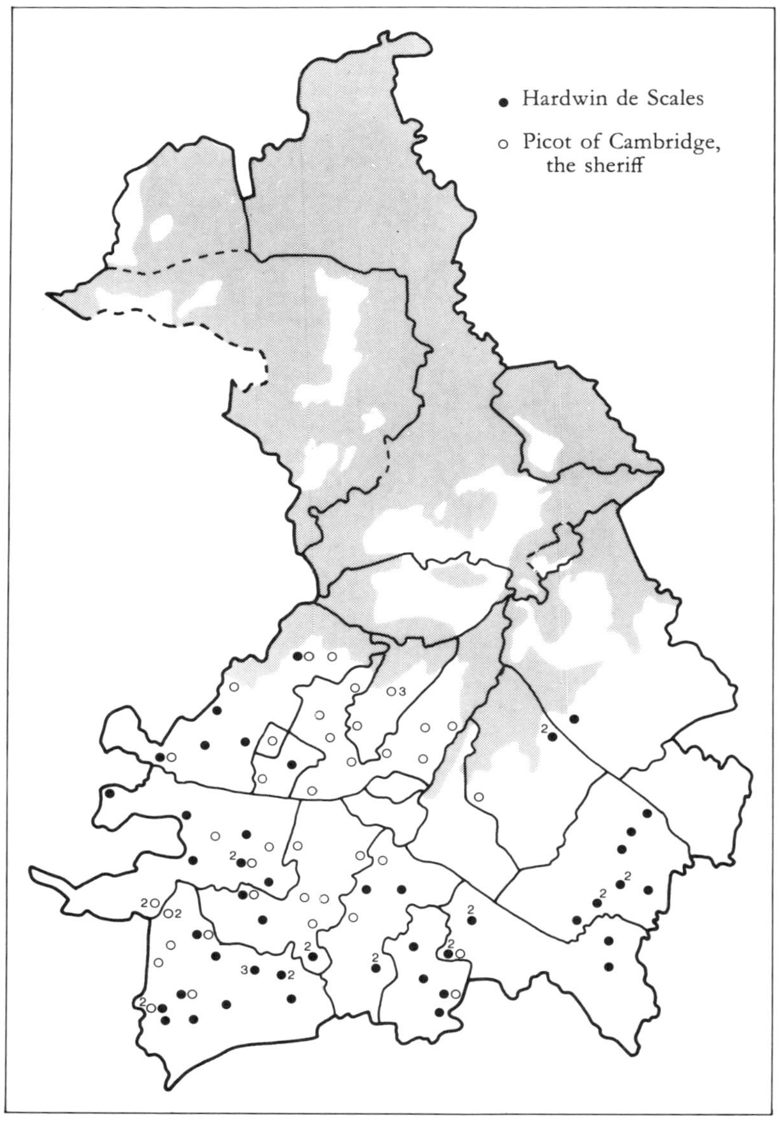

MAP 4: Comital holdings in 1086

MAP 5: The holdings of Hardwin de Scales and Picot in 1086

The figures indicate the number of holdings in a vill, if more than one.

Other Fenland abbeys were among the Domesday property holders. Crowland had holdings in three places north-west of Cambridge (Cottenham, Oakington and Dry Drayton) together with a render of 4,000 eels from Wisbech. Ramsey also took eels from there and, in addition, had sizeable holdings, mainly in Papworth Hundred in the contiguous places of Elsworth, Knapwell and Boxworth, and in nearby Over, Fen Drayton and Graveley; the abbot also had a ten-hide estate in Burwell, over eight hides in Girton, and other holdings in Bourn, Longstowe and Chatteris, where surprisingly, the Abbess of Chatteris is not recorded as holding property. The abbess did have six small and scattered holdings elsewhere. The Abbot of St Edmundsbury had only two holdings, both very small, but there was a valuable render of 5,000 eels from Wisbech. Thorney Abbey had only a single holding, in Whittlesey, but it is curious that there is no mention of the vill of Thorney in the record. Another house with a single holding was Saint-Wandrille, a Norman abbey which held six hides in Dullingham.

Of the lay tenants-in-chief, four were of comital rank: the Count of Mortain (the Conqueror's half-brother), Earl Roger of Shrewsbury, Count Alan and Count Eustace. Of these only Count Alan had substantial holdings in the shire, so many in fact that they fill four and a half folios of the Domesday text (ff.193v-195v). With minor exceptions all these properties had previously been held by Eadgifu the Fair (*Pulchra*) as she is frequently described; historians are not agreed upon who exactly she was but to judge from the size of her estate she must have been of considerable importance, perhaps even Harold's wife, as originally suggested by Sir Henry Ellis. The total estate of eighty-two holdings was very extensive and, except in the Fenland, there was hardly a part of the shire where Count Alan did not have land (see Map 4 above). Most of his smaller holdings were subtenanted.

By comparison the three other comital estates were small. The Count of Mortain had only five holdings, four of them near Cambridge in Barton, Grantchester, Girton and Histon. To the south he held Sawston, his most valuable manor which he had already granted to the Norman Abbey of Grestain (f. 193). Earl Roger's twelve holdings were almost all in the south-west of the shire in the hundreds of 'Arringford' and 'Wetherley', and included land in the Mordens, Arrington, Croydon, Meldreth and Melbourn. Count Eustace held a very large and valuable holding of nineteen and a half hides at Ickleton, one at Duxford of over five hides and smaller properties in Trumpington and Grantchester.

The most extensive holdings of tenants-in-chief below the rank of count or earl were those of Picot of Cambridge, the sheriff, and Hardwin de Scales (see Map 5 above). Picot, greatly disliked by the monks of Ely, had forty-four holdings, many of them previously held by sokemen who had been under the abbot. Most of Picot's properties, almost all located in the south-west of the shire, were subtenanted, and he himself held from nine other tenants-in-chief. As the king's representative in Cambridge and with an interest, direct or indirect, in so many holdings, he must have been the best known and, to judge from contemporary comments, the most feared of the tenants-in-chief. Not far behind him in importance was Hardwin de Scales who, like Picot, had acquired much land formerly connected with Ely. As well as his many holdings in the south-west of the shire he had, unlike Picot, a lot of land in the south-east.

No other tenants below comital rank compared with these two. Nobody had more than a dozen holdings except for the Countess Judith, niece of the Conqueror, who held about forty hides scattered widely over the south of the shire; some of this land had been held by her husband, Earl Waltheof, but most had belonged to Harold and to his brother Gyrth.[1]

For Cambridgeshire, as elsewhere, Domesday provides a remarkable record of the new Norman aristocracy under which the shire was to develop in the late eleventh and early twelfth centuries. It also tells us about the framework of the social structure even if there are few details about the ordinary people. Most of the land was worked by villans (40 per cent of the recorded population) and by bordars (29 per cent)—figures which are in line with the national averages of 41 per cent and 32 per cent respectively[2] and which show Cambridge to be a representative shire in this respect. Below them in the hierarchy were landless cottars and slaves (together 27 per cent). Almost all these working men were no doubt of English origin. That we are told little about them is as much a reflection of the nature of feudal society as it is of the Domesday record. That we know about them at all reinforces Loyn's view[3] that 'without Domesday Book our knowledge of eleventh-century England would be vastly poorer'.

[1] *VCH Cambridgeshire*, i. 357.

[2] B. F. Harvey, 'The Life of the Manor', *Domesday Book Studies*, eds. Williams and Erskine, 41.

[3] Loyn, 'General Introduction', 20.

HUNDREDS AND WAPENTAKES

F. R. THORN

UNDER William I, as under the English kings, vills were grouped together for taxation, judicial and other obligations into 'hundreds' or, in former Danish areas, into 'wapentakes'. These administrative units, intermediate in size between the vill and the shire, and laid down before civil parishes came into existence, usually consisted of a single unified tract of territory (in 1086 varying widely between twenty and 300 hides in extent) which could belong to a variety of tenants-in-chief. Often a lord (particularly the king or a church) was paramount in a hundred; or the lordship of the hundred was attached to a particular manor by a system that was developed in the later medieval period. Some hundreds contained a single large manor only, and these and others had but a single tenant-in-chief. A few had isolated detachments and fewer still were ecclesiastical hundreds geographically scattered but owing suit to their church, however remote, and not to some local meeting-place. Vills were sometimes divided by hundred boundaries and the members of large manors were often in several different hundreds. Many of the hundred-names, if not replaced in 1086 by those of manors, refer to the meeting-places, 'moots', which were often at road-junctions, river-crossings, beside barrows or mounds, on hilltops or near isolated trees in a prominent position.

Hundreds cannot be described or mapped on the basis of Domesday Book alone, for the boundaries of estates and hundreds are never indicated, nor can every estate be allocated with certainty to a particular hundred, especially when it is mentioned in passing or is the dependency of some composite manor. The composition of hundreds can be partly restored from internal evidence by noting those places that fall directly beneath a hundred heading in the text and by identifying hundredal groupings which in many counties are inscribed in a standard sequence. However, the later history of the manor and of the hundred as well as geographical probability must also be employed and the hundredal rubrication itself examined, for it can be shown to be sometimes incorrect or deficient. The scribe's not infrequent errors are of only a few types and easily allowed for, and some restoration of missing headings can be made from the evidence of the text; but a decision sometimes has to be made to restore a hundred heading above a place from later evidence alone.

If these restorations are not made, Domesday will seem to allocate such a place to a different hundred, of which it will appear, owing to its geographical position, to be an improbable detachment. Allowance must be made for the fact that places lying close to the boundary of a hundred in 1086 may well be found in an adjacent hundred in the thirteenth-century surveys which are the first to show the composition of hundreds in detail.

Strictly speaking, it is impossible to map eleventh-century hundred boundaries. The hundred is the sum of exploited land and woodland, while 'waste', 'forest', moor and bog are either to be regarded as being outside the hundred, or the hundred boundary through them is ill-defined. Expansion of arable land, assarting, and drainage have all tended to change boundaries considerably. Compared with the number of vills surveyed in Domesday Book, charters with boundary clauses are few, their interpretation difficult and their relation to Domesday estates often indirect. Few estate maps survive from the Middle Ages and the first accurate hundred maps, dating from the early nineteenth century, are at the end of a process of change which may have left the 1086 pattern scarcely recognizable. But by using the evidence, whether certain, probable or supplemented, for the composition of the eleventh-century hundreds, lines can be drawn between manors—which may well contain more than one place and extend over more than one modern parish—according to the hundred in which they probably lay in 1086. In this way it is possible to recover something that approximates to the eleventh-century topography and administrative divisions.[1]

THE HUNDREDS OF CAMBRIDGESHIRE

Although the first record of the name Cambridgeshire appears to date from 1010,[2] the shire itself probably originated in 917 when Edward the Elder received the surrender of a Danish army in Cambridge. That year also saw the liberation and rebuilding of Huntingdon

[1] Apart from works cited in individual articles in the series, documents and discussions concerning the hundredal system will be found in O. S. Anderson, *The English Hundred-Names* (abbr. *EHN*) (Lund, 1934); *Inquisitions and Assessments Relating to Feudal Aids with other Analogous Documents, Preserved in the Public Records Office A.D. 1284–1431* (abbr. *Feudal Aids*), 6 vols. (HMSO, London, 1899–1920); F. Liebermann, *Die Gesetze der Angelsachsen*, 3 vols. (Halle, 1903–16); H. R. Loyn, *The Governance of Anglo-Saxon England, 500–1087* (London, 1984); A. J. Robertson (ed.), *The Laws of the Kings of England from Edmund to Henry I* (Cambridge, 1925); F. M. Stenton, *Anglo-Saxon England* (3rd edn., Oxford, 1971).

[2] D. Whitelock *et al.* (eds.), *The Anglo-Saxon Chronicle: A Revised Translation* (London, 1965), 90; Reaney, *Place-Names of Cambridgeshire* (abbr. *PNCambs.*), 1.

and of Colchester, and the submission of much of East Anglia and Essex and of what was to become Northamptonshire.[1] How far the boundaries of this and adjacent shires corresponded to those areas occupied by individual Danish armies is unclear, but it is likely that the laying out of the shire also involved, at the same time, its division into hundreds and that within these the hidage of vills was estimated in round numbers based mainly on a decimal system.[2] What is entirely uncertain is the extent to which the Danish armies effaced an earlier hidation of which the only trace survives in the large round numbers of the eighth-century Tribal Hidage;[3] or again, how far the invaders had imposed an assessment based on carucates and bovates within an administrative division they called the wapentake. It is also uncertain in the case of Cambridgeshire whether their system, which survived in the counties of the Danelaw until the Domesday survey,[4] was merely converted after their expulsion into the Anglo-Saxon equivalents of hide, virgate and hundred.

In the County Hidage, a document dating from early in the eleventh century, Cambridgeshire is allocated 2,500 hides.[5] If this is a true statement of fact and neither an erroneous nor an ideal figure, a considerable reduction appears to have taken place by 1066, when the county total seems to have been about 1,320 hides;[6] a further reduction in the assessment of some hundreds had taken place by 1086.[7] Despite this major discrepancy, the figures in the County Hidage deserve to be taken seriously. Worcestershire is there allotted 1,200 hides and in 1086 had the equivalent of twelve hundreds; Huntingdonshire, with 800 or 850 hides, clearly consisted in 1086, as no doubt earlier, of four 'double-hundreds';[8] while the Northamptonshire Geld Roll, which dates from early in the reign of William I, shows that Northamptonshire (3,200 hides

TABLE 1: The Hundreds of Cambridgeshire

Modern Name	Form(s) found in Domesday Book	Number on map
'Arringford'	*Erningford*	XIV
Cambridge[1]	*Grantebrige, Grentebrige*	X
Chesterton	*Cestreton-e*[2]	VI
Cheveley	*Cavelai, Chavelai*	XIII
Chilford	*Cildeford*[3]	XVII
Ely (two hundreds)	*Ely*	I–II
Fleamdyke	*Flamidinc, Flamiding, Flamingdice, Flammidinc, Flammiding, Flammindic*	XI
Longstowe	*Stou*	VIII
'Northstowe'	*Norestou, Orneston*[4]	V
Papworth	*Pampesword,*[5] *Papeword-e, Papesword*	IV
'Radfield'	*Radefelle*	XII
'Staine'	*Stanes*	VII
'Staploe'	*Staplehou*	III
Thriplow	*Trepelau, Trepeslau*[6]	XV
Westley[7]	*Weslai*	—
'Wetherley'	*Wederlai, Wedrelai*	IX
Whittlesford	*Witelesfeld, Witelesford*	XVI

[1] Borough assessed as a hundred TRE.
[2] It is not certain how the abbreviated form *Cestret'* (f.202) should be expanded.
[3] In the right column of f.201v this form could be misread as *CILBEFORD* in the facsimile.
[4] Perhaps the result of scribal confusion at an earlier stage in the compilation of DB: for example, on f.202 the scribe wrote *ORNESTON* but later corrected it to *NORESTOU*.
[5] Form influenced by the vill-name Pampisford (*Pampesworde*).
[6] In the left column of f.202 this form could be misread as *TREPESLAO* in the facsimile.
[7] Occurs only once as a hundred-name (f.199), and is probably a scribal confusion; see p.20 below. It has not been treated as a separate hundred in this edition.

in the County Hidage) contained the equivalent of thirty-two hundreds, though some were 'double-hundreds' or 'hundreds and a half'.[9] Moreover, Northamptonshire with 3,200 hides in the County Hidage, 2,663½ in the Geld Roll and approximately 1,356 hides in Domesday Book provides a parallel for the stages of reduction in hidage assessment found in Cambridgeshire.[10]

The analogy with Northamptonshire suggests that Cambridgeshire might have once contained the equivalent of twenty-five hundreds. However, Domesday Book attests the existence of about seventeen hundreds, among them the borough of Cambridge 'which was assessed as a hundred TRE' and was clearly something more than a small walled *burh* without arable land that was conveniently but only notionally assessed for geld in hides;[11] and 'the two hundreds of Ely which meet at Witchford'.[12] Although the hundred courts were clearly involved in the compilation of Domesday,[13] the Book itself says nothing further

[1] Whitelock *et al.* (eds.), *Anglo-Saxon Chronicle*, 65–6.

[2] J. H. Round, *Feudal England* (London, 1895), 44–54, used several Cambs. hundreds for his demonstration that assessment of the vill was imposed from above, as a subdivision of the hundred, and was often in units of 5 or 10 hides. The same pattern is evident from the much more detailed analysis in Hart, *Hidation of Cambridgeshire*.

[3] W. de G. Birch (ed.), *Cartularium Saxonicum: A Collection of Charters Relating to Anglo-Saxon History*, i (London, 1885), 414–16, no. 297; F. W. Maitland, *Domesday Book and Beyond* (Cambridge, 1897), 506–7; Stenton, *Anglo-Saxon England*, 295–6; W. J. Corbett, 'The Tribal Hidage', *TRHS* ns 14 (1900), 187–230; C. R. Hart, 'The Tribal Hidage', *TRHS* 5th ser., 21 (1971), 133–57.

[4] Leics., Derby., Notts., Rut., Yorks. and Lincs. are divided into wapentakes. In the portion of Northants lying to the east of Watling Street that was occupied by the Danes, the term 'wapentake' is used once in DB for Upton Hundred, and usually for Witchley Hundred which lay north of the river Welland and was later joined to Rutland. Whether the Danes were in fact responsible for the carucation of these counties is uncertain; see the Derby. and Notts. 'Hundreds and Wapentakes' articles in this series.

[5] Maitland, *Domesday Book and Beyond*, 456.

[6] Maitland's total is 1,233 hides (ibid.), which excludes the 'hundred' of Cambridge borough. Baring calculates 1,315 hides ('Hidation of Some Southern Counties', 294). The total of Hart's additions is 1,220 hides without the borough of Cambridge (*Hidation of Cambridgeshire*, 26).

[7] See pp.23–4 below.

[8] Thorn, 'Hundreds and Wapentakes', *Worcestershire Domesday*, 32–3; *idem*, 'Hundreds and Wapentakes', *Huntingdonshire Domesday*, 29.

[9] Thorn, 'Hundreds and Wapentakes', *Northamptonshire and Rutland Domesday*, 36.

[10] See C. R. Hart, *The Hidation of Northamptonshire*, Dept. of Eng. Local Hist. Occasional Papers, 2nd ser., 3 (Leicester, 1970).

[11] Later maps show a substantial *banleuca*, not in other hundreds, attached to the *burh*, e.g. R. G. Baker, *Map of the County of Cambridge and the Isle of Ely, surveyed by R. G. Baker in the years 1816, 17, 18, 19 and 20* (Bluntisham, 1821). There is mention of pasture and mills and of burgesses having ploughs in the borough entry (f.189), but no arable extents are given.

[12] GDB 191v.

[13] References to the hundred courts are to be found on ff.189v, 190, 190v(x3), 191(x2), 191v(x2), 193, 196v, 197(x3), 197v, 198, 198v(x2), 199, 199v(x5), 201v(x3), 202(x3).

about the organization of the hundreds and there is virtually no evidence before 1086 for their existence; only the two hundreds of Ely are attested earlier.[1]

Domesday Book is sometimes misleading concerning the number of hundreds that lay in a county in 1086. In the case of Cambridgeshire it contains a single heading for a hundred of Westley in the fief of Hardwin de Scales above an entry for West Wratting, which follows one for Stetchworth rubricated as being in 'Radfield' Hundred.[2] This 'hundred' is evidently named from the vill of Westley Waterless, which elsewhere in Domesday Book and in the Inquisitio Comitatus Cantabrigiensis is found among 'Radfield' Hundred places as is Balsham which succeeds West Wratting. It is most probable that the vill of Westley Waterless was called a hundred by mistake, maybe because the scribe was working through material arranged vill by vill within each hundred.[3] Or perhaps, more specifically, it was a result of a check on the holdings of the Abbey of Ely where Westley Waterless follows two entries for Stetchworth and precedes two for West Wratting: Hardwin had an interest in both Stetchworth and West Wratting.[4] It is, however, just possible that Westley was an alternative name for 'Radfield', for the moot site of the hundred was adjacent.[5]

The status of Thorney is also uncertain. It was not a hundred, but, like other island monasteries, it enjoyed such extensive privileges that it was almost a kingdom in itself.[6] With the king as its protector and subject to the power of neither layman nor bishop, it seems to have owed no geld nor service to any hundred and to have possessed a court of its own; thus, though it lay geographically within the two hundreds of Ely, it seems to have been outside the hundredal system.[7]

In most counties, reconstruction of the contents of each hundred depends on a study of the rubrication supplied by Domesday Book, then on the identification of blocks of vills grouped by hundreds within each fief, followed by a check from later evidence. Cambridgeshire is fortunate in possessing two 'satellite' documents, the Inquisitio Eliensis and the Inquisitio Comitatus Cantabrigiensis,[8] drawn from material that was itself related to the inquiry which produced Domesday Book. The Inquisitio Eliensis (hereafter IE) is a survey of the lands held by the Abbey of Ely in six counties—Cambridgeshire, Essex, Hertfordshire, Huntingdonshire, Norfolk and Suffolk. It survives in three versions, copied in the second half of the twelfth century, and seems to have been extracted for the abbey's own purposes from the body of material collected for the Domesday survey that was subsequently abbreviated to form Great Domesday Book: it thus contains lists of jurors, some pre-Conquest holders, a few place-names, the amount of hides in demesne and details of livestock which were deliberately eliminated, or in some cases accidentally disappeared, in the excerpting process. It also contains summaries of the holdings of Hardwin de Scales, Guy de Raimbeaucourt and Picot the sheriff who are shown by Domesday Book to have been in illegal possession of some of the abbey's lands.[9] The value of the IE for the reconstruction of the 1086 hundreds is that its hundredal rubrication is meticulous. Although the places are not entered in an order identical to that of Domesday for Cambridgeshire, they are in hundred groups[10] and this serves as a check on the accuracy of Domesday Book, not only in the fief of Ely Abbey but in other fiefs, for the IE also records a number of lands alienated from the Church that in Domesday Book are listed under other tenants-in-chief.[11] In this way a few hundredal headings can be restored.[12]

The Inquisitio Comitatus Cantabrigiensis (hereafter ICC) is similarly a late twelfth-century copy of the material from which Great Domesday Book was compiled, at a time when it was arranged by hundred, vill and landholder and before it was rearranged in the

[1] P. H. Sawyer (ed.), *Anglo-Saxon Charters: An Annotated List and Bibliography*, R. Hist. Soc. Guides and Handbooks, 8 (London, 1968), no. 779; see also no. 1051 (a confirmation by Edward the Confessor), and *VCH Cambridgeshire*, ii (1948), 1–7.

[2] GDB 199.

[3] Many vills appear in the same relative order in different fiefs (see below) as a result of being extracted from material similar to that contained in the Inquisitio Comitatus Cantabrigiensis (see n.8 below). Stetchworth, for example, appears immediately before Westley Waterless in Chs. 5 and 14; see Rumble (ed.), *Domesday Book: Cambridgeshire*, note to 26,51.

[4] GDB 190v.

[5] See Anderson, *EHN*, 101; Reaney, *PNCambs.*, 113; and Table 3, p.26 below. Alternative names for hundreds are found in other counties: for example, the Hants hundred of Odiham appears to be named *Odiham* and also *Edefele* and variants. Documents for Som. and Devon., contemporary with DB, show different names for some hundreds; see the relevant 'Hundreds' articles in this series. The drawing of a hand in the margin beside this entry, dating perhaps from the late sixteenth century and pointing upwards, may be an attempt to indicate that West Wratting was in fact part of the preceding 'Radfield' Hundred.

[6] See Sawyer (ed.), *Anglo-Saxon Charters*, no. 792, and *VCH Cambridgeshire*, ii. 210–17; iv (1953), 219–21.

[7] Many island monasteries enjoyed remarkable liberties, e.g. Ramsey in Hunts., Crowland in Lincs., and Athelney in Som. Thorney, however, does not even appear in the normal feudal lists, e.g. the *Nomina Villarum* of 1316 (*Feudal Aids*, i (1899), 152–7); *Rotuli Hundredorum*, 2 vols. (Record Commission, London, 1812–18); R. E. Glasscock (ed.), *The Lay Subsidy of 1334*, Brit. Acad. Records of Social and Economic Hist. ns 2 (London, 1975), 23–8.

[8] Hereafter abbr. IE and ICC; published in Hamilton (ed.), *Inquisitio Comitatus Cantabrigiensis . . . Subjicitur Inquisitio Eliensis*. There are valuable discussions of one or both documents in Round, *Feudal England*, 1–27, 123–42; V. H. Galbraith, *The Making of Domesday Book* (Oxford, 1961), 123–45; S. P. J. Harvey, 'Domesday Book and its Predecessors', *EHR* 86 (1971), 753–73; H. B. Clarke, 'The Domesday Satellites', *Domesday Book: A Reassessment*, ed. P. H. Sawyer (London, 1985), 50–70; Rumble (ed.), *Domesday Book: Cambridgeshire*.

[9] Cambs. Chs. 26, 31–2. These chapters appear erroneously as numbers 24, 29–30 in the text; see the 'Notes to the Translation', p.43 below.

[10] The order of the groups (Hamilton (ed.), *IE*, 101–21) is 'Staploe', Cheveley (an entry for Woodditton alienated from the Church, held by the king in DB), 'Staine', Fleamdyke, Chilford, 'Radfield', Thriplow, 'Arringford', 'Wetherley', Longstowe, Papworth, 'Northstowe', Chesterton, the two hundreds of Ely, followed by Cambridge borough.

[11] For example, under Thriplow Hundred, in addition to listing Thriplow itself, Hauxton, Harston, Great Shelford and Stapleford, which are in the fief of the abbey in DB, the IE includes Trumpington, held by William de Warenne in DB (f.196v).

[12] For example, the 'Arringford' hundred head which has to be restored above Whaddon (f.191) and the 'Wetherley' hundred head which must be inserted above Shepreth (f.191v) are both entered above these places in the IE.

feudal order of landholder, hundred, manor. It is incomplete and fragmentary, for it lacks entirely the hundred of Chesterton and the two hundreds of Ely, and only portions of the hundreds of Papworth, Longstowe and 'Northstowe' survive. Its additions to Domesday Book are of the same type and contain largely the same material as those of the IE,[1] but because it describes the county hundred by hundred and, within each, brings together the constituents of each vill which are scattered in different chapters of Domesday Book, the composition of those ten hundreds that it describes in full can be determined with complete certainty.[2]

The evidence of the Cambridge and the Ely Inquisitiones supplements the ample material of Domesday Book itself. There is an abundance of hundred heads; moreover, it is rare for the same hundred-name to occur more than once in each fief, which suggests that all the manors of a fief-holder that lay in a given hundred have been entered together as a single block: on closer inspection this proves indeed to be the case. Furthermore, as in a significant number of counties, there is evidence of a consistent order of hundreds within each fief.[3] The fief of Count Alan of Brittany (Chapter 14) contains fourteen of the sixteen purely territorial hundreds of Cambridgeshire;[4] only the two hundreds of Ely are, not surprisingly, omitted.[5] With the inclusion of a few restored hundred heads, ten chapters show an exact correspondence with the order of this chapter;[6] a further two (26 and 41) contain two sections, each of which is in the same order as Chapter 14, as if the scribe, using a pile of hundredal returns, had begun part-way down.[7] Five other chapters (5, 7, 19, 29, 32) have one section that is in the standard order,[8] while Chapters 9 and 18 are also similar to Chapter 14's order, apart from including returns for the two hundreds of Ely.[9] As many as nineteen chapters contain lands in only one hundred and so can be discounted in this connection, while Chapters 1, 6, 11, and 17 show a different order.[10]

The order of the hundreds in the ICC and in the fief of Count Alan is basically the same except that Count Alan's fief in Domesday Book begins at a different point in the sequence, with Fleamdyke Hundred which is the fifth hundred to be entered in the ICC. It then finishes with the four hundreds that begin the sequence in the latter document. Among these four, however, 'Staploe' (first in the ICC) comes after, not before, Cheveley and 'Staine' hundreds in the fief of Count Alan. Furthermore, apart from a difference in the position of 'Radfield' Hundred (sixth in the IE, fourth in the ICC), both Inquisitiones show the same order of hundreds; while for the first three and the last six hundreds, the separate list of jurors in the IE has the same order as set out in the IE proper.[11]

Thus it seems probable that each fief in Great Domesday Book, or in the predecessor 'circuit volume',[12] was extracted from the material of which the ICC was a copy. The scribe, while generally keeping to its sequence of hundreds (probably because he kept the hundredally arranged material in the same order in a pile), did not always begin with the same one. Tidy administrative order is shown also in other ways: at their first appearance, in Chapter 5, the two hundreds of Ely are distinguished from each other: 'So far one hundred, now the other'.[13] In Chapters 6 and 7 the constituents of the first hundred of Ely also precede those of the second.[14] Even within other hundreds, where constituent parts of the same vill appear in different fiefs, many are entered in the same position relative to other vills and in the order of their inscription in the ICC.[15]

With such a wealth of evidence it is easy to check—both for deficiency and for accuracy—the hundredal rubrication that Domesday Book supplies.[16] Error seems likely in only two entries: in the case of the Westley hundred heading supplied above West Wratting

[1] Most significant additions from both 'satellites' to the material given in DB are listed in Rumble (ed.), *Domesday Book: Cambridgeshire*. Additional and discrepant place-name information is given in Table 2, p.25 below.

[2] The hundreds appear in the ICC in the following order: 'Staploe', Cheveley, 'Staine', 'Radfield', Fleamdyke, Chilford, Whittlesford, Thriplow, 'Arringford', 'Wetherley', Longstowe (fragmentary), Papworth (fragmentary), 'Northstowe' (fragmentary).

[3] This has been studied by P. H. Sawyer, 'The "Original Returns" and Domesday Book', *EHR* 70 (1955), 177–97; see esp. p.181.

[4] The order of hundreds in Ch. 14 is: Fleamdyke, Chilford, Whittlesford, Thriplow, 'Arringford', 'Wetherley', Longstowe, Papworth, 'Northstowe', Chesterton (restored), Cheveley, 'Staine', 'Staploe' and 'Radfield'. It mentions the borough of Cambridge on f.194 in the middle of a series of entries for Chilford Hundred.

[5] The doubtful hundred of Westley does not appear.

[6] Chs. 3, 12, 13, 15, 21, 25, 31, 38, 39, 44.

[7] In Ch. 41 only an added and unrubricated Papworth hundred heading interrupts the end of the second section, intervening between 'Northstowe' and Chesterton. Ch. 26 terminates with 5 entries out of hundred order, written shortly after the rest of the fief (perhaps added when the hundredal schedules were checked through), but before the scribe began to enter the next fief. One of these 5 misplaced entries (for Swaffham Prior) has a hundred head added in the margin, and the next (for Babraham) has one that is unrubricated and in error (see p.22 below). Ch. 22 is arranged in the same way as Ch. 14, except that 'Staploe' Hundred is inserted between Thriplow and 'Arringford' Hundreds.

[8] The first 3 hundreds in Ch. 5 are the same as in Ch. 26, but entered in reverse order (i.e. 'Radfield', 'Staploe', 'Staine'); thereafter it keeps to the arrangement of Ch. 14 with the addition of the two hundreds of Ely at the end.

[9] If Ch. 14 represents the order in which the hundredal material was arranged, the Ely Hundreds would, to judge from their position in other fiefs, have occupied the last or penultimate positions after 'Staploe' or 'Radfield' Hundreds respectively.

[10] Many counties in DB have similar chapters whose order differs from the regular scheme of the county.

[11] Chilford Hundred is missing from the list of jurors in the IE and Whittlesford Hundred from the IE proper, while the hundreds in the middle of these two corresponding sections are entered in reverse order to each other. The parallels and differences are tabulated in Hart, *Hidation of Cambridgeshire*, 16.

[12] For the three eastern and the five south-western counties, 'circuit volumes' (LDB and Exon respectively) have survived; the existence of others is only assumed.

[13] GDB 192.

[14] All the places in other fiefs that lay in the two hundreds of Ely have portions entered in Ch. 5, where the division between the 2 hundreds is made clear.

[15] Hart, *Hidation of Cambridgeshire*, 18–19, tabulates the evidence for 4 hundreds. This phenomenon is found in other counties, e.g. Bucks.; see Thorn, 'Hundreds and Wapentakes', *Buckinghamshire Domesday*, p.30, n.7.

[16] There is also one 'continuation head' (*in hoc eodem hundredo*, 'in this same hundred') supplied, as often in other counties, above an unnamed holding (f.194v).

already mentioned,[1] and in the case of the unrubricated Fleamdyke Hundred above Babraham on f.199, where Chilford Hundred would be expected.[2] Fleamdyke Hundred in fact comes immediately before Chilford in the standard sequence, which was no doubt firmly fixed in the scribe's mind and thus caused the error.[3] A further nine hundred headings need to be restored to harmonize the hundred of the places concerned with that given by Domesday Book itself elsewhere, by the satellite surveys and by later evidence.[4]

On this basis hundreds can be confidently reconstituted and mapping can begin with more assurance than is the case in many counties, by drawing the hundredal boundaries between places that Domesday Book allots to adjacent hundreds. The Domesday inquiry did not, however, set out to survey every settlement that lay in England in 1086. Many habitation-places with separate names and, indeed, large areas containing several settlements and sometimes corresponding to entire later parishes are ostensibly omitted, but their size, value, population and resources are in fact entered in the details of an adjacent estate that encompassed them. Thus there is no mention of Newton in Thriplow Hundred,[5] of Coton in 'Wetherley',[6] or of Brinkley in 'Radfield' Hundred.[7] They can only be assigned to their correct hundreds on the basis of later evidence. In the two hundreds of Ely the settlements of (and later parishes named from) Elm, Tydd St Giles, Newton, Leverington, Upwell, Manea, Mepal and Coveney are not named in Domesday Book.[8] Though all these places are named in the fourteenth-century documents and probably existed in 1086 as constituents of named Domesday manors, the difficulty of settlement in this Fenland area, where it had to be confined to higher ground or to islands, led to its paucity. Not only are settlements too far apart for lines to be drawn with certainty between them, but also the topography has greatly changed since the labour of hundreds of years finally drained the Fens.[9] In 1086 the Wash would have been larger and much of the Fenland would have been marsh, mere or swamp, communication being by boat or causeway. The 1086 settlements, which would then have been on islands, cannot have had the extent of their later parishes: in the great expanse of the two hundreds of Ely—almost a separate county—there were only eighty hides in 1086 and less than 140 ploughlands.[10] Boundaries through reeds and mire and water must have been notional: when they ultimately came to be defined they were often run along new ditches, many of recent date, or the old limits were realigned when the rivers that had served as boundaries were straightened or changed in course. Thus the mapping of boundaries in this area of the county can only give an approximate idea of the areas associated with each settlement. Moreover, the interlacing of the two hundreds of Ely creates its own problems, as does their subsequent division into three and then four hundreds.[11] Elsewhere in the county, however, the hundreds seem to have had the same constituents in the late eleventh century as they did in the mid nineteenth and this suggests that most of the boundaries remained constant.[12]

The hundredal pattern thus revealed is one of contrasts. The two hundreds of Ely, dominated but not entirely held by Ely Abbey, consisted of amorphous and interpenetrating areas, much of their surface being unsuitable for cultivation, while they were separated from the rest of the county by the Great Ouse river and a succession of fens. South of this line lay a series of more typical hundreds, many of roughly similar size and all containing a variety of tenants-in-chief. Cambridge borough, forming a partly notional hundred with its dependent land, stood in the centre of this group of hundreds, in which the only unusual feature was the intermixing of the lands of 'Northstowe' and Chesterton Hundreds which at first sight might appear to be a disruption, probably for tenurial reasons, of a simpler, earlier pattern. Many of these southern hundreds took their boundaries from topographical features, especially from the river Cam and its tributaries, from dykes and from Roman roads. Thus 'Arringford' Hundred was mainly bounded by the river Cam (or Rhee) and the Icknield Way, which also forms the county boundary. The northern boundary of Chilford Hundred (except near West Wickham) was

[1] See p.20 above.

[2] It is clearly in Chilford Hundred in Hamilton (ed.), *ICC*, 36.

[3] Similar errors are found elsewhere, e.g. in Notts. (f.290v).

[4] The following hundred heads need to be inserted, as in Rumble (ed.), *Domesday Book: Cambridgeshire* (in which different name-forms have been used for some hundreds): Armingford above Whaddon, f.191; Wetherley above Shepreth, f.191v; Staploe above Soham, f.192; Papworth above Over, f.193; Wetherley above Orwell, f.193v; Chesterton above Dry Drayton, f.195; Whittlesford above Duxford, f.196v; Wetherley above Shepreth, f.198v; and Armingford above Meldreth, f.199v. The most important later evidence is contained in *Feudal Aids*, *Rotuli Hundredorum*, and Glasscock (ed.), *Lay Subsidy of 1334*, and in *The Book of Fees*, 2 vols. and Index (HMSO, London, 1920–31).

[5] NGR TL 4349. It was probably part of Hauxton in 1086.

[6] NGR TL 4058. It was probably part of Grantchester in 1086.

[7] NGR TL 6254. It was probably part of Carlton in 1086.

[8] NGR TF 4706, TF 4216, TF 4414, TF 4411, TF 5002, TL 4889, TL 4480, TL 4882 respectively. On Upwell, partly in Norfolk, see p.23, n.7 below.

[9] The major work on this topic has been done by H. C. Darby, *The Medieval Fenland* (Cambridge, 1940) and *The Draining of the Fens*, Cambridge Stud. in Economic Hist. (Cambridge, 1940). It is probable that Whittlesey, March and Doddington, Chatteris, Littleport, Stuntney and Hainey all lay on separate islands, in addition to the bulk of the abbey's manors which lay on the main island or islands of Ely.

[10] Tabulated in Hart, *Hidation of Cambridgeshire*, 67. On the possibility that the hidage had once been larger, see ibid. 34, and p.24, n.4 below.

[11] See Table 3, p.26, n.4 below. It is possible that the division between the two hundreds of Ely was purely fiscal, as suggested by Miller, *Abbey and Bishopric of Ely*, 31. Topographically, however, there appears to be a distinction between an inner hundred (centred around Ely itself and having only Wisbech as an outlier) and an outer hundred, mostly consisting of scattered islands.

[12] This reconstruction has been checked against Baker, *Map of the County of Cambridge*, and largely agrees with the map in Rumble (ed.), *Domesday Book: Cambridgeshire*, and those in the *VCH Cambridgeshire* 'topographical' volumes so far published: vols. iv, v (1973), vi (1978) and viii (1982). The boundaries between the two hundreds of Ely are much less well evidenced and so open to differing interpretation.

'Wool Street',[1] a Roman road. Fleamdyke Hundred was partly bounded by the dyke that named it, partly by 'Wool Street' and by the Little Wilbraham river. Longstowe was delimited on its northern edge by the road from Cambridge to St Neots,[2] and on its southern edge by another ancient track, the Mare Way. 'Radfield' Hundred was sandwiched between the Icknield Way, the Devil's Ditch (formerly the Devil's Dyke) and 'Wool Street'. The western edge of Thriplow Hundred was the river Cam (or Rhee), its northern edge 'Wool Street'; 'Wetherley' Hundred was partly shaped by the river Cam (or Rhee) and the Mare Way.

There are a few incidental complications to this essentially straightforward pattern. Nine acres of land in Risbridge Hundred (Suffolk) were assessed in Weston Colville,[3] while conversely Babraham and Hinxton were dependent on Great Chesterford in Essex and part of Shelford on Newport in the same county.[4] A part of Papworth and a part of Boxworth were assessed in Fenstanton in Huntingdonshire.[5] Although no vills appear to have been divided by hundredal boundaries, the laying out of the county boundary did split some land-units. Stanground lay partly in Cambridgeshire, partly in Huntingdonshire;[6] Outwell and Upwell were divided with Norfolk;[7] and the land-unit of Tydd was split between Cambridgeshire and Lincolnshire.[8] Papworth Everard lay entirely in Cambridgeshire, Papworth St Agnes partly in Huntingdonshire and partly in Cambridgeshire.[9] It is quite possible that adjustments had already been made by 1086 to the county boundary here and south of Papworth. Westerly loops reach out to include Graveley, Eltisley, Croxton and Little Gransden in Cambridgeshire, while an eastwards bulge appears to take Great Gransden into Huntingdonshire. In fact, it is possible that both Great and Little Gransden formerly lay in Huntingdonshire and that the latter was attracted into Cambridgeshire because of the Abbot of Ely's demesne there.[10] While most changes to the county boundary date from the nineteenth and twentieth centuries, it is medieval changes that are most difficult to detect and to map, especially when they do not involve the transfer of a settlement site from one county to another. The chance survival of a specification of the medieval bounds of Normancross Hundred in Huntingdonshire shows how that county ran eastwards across the Bedford Level, skirting Whittlesey (Cambs.) and reaching Flood's Ferry,[11] before turning back to Benwick,[12] despite the fact that the modern county boundary runs along the apparently ancient feature of 'Cnut's Dyke' (now Oakley Dike).[13]

In 1066 there were about 1,320 hides in the county including the 100 hides of Cambridge borough.[14] Though well short of the total of 2,500 in the County Hidage, they show clear signs of being part of an artificial system of assessment. Most of the pre-Conquest hundreds amount to exact round figures and among these 'Staine' and Cheveley Hundreds total fifty hides each, while 'Arringford' and Longstowe were exact units of 100 hides.[15] Within most hundreds many vills contain five or ten hides, or can be grouped together to form units of twenty-five or thirty hides. 'Radfield' Hundred contained six vills, each of ten hides, and two of five hides.[16] 'Wetherley' Hundred consisted of four units of twenty hides, Longstowe of four units of twenty-five, 'Arringford' of ten units of ten hides.[17] Between 1066 and 1086, however, six hundreds had their geldable hidages reduced. Domesday Book is selective or arbitrary in the omission of such details and the information about the reduction is only reliably obtainable from the ICC, which is itself fragmentary for some of these hundreds. Generally the reassessment when it took place was applied uniformly across the vills of a hundred so that in many cases their relative size in hides did not change. 'Staploe' Hundred appears to have had its hidage reduced from ninety to

[1] 'Wool Street' is a name in local use for the portion of the Roman road that passes through the parishes of Fulbourn, Babraham, Little Abington, Linton, West Wickham, and Horseheath; it is also known as the 'Via Devana' (an antiquarian invention), although neither name occurs on current maps. See Reaney, *PN Cambs*, 30,32.

[2] The A45 trunk road.

[3] LDB 292v.

[4] GDB 189v, 190(x3); see LDB 3v, 7.

[5] GDB 197, 197v.

[6] NGR TL 2097. Only the Hunts. part is mentioned (f.205). The division lasted until 1974.

[7] NGR TF 5103, TF 5002 respectively. They are mentioned only in the Norfolk folios (LDB 160, 215v, 136, 206v, 230v, 231v, 276). The Cambs. portions were unnamed parts of the Ely Hundreds (Glasscock (ed.), *Lay Subsidy of 1334*, 28). The village centres and churches lay and continue to lie in Norfolk.

[8] Tydd St Giles (NGR TF 4216) was an unnamed part of Wisbech in Cambs. (see Glasscock (ed.), *Lay Subsidy of 1334*, 28); Tydd St Mary (TF 4418) is surveyed in the Lincs. folios (GDB 338(x2), 351v, 368). The county boundary still divides them. See Owen, 'A Fenland Frontier'.

[9] The Hunts. portion is on GDB 206v.

[10] See *VCH Cambridgeshire*, v. 1. It is possible that this fretworked border is due to a division on territorial lines of a short-lived single unit of 3,200 hides (the same size as Northants) into the counties of Hunts. (800 hides) and Cambs. (2,400 hides).

[11] NGR TL 3593.

[12] NGR TL 3490.

[13] 'Cnut's Dyke' (now Oakley Dike) passed through NGR TL 2593. On the bounds of Normancross Hundred, see *VCH Huntingdonshire*, iii (1936), 129–31.

[14] See p.19, n.6 above.

[15] The pre-Conquest hidage figures for the Cambs. hundreds are: 'Arringford', 100; Chesterton, 120; Cheveley, 50; Chilford, 54½; Fleamdyke, 46; Longstowe, 100; 'Northstowe', 111; Papworth, *c.*100; 'Radfield', 70; 'Staine', 50; 'Staploe', 90; Thriplow, 90; 'Wetherley', 80; Whittlesford, 80; Ely, 40 + 40; Cambridge borough, 100. These figures are taken from Hart, *Hidation of Cambridgeshire*, 20–6, and agree with the published *VCH Cambridgeshire* 'topographical' volumes and with Round, *Feudal England*, 44–55. 'Northstowe' Hundred may correctly be 110 hides. Papworth Hundred's 100 hides are made up by assuming a deficiency of 3 hides and 3 virgates in Boxworth. Picot's unnamed 1 hide held under the king's hand (f.190) cannot be allocated to any hundred.

[16] The exact figures in DB are: Balsham, 10 hides; Burrough Green, 5 hides; Carlton, 9 hides, 3 virgates, 6½ acres; Dullingham, 10 hides; Stetchworth, 10 hides, ½ virgate; West Wratting, 10 hides; Westley Waterless, 4 hides, 3 virgates, 25 acres; and Weston Colville, 10 hides. There are slight differences in the figures in the ICC from which Hart was working.

[17] Moreover, in 1066 Cheveley Hundred was made up of five units of 10 hides as follows: Silverley, 6½ and Ashley, 3½; Saxon Street, 5 and Woodditton (Ch. 14), 5; Woodditton (Ch. 1), 10; Kirtling, 10; Cheveley (Ch. 1), 8 hides, 40 acres and Cheveley (Ch. 14), 1½ hides, 20 acres. This regularity can help identify unnamed holdings: it is evident that Countess Judith's 3 virgates in Longstowe Hundred (f.202) were part of Hatley St George and that her 3 hides in 'Northstowe' Hundred (f.202) were part of Madingley.

sixty hides, Cheveley from fifty to twenty-five, 'Arringford' from a hundred to eighty, Longstowe from a hundred to perhaps sixty hides. The hidages of Papworth and 'Northstowe' Hundreds were also reduced, but because the record in the ICC is incomplete it is not clear by how much.[1]

The essential simplicity of these across-the-board reductions may be the key to explaining the difference between the 2,500 hides of the County Hidage and the 1,320 or so hides that lay in the county in 1066. If the hidage, as a measure of taxation, could be halved in some hundreds between 1066 and 1086, as in Northamptonshire,[2] could not this have already taken place across more or the whole of the territory of this county at an earlier stage? Were the half-hundreds of 1066 (Cheveley, Chilford, Fleamdyke, 'Staine') once full hundreds, and those 1066 hundreds that contained seventy or eighty hides ('Radfield', 'Wetherley', Whittlesford) formerly hundreds and a half? Had some of the others in fact once been double-hundreds? In the case of Huntingdonshire, a simple pattern of hundreds apparently lasted from the creation of the shire until 1086.[3] In the case of Northamptonshire, as shown above, the existence of the Geld Roll allows the successive stages of a complicated evolution from an original 3,200 hides to the much smaller total in Domesday Book to be understood. However, for Cambridgeshire this key is lacking and there are yet further questions to be answered. Was the original total for the county perhaps 2,400 hides, the extra hundred hides being accounted for either by the borough of Cambridge or by the creation *c.*970 of the two hundreds of Ely and their addition to the shire?[4] Were there perhaps at one time fewer hundreds with, for example, the interlaced Chesterton and 'Northstowe' originally one and Chilford and Fleamdyke forming another?[5] Is the shortage in the 1066 figures for 'Wetherley', Thriplow, Fleamdyke and 'Northstowe' Hundreds which surround Cambridge due to portions of them having been drawn out to form the hundred of Cambridge borough?[6] It is even possible that the shire, without the two hundreds of Ely, was once 'quartered', like Huntingdonshire and perhaps Northamptonshire,[7] with original units of 600 hides reduced to 300. In this case, Papworth, Chesterton and 'Northstowe' Hundreds would have formed one quarter,[8] Longstowe, 'Wetherley' and 'Arringford' another,[9] Thriplow, Whittlesford and Fleamdyke-Chilford a third,[10] leaving 'Staine', 'Radfield', 'Staploe' and Cheveley as the fourth.[11] The uniformity of these larger units would contrast with the irregularity of some of their subdivisions, which could have followed tenure rather than geography. Yet, despite its detached parts, Chesterton Hundred had a simple taxation structure: one main unit of sixty hides and two detachments of thirty hides,[12] although 'Northstowe' Hundred which is intermixed with it had no such clear pattern.[13]

But the manipulation of figures alone is an unsafe procedure[14] and amidst such speculation about the original pattern of the hundreds one can be certain only that the two hundreds of Ely were already in existence in 970 when King Edgar confirmed a number of lands and privileges on the abbey.[15] What is less certain is how ancient was the abbey's liberty and how large was its initial endowment of lands. Even if most of its immunities within its own island dated back to St Ætheldreda's concession of 673, the formation of the two hundreds was probably no earlier than the tenth century and represented a new grouping of isolated fenland holdings.[16]

Whereas in the shires of Wessex there is strong reason to suppose that the hundredal system arose by the fission of a series of *regiones*, each centred on an important royal vill, and that royal holdings continued

[1] In 'Arringford' Hundred, for example, each five-hide holding was reduced to 4 hides and each ten-hide holding to 8; see Hart, *Hidation of Cambridgeshire*, 22.

[2] See Hart, *Hidation of Cambridgeshire*, 38, and p.19 above.

[3] See Thorn, 'Hundreds and Wapentakes', *Huntingdonshire Domesday*, 26, 29.

[4] See n.16 below. In view of the nature of the land, it seems improbable that the two hundreds of Ely ever contained 100 hides each; an original assessment of 50 hides each is possible, but unproven.

[5] Together Chilford and Fleamdyke 'Hundreds' totalled 100½ hides in 1066. A joint moot—at Mutlow Hill—is a possibility; but Mutlow might have served a larger grouping (see Table 3, p.26, n.5 below).

[6] 80, 90, 46, 111 hides respectively, which might have once been 100, 100, 50 and 150 hides.

[7] Of the 32 hundreds in Northants shown to exist by the Geld Roll (p.19, n.9 above), there were the equivalent of 8 hundreds based on Oundle ('Huxloe', Navisford, 'Navisland', Polebrook, Upton and Willowbrook, of which 'Navisland' and Upton were double-hundreds), and another 8 lay south-west of Watling Street ('Alboldstow', 'Alwardsley', Cleyley, Foxley, 'Gravesend', Sutton, Towcester, Warden). Glos. may also once have been quartered.

[8] 331 hides in 1066.

[9] 280 hides in 1066.

[10] 270½ hides in 1066. All could have met at Mutlow Hill (Table 3, p.26, n.5 below).

[11] 260 hides in 1066. Corbett, 'Tribal Hidage', 206, proposes a similar fourfold division based on units of 330 hides. *VCH Cambridgeshire*, i. 341, by contrast proposes a threefold division of the shire, which, if it had once been combined with Hunts. (see p.23, n.10 above), would produce a larger, quartered unit.

[12] Cottenham, Westwick and Histon amounted to 60 hides, the detachment of Dry Drayton and Childerley to 30, and the detachment of Chesterton also to 30 hides.

[13] It may have consisted of the odd pattern of four units of 15 hides, one of 10, two of 12 and one of 16, but the ICC for this hundred is fragmentary. See Hart, *Hidation of Cambridgeshire*, 24–5. It seems likely that the moot of 'Northstowe' Hundred was in Dry Drayton (Table 3, p.26, n.6 below), which, however, lay in Chesterton Hundred. A parallel to this is Foxley in Northants which named a hundred, but did not lie within it.

[14] Hart's reconstruction of the original hidation (*Hidation of Cambridgeshire*, 30–8) is a gigantic leap ahead of the evidence presently available. He asserts, for example, that the early halving of assessment dates from 942, when, according to the Anglo-Saxon Chronicle, King Edmund 'redeemed' the Five Boroughs, but the Five Boroughs did not include Cambridge, and his theory requires a much earlier date for the County Hidage than is usually accepted.

[15] Sawyer (ed.), *Anglo-Saxon Charters*, no. 779.

[16] The Isle of Ely Hundreds had no natural connection with Cambs. and in particular the area around Wisbech may well have once been more closely allied with Norfolk. Wisbech is described in the *Liber Eliensis* (144) as *quarta pars centuriatus insulae*, 'a quarter of the hundredal system of the Isle' and such 'ferdings' are found in the hundreds of Suffolk and Norfolk. Wisbech also appears to have had its own hundredal moot at a lost 'Modich' and was associated in the thirteenth century with Ely's Norfolk manors. See *VCH Cambridgeshire*, iv. 1–6; Miller, *Abbey and Bishopric of Ely*, 31–3; Blake (ed.), *Liber Eliensis*, *passim*.

to dominate and in some cases to name hundreds,[1] no such pattern seems very likely in Cambridgeshire. Although the king had important manors in half-a-dozen hundreds,[2] it is not clear whether any hundreds were appurtenances of particular manors, or whether (except in the case of the two hundreds of Ely) the lordship of the hundred belonged to an individual.[3] Cambridge Hundred was of course dominated by its borough, and Chesterton was named from a royal vill. A royal manor was among one of the holdings in Cheveley and the moot site of Fleamdyke Hundred lay in Fulbourn where the king had a manor. The exact location of some moot sites is unknown, but others lay in Domesday manors that in themselves appear to have had no particular importance.[4] By the fourteenth century, however, the lordship of all the hundreds, apart from the two Ely Hundreds and Cambridge borough, was in royal hands, while their extents (apart from Ely) seem to have remained the same. By this time the constituents of the two Ely Hundreds had been redistributed between three, known as the Isle of Ely, Witchford and Wisbech Hundreds.[5]

[1] Stenton, *Anglo-Saxon England*, 300–1.

[2] In Wessex, demesne manors of King Edward play an important part in the hundredal structure. In Cambs. the manors of King Edward are Soham, Fordham and Isleham in 'Staploe' Hundred; Cheveley which named Cheveley Hundred; Great Wilbraham in 'Staine' Hundred; Comberton and Haslingfield in 'Wetherley' Hundred; Kingston in Longstowe Hundred; and Chesterton which named Chesterton Hundred.

[3] On this, see H. M. Cam, *Liberties and Communities in Medieval England: Collected Studies in Local Administration and Topography* (Cambridge, 1944; repr. London, 1963), 64–90.

[4] See Table 3, p.26 below.

[5] See Table 3, p.26 below.

TABLE 2: Additional or discrepant place-name information from the Inquisitio Comitatus Cantabrigiensis

Domesday name and folio number	Modern form of Domesday name	Identification in ICC	Form adopted in this edition
Ichelintone, 190[1]	Ickleton	Litlington	Ickleton
Weslai, 190v	Westley Waterless	Burrough Green and Westley Waterless	Westley Waterless
Coeia, 190v	Quy (in Stow cum Quy)	Quy and Stow	Stow cum Quy
Harduic, 191v[2]	Hardwick	Toft	Hardwick
(Unnamed), 195v	(Unnamed holding of 4 hides)	Wilbraham	(Great Wilbraham)
(Unnamed), 195v	(Unnamed holding of 1 hide)	Quy and Stow	(Stow cum Quy)
Weslai, 195v	Westley Waterless	Burrough Green and Westley Waterless	Westley Waterless
Burch, 195v	Burrough Green	Burrough Green and Westley Waterless	Burrough Green
(Unnamed), 195v	(Unnamed holding of 1½ hides)	Weston Colville	(Weston Colville)
(Unnamed), 197v	(Unnamed holding of half a hide)	Burwell	(Burwell)
Weslai, 197v	Westley Waterless	Burrough Green and Westley Waterless	Westley Waterless
Inchelintone, 198 (second mention)[3]	Ickleton	Litlington	Ickleton
Wiborgham, 199v[2]	Little Wilbraham	Second holding separately named as Quy and Stow	Not separately identified
Coeia, 200[4]	Quy (in Stow cum Quy)	Quy and Stow	Stow cum Quy
Bertone, 201v	Barton	Comberton	Comberton[5]
Weslai, 202	Westley Waterless	Burrough Green and Westley Waterless	Westley Waterless

[1] The scribe may have misread *Lidlintone* as *Ichelintone*.

[2] Hardwick, Little Wilbraham: two holdings. In each case, the second holding is not separately named by DB, but is indicated only as *in eadem villa* ('in the same vill').

[3] The scribe may have misread *Litlingetona* as *Inchelintone*.

[4] Stow cum Quy: two holdings, the second not separately named by DB. It is indicated in DB only as *ibidem* ('in the same place').

[5] The Domesday form (*Bertone*), which points to Barton in the same hundred (entered directly after Comberton in ICC), is clearly an error for *Cumbertone* (Comberton).

TABLE 3: The Domesday Hundreds of Cambridgeshire, showing the places from which they were named, and their approximate relationship to the fourteenth-century hundreds

Modern Name and number on map	Place from which named, with NGR if known and if not indexed below	Approximate relationship to the hundreds of the fourteenth century[1]
'Arringford', XIV	Named from a ford on Ermine Street, possibly near Kneesworth (TL 3444)[2]	Continued as 'Arringford'
Cambridge, X	Domesday borough (royal)	Ceased to be regarded as a hundred; the town itself continued as a borough, and the lands of the former hundred became its dependencies
Chesterton, VI	Domesday manor (royal)	Continued as Chesterton
Cheveley, XIII	Domesday vill (the king/Count Alan)	Continued as Cheveley
Chilford, XVII	Named from a ford over the river Bourn (TL *c.*5547) in Linton parish[3]	Continued as Chilford
Ely, I-II	Domesday manor (Abbey of Ely)	Divided into three hundreds: Isle of Ely, Witchford, and Wisbech[4]
Fleamdyke, XI	Named from the Fleam Dyke (TL 5355–TL 5553)[5]	Continued as Fleamdyke
Longstowe, VIII	Domesday vill (Abbey of Ramsey/ Count Alan/Hardwin de Scales)	Continued as Longstowe
'Northstowe', V	Name lost, but the site was probably in or near Dry Drayton[6]	Continued as 'Northstowe'
Papworth, IV	Domesday vill of Papworth Everard/ Papworth St Agnes, partly in Hunts. in 1086; the Cambs. portion was divided between six tenants-in-chief	Continued as Papworth
'Radfield', XII	Name lost; the site was in Burrough Green and Dullingham parishes (TL 6355, TL 6357), near Westley Waterless[7]	Continued as 'Radfield'
'Staine', VII	Name lost, site unknown[8]	Continued as 'Staine'
'Staploe', III	Name lost; the site was in Burwell parish (TL 5866)[9]	Continued as 'Staploe'
Thriplow, XV	Domesday vill (Abbey of Ely/Geoffrey de Mandeville/Hardwin de Scales)[10]	Continued as Thriplow
'Wetherley', IX	Name lost, but the site was probably in Harlton parish (TL 3852)[11]	Continued as 'Wetherley'
Whittlesford, XVI	Domesday vill (Count Alan/Hardwin de Scales/Countess Judith)[12]	Continued as Whittlesford

[1] Information is derived from *Feudal Aids*, i, and Glasscock (ed.), *Lay Subsidy of 1334*.

[2] 'Arringford' shares a common first element with Arrington (TL 3250) which lay in the adjacent hundred of 'Wetherley'. 'Arringford' is the 'ford of the *Earningas*', the latter being a tribal name that may have denoted a considerable area. The most obvious fording place is on Ermine Street (now the A14 road), at what is now Arrington Bridge, by Wimpole Lodge (TL 3248), but that is exactly on the hundred boundary. A more likely site is near Kneesworth where Ermine Street crossed a tributary of the Cam. 'Arringford' had been granted in the tenth century to the Abbey of Ely with Melbourn (Sawyer (ed.), *Anglo-Saxon Charters*, nos. 776, 779) which is adjacent to Kneesworth. In later times at least, the moot was at 'Mutlow', now Mettle Hill (TL 3645) in Meldreth parish, adjacent to the boundary of Kneesworth parish. There was also a lost 'Mootelowfurlong' in the adjacent parish of Bassingbourn. See Reaney, *PNCambs.*, 50, 70; Anderson, *EHN*, 103; *VCH Cambridgeshire*, viii. 1.

[3] The name survives in Chilford Hall (TL 5648) and Little Chilfords (TL 5547) which do not stand at the moot site: this was at a ford between Linton and Little Linton; Reaney, *PNCambs.*, 99, 110; Anderson, *EHN*, 101; *VCH Cambridgeshire*, vi. 1.

[4] The Isle of Ely Hundred grouped together Ely, Littleport and Little Downham; Wisbech became a separate hundred, with six members listed in 1334 (Glasscock (ed.), *Lay Subsidy of 1334*, 28), none of them named in DB; Witchford Hundred, named from the place at which the two hundreds of Ely met in 1086 (f.191v), comprised the remaining places and was later itself divided (into the hundreds of North and South Witchford).

[5] On this stretch, the Dyke forms the boundary between Fleamdyke and 'Staine' Hundreds. The moot was possibly in Fulbourn beside the dyke at Mutlow Hill (OE *(ge)mot*, *hlaw*, 'moot-hill') where it crosses the Icknield Way (TL 5354). It is not central to the hundred and might once have been a joint meeting-place for Fleamdyke, 'Radfield' and 'Staine' Hundreds: Reaney, *PNCambs.*, 140; Anderson, *EHN*, 100.

[6] Reaney, *PNCambs.*, 176; Anderson, *EHN*, 105. Dry Drayton itself was a detached part of Chesterton Hundred in 1086 and later, but it is possible that these two interlaced hundreds were once combined: see p.24 above.

[7] It survived as a field-name until the nineteenth century: Reaney, *PNCambs.*, 113, 120; Anderson, *EHN*, 101; *VCH Cambridgeshire*, vi. 125. On the possible hundred of Westley, see p.20 above.

[8] Reaney, *PNCambs.*, 129, 138; Anderson, *EHN*, 99.

[9] It probably lay in the east of the parish, towards Exning: Reaney, *PNCambs.*, 187; Anderson, *EHN*, 98.

[10] There was formerly a 'Motlowe' in Newton parish near Thriplow, which may represent the moot site: Reaney, *PNCambs.*, 82; *VCH Cambridgeshire*, viii. 152.

[11] It lay near May Pole Farm (TL 368515) in Harlton parish: *VCH Cambridgeshire*, v. 137; see Reaney, *PNCambs.*, 69; Anderson, *EHN*, 104.

[12] Lost places called 'Muttlow Moor' in Whittlesford parish and 'Mitlowedene' in Duxford parish probably represent the moot site, which may have been on the border of the two parishes: Reaney, *PNCambs.*, 92; *VCH Cambridgeshire*, vi. 199.

BIBLIOGRAPHY

INDICES

TO THE DOMESDAY FOLIOS

BIBLIOGRAPHY

The following bibliography, arranged in date order, is derived by kind permission from D. Bates, *A Bibliography of Domesday Book*, published by Boydell and Brewer Ltd. for the Royal Historical Society, 1986. Dr Bates has added certain entries to this county list in order to update it, and to include appropriate references which are cited in the 'General Studies' section of his original work.

CAMBRIDGESHIRE

1. H. Ellis (ed.), *Libri Censualis, vocati Domesday Book, Additamenta ex. Codic. Antiquiss. Exon Domesday; Inquisitio Eliensis; Liber Winton; Boldon Book* (London, 1816). The edition of Inquisitio Eliensis, like that in 3, was based on what is now regarded as an inferior MS, Trinity College, Cambridge MS o.2.1, instead of the better Trinity College, Cambridge MS o.2.41.
2. H. James (director), *Domesday Book: or the Great Survey of England of William the Conqueror, A.D. MLXXXVI. Facsimile of the Part Relating to Cambridgeshire.* Photozincographed by Her Majesty's Command at the Ordnance Survey Office, Southampton (Southampton, 1862).
3. N. E. S. A. Hamilton (ed.), *Inquisitio Comitatus Cantabrigiensis . . . Subjicitur Inquisitio Eliensis* (London, 1876). For a translation, see 24.
4. B. Walker, 'On the Measurements and Valuations of the Domesday of Cambridgeshire', *Communications of the Cambridge Ant. Soc.* 5 (1884), 93–129 and supplement.
5. B. Walker, 'On the *Inquisitio Comitatus Cantabrigiensis*', *Communications of the Cambridge Ant. Soc.* 6, no. 1 (1887), 45–64. Provides a tabulation of comparative hidation in Inquisitio Comitatus Cantabrigiensis and DB of the holdings of bordars and cottars.
6. J. H. Round, 'Ely and her Despoilers (1072–75)', *Feudal England* (London, 1895; 2nd edn., 1964), 459–61 (1st edn.), 349–50 (2nd edn.).
7. H. Barber, 'Place-Names of East Anglia', *East Anglian*, ns 6 (1895–6), 65–9, 93–5, 124–7, 196–9, 237–40, 281–5; ns 7 (1897–8), 9–11, 29–31, 41–4, 52–5, 157–60, 181–4, 204–6. Included little more than the DB names.
8. F. W. Maitland, *Township and Borough* (Cambridge, 1898; repr. 1964). Relates to Cambridge.
9. F. H. Baring, 'The Hidation of Some Southern Counties', *EHR* 14 (1899), 290–9. See further 40.
10. N. Neilson, *Economic Conditions on the Manors of Ramsey Abbey* (Philadelphia, 1899).
11. W. W. Skeat, *The Place-Names of Cambridgeshire* (London, 1901; 2nd edn., 1911). Selective. Superseded by 26.
12. L. Guilloreau, 'Les Possessions des Abbayes Mancelles et Angevines en Angleterre d'après le Domesday Book', *Revue Historique et Archéologique du Maine*, 60 (1906), 5–23.
13. C. H. and H. G. Evelyn-White, *The Cambridgeshire Portion of the Great Survey of England* (London, Norwich, Cambridge, 1910). Reprinted from *East Anglian*, ns 11 (1905–6), 65–71, 92–5, 110–11, 116–19, 134–7, 150–3, 174–5, 180–1, 204–5, 218–19, 232–5, 248–51, 262–5, 282–5, 292–5, 314–17, 328–33, 342–7, 362–5, 380–5; ns 12 (1907–8), 4–9, 26–9, 40–5, 58–61, 74–7, 84–7, 100–3, 120–3, 140–1, 150–1, 170–3, 188–91, 206–7, 220–1, 236–7, 248–9, 272–5, 286–9, 318–19, 328–9, 346–9. Gives a text with abbreviations extended and a translation which is not entirely reliable.
14. D. Stokes, 'The Old Mills of Cambridge', *Proc. of the Cambridge Ant. Soc.* 14 (1910), 180–233. See pp.181–3 for the DB mills.
15. W. Farrer, *Feudal Cambridgeshire* (Cambridge, 1920). Important for Cambs. DB manors and their descent.
16. A. Gray, *The Town of Cambridge: a History* (Cambridge, 1925). See Ch. 4 for DB Cambridge.
17. G. H. Fowler, 'An Early Cambridgeshire Feodary', *EHR* 46 (1931), 442–3.
18. G. H. Fowler, 'Fenland Waterways, Past and Present. South Level District. Part 1', *Proc. of the Cambridge Ant. Soc.* 33 (1931–2), 108–28. See Appendix IV for the fisheries of Cambs. DB.
19. H. M. Cam, 'The Origin of the Borough of Cambridge', *Proc. of the Cambridge Ant. Soc.* 35 (1933–4), 33–53. Reprinted in H. M. Cam, *Liberties and Communities in Medieval England: Collected Studies in Local Administration and Topography* (Cambridge, 1944; repr. London, 1963), 1–18.
20. F. M. Page, *The Estates of Crowland Abbey* (Cambridge, 1934). For DB estates in five counties. See also 43.
21. H. C. Darby, 'The Domesday Geography of Cambridgeshire', *Proc. of the Cambridge Ant. Soc.* 36 (1934–5), 35–57.
22. L. F. Salzman, 'Introduction to the Cambridgeshire Domesday', *VCH Cambridgeshire and the Isle of Ely*, ed. L. F. Salzman, i (London, 1938), 335–57.
23. J. Otway-Ruthven, 'Translation of the Text of Cambridgeshire Domesday', ibid. 358–99.
24. J. Otway-Ruthven, 'Translation of *Inquisitio Comitatus Cantabrigiensis*', ibid. 400–27.
25. H. C. Darby, *The Medieval Fenland* (Cambridge, 1940; repr. Newton Abbot, 1974).
26. P. H. Reaney, *The Place-Names of Cambridgeshire and the Isle of Ely*, EPNS 19 (Cambridge, 1943).
27. H. C. Darby, 'Domesday Cambridgeshire', *VCH Cambridgeshire and the Isle of Ely*, ii (London, 1948), 49–58. An abbreviation of 21 with maps of population, mills, woodland, etc.
28. B. Dodwell, 'East Anglian Commendation', *EHR* 63 (1948), 289–306.
29. R. S. Hoyt, *The Royal Demesne in English Constitutional History, 1066–1272* (Cornell, 1950). Has a valuable appendix on the geld exemption of manorial demesne and *Terra Regis* in Cambs.
30. E. Miller, *The Abbey and Bishopric of Ely* (Cambridge, 1951).
31. H. C. Darby, *The Domesday Geography of Eastern England* (Cambridge, 1952; 2nd edn., 1957; 3rd edn., 1971). Changes in later editions, though small, should be taken note of.
32. J. A. Raftis, *The Estates of Ramsey Abbey* (Toronto, 1957).
33. R. Welldon Finn, 'Some Reflections on the Cambridgeshire Domesday', *Proc. of the Cambridge Ant. Soc.* 53 (1959), 29–38. Mostly devoted to the transfer of estates from English to Normans.
34. E. O. Blake (ed.), *Liber Eliensis*, Camden Soc. 3rd ser., 92, R. Hist. Soc. (London, 1962). See pp.419–32 for the Abbey of Ely's estates in this and six other counties.
35. M. Spufford, *A Cambridgeshire Community: Chippenham from Settlement to Enclosure*, Dept. of Eng. Local Hist. Occasional Papers, 20 (Leicester, 1965).

36. C. R. Hart, *The Early Charters of Eastern England* (Leicester, 1966). For the DB estates of Thorkil of Harringworth in five counties.

37. E. Miller, 'Some Twelfth-Century Documents concerning St Peter's Church at Babraham', *Proc. of the Cambridge Ant. Soc.* 59 (1966), 113–23. Second part of the article is mainly devoted to DB Babraham and its tenants.

38. C. Taylor, *The Cambridgeshire Landscape* (London, 1973).

39. C. R. Hart, 'Hereward "the Wake"', *Proc. of the Cambridge Ant. Soc.* 65 (1974), 28–40. For well-known material on Hereward's DB lands and for the holdings of Thorkil of Harringworth in five counties.

40. C. R. Hart, *The Hidation of Cambridgeshire*, Dept. of Eng. Local Hist. Occasional Papers, 2nd ser., 6 (Leicester, 1974). Of fundamental importance for the structure of Cambs. DB. Discussion bears on wider questions about the making of DB.

41. A. E. B. Owen, 'Medieval Saltmaking and the Coastline in Cambridgeshire and North-West Norfolk', *Salt: the Study of an Ancient Industry*, eds. K. W. de Brisay and K. A. Evans (Colchester, 1975), 42–4.

42. H. C. Darby, *Medieval Cambridgeshire* (Cambridge, 1977).

43. S. Raban, *The Estates of Thorney and Crowland. A Study in Medieval Monastic Land Tenure*, Univ. of Cambridge Dept. of Land Economy Occasional Paper 7 (Cambridge, 1977).

44. A. Rumble (ed., from a draft translation by J. Fellows and S. Keynes), *Domesday Book: Cambridgeshire* (Chichester, 1981). Contains text, translation, valuable notes and the names of the hundred-juries from Inquisitio Comitatus Cantabrigiensis and Inquisitio Eliensis. Also comparisons with and discussion of Inquisitio Comitatus Cantabrigiensis and Inquisitio Eliensis.

45. A. E. B. Owen, 'A Fenland Frontier: The Establishment of the Boundary between Cambridgeshire and Lincolnshire', *Landscape Hist.* 4 (1982), 41–6.

The following volumes are those of the Alecto County Edition of Domesday Book which have been published to date. Included for convenience are the names of the authors who have contributed the 'Introductions' to each volume. All the articles on 'Hundreds and Wapentakes' are by F. R. Thorn.

1. A. Williams and R. W. H. Erskine (eds.), *The Northamptonshire and Rutland Domesday* (London, 1987).

D. N. Hall, 'An Introduction to the Northamptonshire Domesday', ibid.

T. D. Cain, 'An Introduction to the Rutland Domesday', ibid.

2. A. Williams and R. W. H. Erskine (eds.), *The Berkshire Domesday* (London, 1988).

N. A. Hooper, 'An Introduction to the Berkshire Domesday', ibid.

3. A. Williams and R. W. H. Erskine (eds.), *The Buckinghamshire Domesday* (London, 1988).

J. Bradbury, 'An Introduction to the Buckinghamshire Domesday', ibid.

4. A. Williams and R. W. H. Erskine (eds.), *The Cornwall Domesday* (London, 1988).

I. N. Soulsby, 'An Introduction to the Cornwall Domesday', ibid.

5. A. Williams and R. W. H. Erskine (eds.), *The Herefordshire Domesday* (London, 1988).

C. P. Lewis, 'An Introduction to the Herefordshire Domesday', ibid.

6. A. Williams and R. W. H. Erskine (eds.), *The Worcestershire Domesday* (London, 1988).

A. Williams, 'An Introduction to the Worcestershire Domesday', ibid.

7. A. Williams and R. W. H. Erskine (eds.), *The Gloucestershire Domesday* (London, 1989).

A. Williams, 'An Introduction to the Gloucestershire Domesday', ibid.

8. A. Williams and R. W. H. Erskine (eds.), *The Hampshire Domesday* (London, 1989).

B. J. Golding, 'An Introduction to the Hampshire Domesday', ibid.

9. A. Williams and R. W. H. Erskine (eds.), *The Huntingdonshire Domesday* (London, 1989).

D. R. Roffe, 'An Introduction to the Huntingdonshire Domesday', ibid.

10. A. Williams and R. W. H. Erskine (eds.), *The Somerset Domesday* (London, 1989).

G. A. Loud, 'An Introduction to the Somerset Domesday', ibid.

11. A. Williams and R. W. H. Erskine (eds.), *The Surrey Domesday* (London, 1989).

J. Blair, 'An Introduction to the Surrey Domesday', ibid.

12. A. Williams and R. W. H. Erskine (eds.), *The Wiltshire Domesday* (London, 1989).

N. A. Hooper, 'An Introduction to the Wiltshire Domesday', ibid.

INDEX OF PLACES

NOTES

In this edition, the place-names found in the translation, on the county map, and in the following Index of Places are all interrelated and have been established according to strict editorial policy. The central source for each of these three elements has been a specially compiled card-index containing a card for every mention of a place-name in Domesday Book: this index itself has been adjusted as research progressed. Thus the separate disciplines of identification, map-making, indexing, and rendering the Latin into readable English have all contributed to this compendium of Domesday place-names and to the manner of the presentation of each category. However, a word of caution is appropriate here, because the reader should be aware that the simple exchange of a Domesday name for even the most obvious modern equivalent does not necessarily mean that the original settlement lay precisely at that location, nor that it had a similar territorial form.

It is important to realize that the place-names of Domesday Book do not represent modern religious, social, administrative or agricultural units such as parishes, townships, villages, hamlets or farms, except by coincidence. They stand for estates or taxable units that may not in reality have been either independent or self-supporting. No bounds are given and these estates, depending on their size, may well have extended over more than one modern parish, be interlaced with other holdings, or possess a number of widely scattered members. Most Domesday estates will have contained several settlements, all of which had names in 1086, but which the survey leaves unnamed and whose statistics it engrosses with others. Frustratingly, Domesday says nothing that allows us to determine the centre, the extent, or the form of the estate.

Many Domesday estate-names will doubtless have been those actually current in the locality concerned; but others are 'book-names'—administrators' designations and often very general in scope—such as the name of a valley, hill, river or tract of land. These were probably known by more specific names on the ground, but Domesday Book does not record them. Especially where a vill is shown to have been in divided ownership in 1086, or where the Domesday unit is the fragment of some great multiple estate of pre-Conquest times, Domesday may well retain the 'charter' or 'book' name of its more extensive predecessor even though other evidence may indicate that a more precise appellation was almost certainly in use at the time.

The Domesday name may now be represented by a parish name, or by that of a township, hamlet or isolated farm. It may no longer survive as a settlement-name at all, but only as that of a river, wood, hill, road or bridge. The name may even have become lost before it appeared on any map; and finally it may have escaped identification altogether, either because the place designated scarcely survived the eleventh century or because the form in which Domesday transmits the place-name is corrupt and so far unintelligible.

A Domesday place can only be considered to be satisfactorily identified when the proposed name has passed a number of tests. Is the evolution of the 1086 name-form to the suggested modern equivalent philologically acceptable? Does it lie in the hundred indicated or implied by the text, or reconstructed from it? Do the details of land, equipment, resources and industry given by the entry in Domesday Book accord with what could have been practicable within the proposed area? Can the estate be identified among the possessions of the 1086 holder's heir or successors in later centuries? In practice, by no means all published identifications satisfy these requirements and the accuracy and reliability of identifications varies considerably from county to county. Much depends on the quality of the work of the eighteenth- and nineteenth-century 'antiquarian' pioneers and of the sections on Domesday in the relevant volume of the *Victoria County Histories*. The standard of more recent work, the existence of a county volume among the publications of the English Place-Name Society, or of 'topographical' volumes from the *Victoria County History* make the identifications of some counties more secure than those of others. The evidence so gathered will have been reviewed for H.C. Darby's monumental series on Domesday Geography (1952–77) and for the Phillimore edition of Domesday Book (1975–86), but with varying thoroughness. For the present publication, it has been impractical to re-examine every item of this complex and widely scattered evidence afresh, but in cases where modern published identifications conflict or where there are other obvious reasons for doubt, the evidence has been rescrutinized.

In the following Index of Places, a system of square-bracketed editorial additions and of single or double inverted commas imply varying degrees of certainty in identification, and are set out in the key below. A further key precedes the translation in this volume and contains the related conventions employed there. Among the symbols on the county map, of which this index is also the gazetteer, will be found a system of circles, complete, broken or interlinked, which serves the same function, besides a full treatment of the county and hundred-boundaries in 1086.

By far the greater part of the evidence for the identification of place-names is derived from Great Domesday Book itself. However, occasionally a holding was entered without its eleventh-century name, or the name given has been replaced by a later one, and where possible these have been supplied from the testimony of certain other documents that are directly related to the making of Domesday Book or to its use. Such documents deemed admissible as evidence in this context are, for example, the Exon Book for the south-western counties, Evesham A for Worcestershire, and the Herefordshire Domesday. In this volume the two sources accepted for identification other than the Domesday folios are the Inquistio Comitatus Cantabrigiensis and the Inquisitio Eliensis.

F.R.Thorn

GENERAL

1. Scope of Index

The Index refers to all place-names found in the text written at the time of the compilation of Great Domesday Book, 1086–7, including all contemporary corrections, notes and additions in the margins. Insertions added to the MS in medieval and later times are not indexed, but identifications are incorporated which have been assisted by the evidence of any secondary documents that might exist as indicated in the introduction to these notes above.

Only references to the folios and translation supplied with this volume are indexed. A section listing any named holdings in this county which are recorded in the folios of other shires will be found on the associated county map.

2. Use of suprascript numbers

Where a place-name occurs more than once on a folio, its incidence is indicated by a suprascript number.

Note that occasionally a named entry can be followed immediately by further reference(s) to the same vill, usually designated by terms such as *ibi*, 'there'; *ibidem*, 'in the same place'; *in eadem villa*, 'in the same vill'. Such entries are not indexed as the place-name itself is absent.

3. Use of "..."

Double inverted commas indicate a name found only in Domesday Book and for which there is no known later equivalent, or of which the form may be corrupt. The name so enclosed is printed in Roman type.

4. Use of '...'

Single inverted commas indicate the latest or most typical known form of a name which remained in use beyond the eleventh century, but which either has not survived into modern times at all, or which only appears on twentieth-century maps as the name of a feature such as a river, hill, wood etc., rather than a place of habitation. This also applies to names without a continuous history and which have only recently been revived for antiquarian reasons.

MODERN PLACE-NAMES (ROMAN TYPE)

5. Authority

The modern place-names are consistent with those marked on the particular 1:100,000 Ordnance Survey grey base-map employed as the background for each associated county map. Note that place-names can vary from edition to edition of OS maps and their absence from this particular map does not mean they are necessarily lost.

6. Modern counties

Throughout this edition the county-boundaries are regarded as those that existed prior to the restructuring of the counties in 1974.

7. National Grid Reference

Four-figure National Grid References are given for modern place-names which represent settlements recorded in Domesday Book. Note that these NGRs do not necessarily pin-point the precise location of such settlements in 1086 for the reasons set out in the introduction to these notes above.

8. Common prefixes and suffixes: Great, Little, etc.

Modern places which are distinguished by common prefixes such as Old, Great and Little, Upper, Middle and Lower, Nether and Over, East and West, North and South have their main entry indexed under the relevant place-names, in the same way as those with distinguishing suffixes such as All Saints, St Andrews and Abbots.

9. Use of 'or', 'and'

Where a place is designated by two or more prefixes or suffixes and linked by 'or', e.g. Great or Little, All Saints or St Andrew, it is uncertain which of these two modern places represents the holding in question or whether both did so. Where prefixes are linked by 'and', e.g. East and West, St Peter and St Martin, the inference is that both modern places lie within the territory of a single estate of 1086.

10. Use of 'in', 'near'

In the event of two or more places in one county having the same name, they are distinguished by the addition of the parish-names in square brackets, e.g. [in Compton]. The only exception is when the parish- and place-name are the same, or where the place-name forms part of the parish-name. In these cases one will be followed by the parish-name, [in Compton], while the other will be related to a prominent nearby town or feature, [near Wallingford].

11. Choice of representative names distinguished by affixes

In a given locality a single place-name in Domesday Book may now be represented by a number of variant names distinguished by different prefixes or suffixes. Where a major derivative name signifying a village or hamlet still exists, such as Great, Little, Higher, Lower, St Mary, St Peter, this is preferred to minor or dependent variant names, such as Park, Moor, Gate, Green, Manor. Similarly minor settlement-names, where only they survive, are preferred to non-settlement names such as those of fields, hills, woods, streams, marshes.

Where the name in Domesday Book is represented on modern maps only by the name of a minor feature, the principal element alone is used in the index and in the translation, so that Weston Farm, Lodge, Hall, Bridge, Wood etc., appear only as Weston.

12. Places now 'lost'

A number of places named in Domesday Book either no longer exist as distinct settlements or have disappeared altogether due to urban development, inundation by reservoirs, coastal erosion, rural depopulation, and other causes. These 'lost' places are treated variously, both in the translation and in this index, according to the circumstances that have caused them to disappear.

a. Places which have been absorbed into an area of urban development, but have given their name to a distinct suburb or district. These are designated as 'in' the relevant town or city which is enclosed in square brackets, e.g. Knowle [in Bristol].

b. Places absorbed into urban development, as above, but of which the name has not survived as that of a distinct suburb or district. These are designated as 'in' the relevant town or city in square brackets, also as above, but the place-name is enclosed within single inverted commas, e.g. 'Tessall' [in Birmingham].

c. Places now lost underwater have their names enclosed in single inverted commas and are followed by an indication of their former whereabouts in square brackets if known, e.g. 'Syndercombe' [in Clatworthy Reservoir].

d. Names of places lost in rural areas are enclosed in single or double inverted commas as set out in 3 and 4 above. However, they may also be designated as being 'in' the parish to which they belonged when this is known. e.g. "Sortelai" [in Quainton], 'Ashden' [in Compton].

e. Those lost places which can be reliably located have been plotted on the accompanying county map. Those which can only be approximately located are included in the Index and the translation but are not mapped.

13. Use of names other than Domesday derivatives

All modern names used in this edition are derived from those of 1086 with only the following exceptions:

a. Where the name of the Domesday Book estate has been entirely superseded by a more recent name that covers the same extent, e.g. Reigate (Surrey) for 'Churchfield'; Padstow (Corn.) for *Lanwenehoc*.

b. Where the later name of the Domesday Book estate is derived from the TRE or TRW holder or his title, e.g. Dodington (Som.) for 'Stowey'; Bishopstone (Herefs.) for 'Mansell'.

c. Where it is now possible to identify places which were sited along the banks of a river and which bear only the river name in Domesday Book, as with many settlements on the Ottery (Devon) and the Piddle (Dorset).

d. Where the holding is unnamed in Domesday Book, but its name can be reliably established from any other contemporary documents, such as those mentioned in the introduction to these notes above.

PLACE-NAMES IN DOMESDAY BOOK *(ITALIC TYPE)*

14. Variant forms

All variant forms found in these county folios of Domesday Book are indexed.

15. Abbreviation

Place-names that are specifically shortened in the MS with abbreviation-marks are given in their extended form.

16. Use of *u, v, w*

Since *u* and *v* are used indiscriminately in this MS, as in others of the period, they are here transposed to be closest to the modern spelling of the place-names. Double-*u* (*uu*) is always transposed as *w*, except in names enclosed in double inverted commas (see 3 above) where the scribe's original orthography is maintained.

17. Use of hyphenated endings

Where the spelling of a name varies only by the addition of a final letter or letters, the shorter version is given followed by the variant ending after a hyphen. Thus *Evelai*, *Evelaia* appears as *Evelai-a*; *Heiford*, *Heiforde* as *Heiford-e*; *Winewic*, *Winewiche* as *Winewic-he*.

OTHER

18. Page and folio references

References to the pages of editorial matter in this volume are printed in **bold**, and are followed by the references to the folio numbers of the facsimile and the translation, which are identical for both.

19. Recto and Verso

Folio numbers without suffix indicate the *recto* of the folio, while suffix 'v' indicates the *verso*.

20. Use of ‡

A double-dagger ‡ before a main entry refers to the errata section printed at the end of these indices, if such is required.

CAMBRIDGESHIRE

EDITOR'S NOTE

A few Cambridgeshire holdings which are not named in Domesday Book can be identified from the Inquisitio Comitatus Cantabrigiensis, see F. R. Thorn, 'Hundreds and Wapentakes' p.20 *passim* and p.25, Table 2 above; and R. E. Glasscock, 'An Introduction to the Cambridgeshire Domesday', pp.3–5 above. Their modern names are therefore supplied in square brackets in the translation, e.g. [Burwell] on f.197v, and the relevant folio numbers are included in this index.

INDEX OF PERSONS AND ECCLESIASTICAL BODIES

NOTES

1. TRE, TRW

Most of the entries in Domesday Book record two distinct categories of landholder: those English or Anglo-Scandinavian owners who held land before the Conquest (TRE, *tempore regis Edwardi*, 'in the time of King Edward'), and those who dispossessed them after 1066 (TRW, *tempore regis Willelmi*, 'in the time of King William')—or more particularly twenty years later at the time of the Conqueror's survey. It is usual for the Church to maintain continuity of ownership throughout both periods, but it is rare for an individual to do so. Since Domesday Book is a description of the situation at the time of its compilation in 1086–7, the circumstances obtaining TRE are invariably entered in the past tense, TRW in the present.

2. Use of * †

Prefixed asterisks * indicate references to the names of English or Anglo-Scandinavian landholders or churches mentioned only in a TRE context. Daggers † signify those which are stated to have continued their tenancy from the TRE to the TRW period. Names found only TRW have no prefixed symbol.

3. The Kings

The references to King Edward and to King William are divided for convenience into categories which encompass various aspects of kingship. The references to King Edward implied by the abbreviation TRE are not indexed. Where the text shows that someone in the TRE period *tenuit de rege Edwardo*, 'held of King Edward', the references are indexed under the category of King Edward 'as lord'.

References to the equivalent TRW phrase *tenet de rege*, 'holds of the king', are not indexed as it was not used systematically and was anyway superfluous because in feudal theory current after the Conquest all land was technically held of the king.

4. Abbeys and Churches

The terms *Abbatia*, 'Abbey', and *Æcclesia*, 'Church' are sometimes used interchangeably in Domesday Book for large monastic institutions. In this index, irrespective of the text, 'Abbey' is always used for the Benedictine houses, both in England and on the continent, while 'Church' is reserved for secular houses, i.e. colleges of priests, non-monastic bishoprics, minsters, etc. Only churches recorded as owning land are indexed here.

5. Personal Names TRE

All TRE names are standardized in accordance with O. von Feilitzen, *The Pre-Conquest Personal Names of Domesday Book* (Uppsala, 1937) with the following exceptions: Alfred, Edgar, Edith, Edmund, Edward, Edwin, Harold, Morcar, Siward, Stigand, Swein and Waltheof.

Old English forms are used in preference to Scandinavian variants. When no Old English form is attested, names are standardized first to their Anglo-Scandinavian, then to their Old Danish, Old Swedish, and finally Old Norse forms.

6. Personal Names TRW

There is no authority equivalent to von Feilitzen for TRW names, and their transposition into modern forms by individual historians has seldom been consistent. For this edition the editors have retained what they perceive to have become the 'accepted' forms of certain names despite inconsistencies. Thus, for example, *Albertus Lotharingensis* becomes Albert of Lorraine, not the Lotharingian, whilst *Walterius Flandrensis* remains Walter the Fleming, not of Flanders, in the style used for most non-Norman continentals. However, a policy of standardization has been established for the aspects of nomenclature which follow.

Modern anglicized forms of Christian names are preferred, e.g. Gilbert for *Giselbertus*, Geoffrey for *Goisfridus*, Hugh for *Hugo*, Ralph for *Radulfus*.

Continental and English toponymics appear in the modern form of the place-name e.g. Robert d'Oilly not *Robert de Oilgi*, Roger of Westerham not *Roger de Oisteram*. As in these examples, 'de' is used for continental places of origin, 'of' for English names.

Continental patronymics are expressed with the prefix 'fitz', e.g. Hugh fitzBaldric. The equivalent English or Anglo-Scandinavian names are expressed as 'son of', e.g. Swein son of Azur. This rule is also applied to patronymics in TRE names.

Ambiguous TRW personal names which are attested in both Anglo-Scandinavian and Continental sources are given their Continental forms unless the manuscript specifically identifies any person so named as English.

TRW names with obscure Latin forms or with no modern equivalent appear in the Index as they do in the manuscript, but without the *-us* ending, e.g. Otbert for *Otbertus*, Winemar for *Winemarus*.

7. Titles

Main entries are indexed under the toponymic, and the personal name(s), where known, are supplied in square brackets, e.g. Mortain, [Robert], Count of; Coutances, [Geoffrey de Mowbray], Bishop of. If these name(s) occur explicitly in the folios of this country, the square brackets are left off.

8. Occupational Names

Examples: Alwine the huntsman, Gilbert the cook, Regenbald the priest. Although Domesday Book describes many of these persons with other descriptive suffixes—for instance Regenbald occurs variously in different counties as 'the priest', 'the chaplain', 'the king's chaplain', and 'of Cirencester'—only that or those which occur in the folios of this particular county are listed here.

9. Cross-indexing

All patronymics, non-titular toponymics, rank-names, bynames and occupational names are cross-indexed with the main entry under the Christian name. Examples:

Main Entry	Cross-reference
Eudo fitzHubert	Hubert, *see* Eudo fitzHubert
Alvred of Lincoln	Lincoln, *see* Alvred of Lincoln
Leofwine Cild	Cild, *see* Leofwine Cild
Alwine Cobbold	Cobbold, *see* Alwine Cobbold
Gilbert the cook	cook, *see* Gilbert the cook

In the case of Abbeys, main entries will be found under the place-name with the dedication cross-indexed: Ramsey, Abbey of St Benedict (main entry); St Benedict, Ramsey, Abbey of.

Secular churches are indexed under Church with a cross-reference to the dedication, and also to the place-name: Church of Saint-Remy of Rheims (main entry); Saint-Remy of Rheims, Church of; Rheims, Church of Saint-Remy of.

10. Folio References

Only one reference to a name is indexed per folio. The frequent use of *idem*, 'the same man', is not indexed as the name itself is not present. References are linked by a hyphen when the consecutive entries for a holder's fief cover more than one folio.

Folio numbers without suffix indicate the recto of the folio, while suffix 'v' indicates the verso.

CAMBRIDGESHIRE

TRANSLATION

TRANSLATION

NOTES TO THE TRANSLATION

SOURCE AND STANDARDIZATION

The translations in the County Edition of Domesday Book are based in the main upon those that appear in the *Victoria Histories of the Counties of England*, of which publication commenced in 1900 and is still in progress. The translator of the relevant county folios of Domesday Book in volume one of *VCH Cambridgeshire* (1938) was Jocelyn Otway-Ruthven. Alecto Historical Editions are grateful to the publishers of *VCH* for permission to make use of this translation.

In order that the translations contained in each of the county volumes can be served by a common system of indices, the text of all sources has been standardized so that place- and personal names as well as technical terms and certain common phrases are consistent throughout. The opportunity has also been taken to correct such errors as may have become apparent as a result of subsequent research.

For a detailed statement of the policies governing the treatment of names, see the notes which precede the 'Index of Places' and the 'Index of Persons and Ecclesiastical Bodies' above.

METHODS OF RELATING THE TRANSLATION TO THE FACSIMILE

Throughout the folios of Great Domesday Book there is considerable variation in the number of lines written per page, in the depth and width of the columns, and in the spaces that separate the numbered chapters. In order to assist the use of the facsimile and this translation together, the type-size and the lay-out of the pages of the translation have been designed to match the configuration of the MS text as closely as possible.

The MS was foliated in the seventeenth century on only the *recto* side of each page. In the translation the *verso* is also foliated with the number followed by v.

● to the left, within the column, signifies the presence of one of the larger rubricated initial letters that commonly begin each entry. This device is provided to enable the reader more easily to relate passages in the translation to those in the facsimile by counting the spots on the former against the more prominent initials in the latter.

Typography

Roman type is reserved for the original text of Great Domesday, including all corrections and marginal additions made to the MS at the time of its compilation in the late eleventh century.

Italic type is used for all matter added subsequently during the Middle Ages and up to recent times.

The use of upper and lower case is the same as in the MS:

FULL CAPITALS represent the large rustic capitals used for county- and chapter-headings, which are all written in red.

Large and Small Capitals represent matter written in black rustic capitals within the text and usually through-lined in red. Those not written in capitals, whether intentionally or in error, are here transposed in lower case.

MARGINALIA

The translations of those passages entirely written in the margin are printed as close as is possible to the position they occupy in the MS, in smaller type where necessary. A complete key to the system of symbols employed here for the marginal notes and signs found in the MS, such as § for the transposition signs, M, B, S, etc. preceding ● in certain counties, and [1], [2], [3], □, ⬚, ☒, etc., is given in Appendix I, 'The Marginalia of Great Domesday Book', in the associated *Domesday Book Studies* volume, pp. 160–2.

EDITORIAL CONVENTIONS

Square brackets are reserved for editorial insertions.

[*sic*] — indicates a scribal error in the MS, here reproduced in the translation. The only exception is incorrect chapter numbering.

[. . .] — signifies a gap in the MS text, either left blank by the scribe for an insertion to be added later, or as a result of erasure. Three full points within the brackets are the standard length in the translations regardless of the actual extent of the gap in the MS.

† 7 hides † — Daggers enclose the tentative translation of a passage, phrase or numeral which is obscure in the MS, owing either to slips of the pen, to unclear alteration by the scribe, or to the worn condition of the parchment.

7 hides — Underlining indicated words or passages marked for deletion in the MS: the same convention is followed in the translation where no correction has been added suprascript. In the latter case, only the corrected text is given.

|it is worth 12*s*.| — Bars within the text enclose the full extent of a passage of which part is written in the margin, where a note will be found to that effect in square brackets.

[?]Weston — The modern equivalent given for a Domesday place-name which is probable, but not certain.

[?Weston] — A place left unnamed in Domesday Book, but which can be tentatively identified from internal evidence or from the evidence of other related documents.

Weston [in Parishbrook] — Where a county contains two or more modern places with the same name, they are differentiated by indicating the parish 'in' which each of them lies.

Weston [near Oldborough] — In the above instance, when one of the place-names is the same or partially the same as the name of the parish in which it lies, giving the awkward Weston [in Weston], its situation is instead indicated as being 'near' a prominent town or feature.

[Great or Little] Weston — The use of 'or' indicates that it is uncertain which of two or more modern places now represent the Domesday place-name, or whether all did so.

[Great and Little] Weston — The use of 'and' indicates that two or more modern places lie within the territory of the same Domesday estate.

Weston [Oxon.] — County abbreviations indicate that a locality recorded in the folios of this county lies within the boundaries of another in modern times. Throughout this edition the modern county boundaries are taken to be those that obtained prior to the restructuring of the counties in 1974.

NOTES TO THE TRANSLATION

Use of Inverted Commas

"CELVERDESCOTE" Double inverted commas indicate a place-name found only in Domesday Book and for which there is no known later equivalent, or of which the form may be corrupt.

Hundred- and wapentake-names are similarly treated, but a typical form is used if there are variants.

'SCULTHORP' Single inverted commas indicate the latest or most typical known form of a name which remained in use beyond the eleventh century, but which either has not survived into modern times at all, or which only appears on twentieth-century maps as the name of a feature such as a river, hill, wood, etc., rather than as a place of habitation. This also applies to names without a continuous history and which have only recently been revived for antiquarian reasons.

Hundred- and wapentake-names which are antiquarian revivals are similarly treated. Single inverted commas also indicate such names derived from places which had disappeared before the compilation of the first OS one-inch maps in the early nineteenth century, either because they never were the names of inhabited communities, or because they had fallen into disuse by that time. In such cases the name-form adopted is the latest, most or a regularized form.

EDITOR'S NOTE

There are considerable discrepancies in the Cambridgeshire folios between the numbering of the initial list of tenants-in-chief on f.189 and that of the chapters in the body of the text. On f.196 the scribe unaccountably added the extra X to the five chapter-numbers inscribed there, making Chs. XV, XVI, XVII and XVIII in the list into XXV, XXVI, XXVII and XXVIII in the text. Over the page, he also misnumbered XIX, the land of Richard fitzGilbert, as XXV, and then left out altogether the chapter-numbers for Robert de Tosny and Robert Gernon (XX and XXI in the list). He then reverted to the previous numbering without the extra X, but as a result of these last two omissions all the subsequent numbering was out by two digits right up to the end of the Cambridgeshire section.

A further anomaly involved two chapters spread over ff.200–201v. In the list, the fief of Picot of Cambridge follows that of Peter de Valognes, while in the text Picot's holdings are enrolled first. In this case the scribe corrected the list by superscribing the letter 'a' above *Picot* and 'b' above *Petrus*; unnecessarily he also added 'c' over *Rannulf*, in the list (as spelled), which is in the correct position.

For the sake of simplicity these scribal errors are noticed here only and are not signalled by [*sic*] in this translation.

• THE BOROUGH of CAMBRIDGE was assessed as a single HUNDRED TRE. In this borough were and are 10 wards. In the first ward [were] 54 messuages; 2 of these are waste. In this first ward Count Alan has 5 burgesses paying nothing. The Count of Mortain has 3 messuages of the land of Iudichael, and there are 3 burgesses who paid 5*s.* $8\frac{1}{2}$*d.* TRE; now they pay nothing. Ralph de Baons-le-Comte has 3 burgesses paying nothing. Roger, the man of Bishop Remigius, [has] 3 burgesses paying nothing. Erchenger has 1 burgess [who] pays nothing. This same 1 ward was reckoned as 2 TRE, but 27 houses have been destroyed for the castle.

In the second ward were 48 messuages TRE; 2 of these are waste. Of these, 13 messuages render nothing; the remaining 32 render all the customs. Of these, Count Alan has 5 burgesses paying nothing, and 9 dwell on the lands of the English.

In the third ward were 41 messuages TRE. Of these, 11 are waste; the remaining 30 render all the customs.

In the fourth ward were 45 messuages TRE. Of these, 24 are waste; the remaining 21 render all the customs.

In the fifth ward were 50 messuages TRE. 1 of these is waste; all the others render their customs.

In the seventh ward were 37 messuages TRE. 3 Frenchmen have [. . .] 3 of these messuages but they pay nothing.

In the eighth ward were 37 messuages TRE. A certain priest holds 1 of these and pays nothing.

In the ninth ward were 32 messuages TRE. Of these, 3 are waste.

In the tenth ward were 29 messuages TRE. Of these, 6 are waste, yet they pay their dues.

• From the customs of this vill, £7 a year, and from land-rent £7 and 2 orae and 2*d.*

TRE the burgesses lent the sheriff their plough-teams 3 times a year; now they are demanded 9 times.

They provided neither cartage-dues nor carts TRE, which they now do because a custom has been imposed. They claim back from Picot the sheriff, however, the common pasture taken from them through and by him.

Picot himself has built 3 mills there, which have taken up the pasture and destroyed many houses and 1 mill of the Abbot of Ely and another of Count Alan. The mills themselves render £9 a year.

The same Picot had £8 and a riding-horse and the arms of 1 knight from the heriot of the lawmen.

Ælfric son of Godric, when he was sheriff, had 20*s.* heriot of 1 of these men.

• I KING WILLIAM
II The Bishop of Winchester
III The Bishop of Lincoln
IIII The Bishop of Rochester
V The Abbot of Ely
VI The Abbot of St Edmundsbury
VII The Abbot of Ramsey
VIII The Abbot of Thorney
VIIII The Abbot of Crowland
X The Abbot of Saint-Wandrille
XI The Abbess of Chatteris
XII The Count of Mortain
XIII Earl Roger
XIIII Count Alan
XV Count Eustace
XVI The canons of Bayeux
XVII Walter Giffard
XVIII William de Warenne
XIX Richard son of Count Gilbert
XX Robert de Tosny
XXI Robert Gernon
XXII Geoffrey de Mandeville
XXIII Gilbert de Ghent
XXIIII Gilbert fitzTurold
XXV Eudo the steward
XXVI Hardwin de Scales
XXVII Hugh de Bernieres
XXVIII Hugh de Port
XXVIIII Aubrey de Vere
XXX Eustace of Huntingdon
XXXI Guy de Raimbeaucourt
XXXII Peter de Valognes, b
XXXIII Picot of Cambridge, a
XXXIIII Ranulph brother of Ilger, c
XXXV John fitzWaleran
XXXVI William fitzAnsculf
XXXVII William de Keynes
XXXVIII Robert Fafiton
XXXVIIII David d'Argentan
XL Two of the king's carpenters
XLI Countess Judith
XLII Azelina wife of Ralph Taillebois
XLIII The wife of Boselin de Dives
XLIIII Erchenger the baker

THE LAND OF THE KING

IN 'STAPLOE' HUNDRED

• SOHAM, the king's manor, is assessed at $9\frac{1}{2}$ hides. There is land for 14 ploughs. There are 16 villans and 16 bordars with 12 ploughs. In demesne [are] 2 ploughs, and 4 slaves, and 2 mills [rendering] 24*s.* From the fisheries, 3,500 eels. [There is] meadow for 14 ploughs, [and] pasture for the livestock of the vill. There are 7 fishermen rendering to the king a gift of fish 3 times a year according to their ability. In all it renders £25 a year, assayed and weighed, and £13. 8*s.* 4*d.* by tale in blanch pennies for wheat, malt, honey and other minor customary dues. TRE it rendered £25 by tale and 3 days' farm in wheat, honey and malt and in everything else. King Edward always had this manor in demesne.

M • FORDHAM, a demesne vill of the king, is assessed at 5½ hides. There is land for 10 ploughs. In demesne [are] 2 ploughs, and there can be 4 more. There are 6 villans and 15 bordars with 15 acres with 4 ploughs. There is 1 slave, and 2 mills [render] 16*s.* and feed 2 pigs a year. [There is] meadow for 6 ploughs, [and] pasture for the livestock of the vill. It renders £10 assayed and weighed and £13. 8*s.* 4*d.* in blanch money for honey, wheat and malt; TRE it rendered £10 by tale, and 3 days' farm in honey, wheat and malt. King Edward always had this manor in demesne. In this vill a certain sokeman, Brunmann, holds 1 hide of the king's soke. TRE this man could give his land to whom he would, but yet he always provided cartage-due or 8*d.* in the king's service, and he paid amercements to the sheriff.

M • ISLEHAM, a demesne vill of the king, is assessed at 6 hides and 40 acres of land. There is land for 10 ploughs. In demesne are 2 [ploughs]; and 16 villans and 10 bordars with 8 ploughs. There are 3½ mills rendering 22*s.* 8*d.* and 1,250 eels, meadow for 10 ploughs, [and] pasture for the livestock of the vill. It renders £10 assayed and weighed and £13. 8*s.* 4*d.* in blanch money for honey, wheat and malt and other minor customary dues. King Edward always had this manor in demesne. In this manor were 4 sokemen of King Edward, and of this land they had 1 hide and 40 acres [and] could give and sell to whom they would, but they always provided cartage-due or 8*d.* in the king's service, and they paid their amercements to the sheriff.

In Cheveley Hundred

M • CHEVELEY, a demesne vill of the king, is assessed at 8 hides and 40 acres. There is land for 12 ploughs. In demesne are 2 [ploughs], and there can be a third. There are 12 villans and 7 bordars with 8 ploughs, and there can be a ninth. [There is] meadow for 1 plough, woodland for 20 pigs, [and] pasture for the livestock of the vill. It renders £10 assayed and weighed and £13. 8*s.* 4*d.* in blanch money, for honey, wheat and malt. TRE it rendered £15 by tale. King Edward always had this manor in demesne.

In 'Staine' Hundred

M • GREAT WILBRAHAM is a demesne vill of the king. There are 2 hides, and land for 8 ploughs. In demesne is 1 [plough], and there can be 3 more. There are 5 villans and 5 bordars with 5 ploughs. There are 2 slaves, and 1 mill [rendering] 10*s.*, and 2 orae from a toll. [There is] meadow for 8 ploughs. It renders £10 assayed and weighed and £13. 8*s.* 4*d.* in blanch money for honey, wheat and malt. The farm of King Edward was £14 by tale for all things pertaining to the farm. This manor was always in the king's demesne.

In 'Wetherley' Hundred

M • COMBERTON is a demesne vill of the king. There are 2½ hides. There is land for 5 ploughs. In demesne are 2 [ploughs], and there can be a third. There are 7 villans and 5 bordars with 2 ploughs. [There is] meadow for 2 ploughs. It renders 100*s.* by tale and rendered as much TRE. This land always belonged to the king's farm. With these 2 hides is half a virgate which a sokeman holds who was not there TRE; and it was then worth 2*s.*; now 12*d.* This man was under Earl Waltheof.

M • In HASLINGFIELD the king holds 7 hides and 1 virgate. There is land for 8 ploughs. In demesne are 2 [ploughs], and there can be a third. There are 11 villans and 9 bordars with 4 ploughs, and there can be a fifth. [There is] meadow for 3 ploughs. [There is] a wood to repair fences, and 2 slaves. It renders £10 assayed and weighed and £13. 8*s.* 4*d.* in blanch money by tale for honey, wheat and malt, and other customary dues. TRE it rendered £10 by tale and, as distinct from this, as much as was necessary in wheat, malt and honey. This land always belonged to the king's farm.

In Longstowe Hundred

• In KINGSTON the king holds 1 hide and 3 virgates. There is land for 2 ploughs. In demesne is 1 [plough]; and 1 villan and 3 bordars with 1 plough. There is 1 slave. It renders 40*s.* by tale; TRE it rendered 60*s.* This land always belonged to the king's farm.

In Chesterton Hundred

• CHESTERTON, a demesne vill of the king, is assessed at 30 hides. There is land for 16 ploughs. In demesne are 3 [ploughs], and there can be 9 more. There are 2 villans and 16 bordars and 6 cottars with 4 ploughs. The priest has 1 virgate of land. [There is] meadow for 8 ploughs. From the fen, 1,000 eels. It renders £15 assayed and weighed and £13. 8*s.* 4*d.* in blanch money for honey, wheat and malt and other customary dues. TRE it rendered £15 by tale and, as distinct from this, as much as was necessary in customary dues.

In Whittlesford Hundred. In Hinxton lies the wara of 1½ hides of the manor of Great Chesterford [Essex] and it is valued in Essex. Earl Ælfgar held this land.

In Cheveley Hundred

M • WOODDITTON was assessed at 10 hides TRE, and now at 1 hide. There is land for 16 ploughs. In demesne [are] 2 ploughs; and 7 villans and 3 bordars with 3 ploughs, and there can be 13 more. There are 3 slaves, pasture for the livestock of the vill, [and] woodland for 300 pigs. From the herbage of the vill, 6*s.* 8*d.* In all it is worth £12; when received, £15; and as much TRE. William de Noyers holds this manor at farm from the king. This manor belonged to the Church of St Æthelthryth of Ely TRE, but Archbishop Stigand took it away, the men of the hundred do not know how.

In 'Staploe' Hundred

• In EXNING [Suffolk] King William has 13½ hides. There is land for 34 ploughs. In demesne are 7 ploughs, and there can be 3 more. There are 35 villans and 34 bordars with 24 ploughs. There are 7 slaves, and 3 mills [rendering] 20*s.* and 7,000 eels, [and] meadow for 4 ploughs. In all it is worth £53; when Godric received it, £12; TRE £56. Eadgifu the Fair held this manor, and in this manor were 7 sokemen, men of the same Eadgifu, and they could depart without her leave but she herself had their soke, and each of them provided cartage-due or 8*d.* in the king's service or [gave] a pledge.

• In Soham King William has 6 hides and 40 acres in his return.

• In Fleamdyke Hundred. In Fulbourn Picot holds 26 sokemen who have 4 hides under the king's hand. There is land for 6 ploughs, and there are [6 ploughs], [and] meadow for the ploughs. They pay £8 a year assayed and weighed, and every year [provide] 12 horses and 12 watchmen if the king should come into the shire. If he should not come [they pay] 12*s.* 8*d.* TRE they rendered nothing to the sheriff but cartage-dues and escort-service, or 12*s.* 8*d.*, and the rest Picot has usurped in defiance of the king.

In Chilford Hundred

• In Babraham Picot holds half a hide and half a virgate from the king. This land pertains to Great Chesterford [Essex] and is valued there at 30*s.* in Essex. Wulfwine held this land under Earl Ælfgar, [and] could not depart nor sell it.

• In Great Abington Picot holds under the king's hand half a virgate, and a sokeman, Sagar, [holds] of him. It is worth 12*d.* Almær held this land TRE and could give and sell it. Aubrey de Vere usurped this in defiance of the king, and Picot proved his right to it against him. Of the livestock which Aubrey took from there he still retains 400 sheep, less 20, and a plough, as the men of the hundred bear witness.

In Thriplow Hundred

• In [?Great] Shelford Peter de Valognes holds 3 hides of the king's farm in Newport [Essex]. There is land for 4 ploughs. In demesne is 1 [plough], and there can be another; and 5 villans and 6 bordars have 2 ploughs. [There is] meadow for 4 ploughs. It renders £4 assayed and weighed and 20*s.* by tale. This land is a Berewick of Newport, but its wara pertains to Cambridge. Earl Harold held this land.

In 'Arringford' Hundred

• In Litlington William the chamberlain and Otto the goldsmith hold $4\frac{1}{2}$ hides and half a virgate from the king at farm. There is land for 10 ploughs. In demesne [are] 2 hides and 3 ploughs. There are 26 villans and 10 bordars with 7 ploughs. There are 6 slaves, meadow for 2 ploughs, [and] woodland for 30 pigs. In all it is and always was worth £22. Earl Ælfgar held this manor. The men of this manor paid wardpenny to the king's sheriff or did ward.

• In Abington Pigotts the king holds half a hide which pertains to Litlington. There is land for 1 plough, and there is [1 plough], and it is valued with the same manor.

• In Abington Pigotts Alwine Coc the beadle holds half a virgate from the king. There is land for half a plough, and there is [half a plough]. It is worth 5*s.*; TRE 10*s.* The same man held it TRE and could neither give nor sell it. It pertained to Ickleton.

In Papworth Hundred

• In Fen Drayton 2 sokemen hold half a hide from the king. There is land for 4 oxen, and meadow. It is and always was worth 2*s.* The same men themselves held and could give and sell it.

In Whittlesford Hundred. In Hinxton lies the wara of $1\frac{1}{2}$ hides of Great Chesterford [Essex] manor and it is valued in Essex. Earl Ælfgar held it.

Picot has under the king's hand 1 hide. 7 sokemen held this TRE and they could sell it.

II. THE LAND OF THE BISHOP OF WINCHESTER

In 'Arringford' Hundred

M • Walkelin, Bishop of Winchester, holds Steeple Morden. It is assessed at 8 hides. There is land for 16 ploughs. In demesne [are] 4 hides, and there are 5 ploughs; and 15 villans and 15 bordars with 11 ploughs. There are 11 slaves, and 1 mill rendering 16*d.* and 2 other mills rendering 32*d.*, meadow for 16 ploughs, [and] pasture for the livestock of the vill. In all it is worth £20; when received, £10; TRE £16. This manor pertains and pertained to the Church of St Peter of Winchester.

• In 'Clopton' [in Croydon] the same bishop holds $3\frac{1}{2}$ hides. There is land for 5 ploughs. In demesne [is] 1 hide and 3 virgates, and there is 1 plough. There are 6 villans and 5 bordars with 3 ploughs, and there can be a fourth. [There is] meadow for 5 ploughs, [and] pasture for the livestock of the vill. It is worth 60*s.*; when received, 40*s.*; TRE £4. This land pertained to the demesne of the Church of St Peter of Winchester.

• In Abington Pigotts Hugh holds $2\frac{1}{2}$ hides and half a virgate from Bishop Walkelin. There is land for 5 ploughs. In demesne [are] 3 ploughs; and 9 bordars, each with 5 acres, with 2 ploughs. [There is] meadow for 5 ploughs, and [rendering] 2*s.* It is worth £7; when received, £3; TRE £8. This manor pertained and pertains to the Church of St Peter of Winchester, and there a sokeman held half a virgate under Archbishop Stigand, and could depart without his leave.

• In Bassingbourn the same bishop holds 1 hide and $2\frac{1}{2}$ virgates. There is land for 3 ploughs. In demesne [is] 1 hide, and there is 1 plough. There is 1 villan and 4 bordars with 1 plough, and there can be another. There are 2 mills rendering 20*s.*, [and] meadow for 1 plough. It is worth 60*s.*; when received, 40*s.*; TRE 60*s.* This land pertained and pertains to the Church of St Peter of Winchester, and there was 1 sokeman, the man of Archbishop Stigand; he held half a virgate and could give and sell it.

III. THE LAND OF THE BISHOP OF LINCOLN

In Whittlesford Hundred

• The Bishop of Lincoln holds 2 hides in Hinxton, and Robert [holds] of him. There is land for 2 ploughs. There is 1 [plough], and there can be another. There are 2 villans and 2 bordars. [There is] meadow for 2 ploughs, and 1 mill rendering 8*s.* It is worth 40*s.*; when received, 20*s.*; TRE £4. Siward held this land from Earl Harold and could give it to whom he would.

In 'Northstowe' Hundred

• In Madingley Picot holds $1\frac{1}{2}$ virgates of land from Bishop Remigius. It is and was worth 5*s.*; TRE 10*s.* Blæcwine, the man of King Edward, held this land and could depart; but the soke remained with Bishop Wulfwig.

In Chesterton Hundred

M • Histon is assessed at $26\frac{1}{2}$ hides. This manor is 1 of the 12 demesne manors of the bishopric of Lincoln. Bishop Remigius holds there 17 hides, less 1 virgate. There is land for 13 ploughs. In demesne [are] 8 hides, and there are 2 ploughs, and there can be a third. There are 18 villans and 18 bordars with 9 ploughs, and there can be a tenth plough. There are 4 cottars and 4 slaves, meadow for 13 ploughs, [and] pasture for the livestock of the vill. In all it is worth £10; when received, £12; TRE £14.

• Of the 26½ hides, Picot holds 9 hides and 3 virgates from the bishop. There is land for 6 ploughs. In demesne [is] 1 plough, and there can be another. There are 10 villans and 19 cottars with 2 ploughs, and there can be another 2. [There is] meadow for 6 ploughs, [and] pasture for the livestock of the vill. It is worth £4; when received, £6; TRE £7. 9 sokemen held this land and could sell, but the soke remained with the bishop.

• In the same vill Bishop Remigius holds 1 hide and 1 virgate and 2 parts of a virgate. There is land for 1 plough, but there is no plough. There is 1 villan and
[1] 1 cottar, [and] meadow for 1 plough. It is worth 5*s.*; when received, 10*s.*; TRE 20*s.* Wulfwine, the man of the Abbot of Ely, held this land and rendered yearly a sester of honey. Bishop Remigius usurped this land in defiance of the abbot, as the hundred bears witness. Picot the sheriff holds it from the bishop.

• In Childerley Roger holds 3 hides from Bishop Remigius. There is land for 2½ ploughs. In demesne is 1 [plough]; and 1 villan and 5 bordars with 1 plough, and there can be half a plough [more]. There is 1 cottar and 3 slaves, [and] a wood for fences. It is worth 50*s.*; when received, 40*s.*; TRE 100*s.* Siward, the man of Earl Harold, held this manor and could sell it.

IIII. THE LAND OF THE BISHOP OF ROCHESTER

In 'Staploe' Hundred

• The Bishop of Rochester holds 1½ hides and 20 acres in Isleham under Archbishop Lanfranc. There is land for 3 ploughs. In demesne [is] 1 plough; and 11 villans with 2 ploughs. There is half a mill [rendering] 2*s.* 8*d.* and 300 eels, meadow for 3 ploughs, and 2,000 eels, [and] pasture for the livestock of the vill. It is and was worth 40*s.*; TRE 60*s.* Wulfwine, King Edward's huntsman, held half a hide and 20 acres of this land, and 12 sokemen, who could all give and sell, had 1 hide under Thurbert.

V. THE LAND OF THE ABBEY OF ELY

In 'Radfield' Hundred

M • The Abbot of Ely holds Stetchworth. He has there 8½ hides and half a virgate. There is land for 12 ploughs. In demesne [are] 3½ hides, and there are 3 ploughs, and there can be 2 more. There are 16 villans and 5 bordars with 6 ploughs, and there can be a seventh. There are 4 slaves, woodland for 260 pigs, [and] pasture for the livestock of the vill. All together it is worth £10; and as much when received; TRE £12. This land pertained and pertains to the demesne of the Church of Ely.

• In the same vill Hardwin de Scales holds 1 virgate of the abbot. There is land for 2 oxen. It was always worth 5*s.* Godwine held this land, but could not sell it. The Abbot of Ely has half a hide of meadow in demesne in the vill itself. Særic d'Auberville took 1½ virgates of the demesne farm of the Abbot of Ely from this manor, and put them in the manor of Saint-Wandrille, as the hundred bears witness.

• In Westley Waterless the abbot holds 3 hides. There is land for 5 ploughs. There are 2 [ploughs], and there can be 3 more. There are 4 villans and 5 bordars and 2 slaves, [and] meadow for 2 oxen. It is and was worth 10*s.*; TRE 100*s.* This land pertains and always pertained to the demesne of the Church of Ely, the hundred bearing witness.

M • The abbot himself holds West Wratting. There are 4½ hides. There is land for 7 ploughs. In demesne [are] 3 hides, and there are 2 ploughs, and there can be 2 more. There are 6 villans and 3 bordars with 3 ploughs. There are 3 slaves, and meadow for 1 plough, woodland for 20 pigs, [and] pasture for the livestock of the vill. All together it is worth £4; when received, 40*s.*; TRE 100*s.* This manor pertains and always pertained to the demesne of the Church of Ely.

• In the same vill Hardwin holds 3 hides from the abbot. There is land for 4 ploughs. In demesne [are] 2 ploughs; and 5 villans and 4 bordars with 2 ploughs. There are 4 slaves, and 4 acres of meadow, [and] woodland for 12 pigs. It is worth £4; when received, 20*s.*; TRE 40*s.* 10 sokemen held this land: they were the men of the abbot, and without his leave they could not sell their land. 6 of them provided cartage-dues and 4 provided escort-service if the king came to the shire. If not, they paid 8*d.* for cartage-due, and 4[*d.*] for escort-service.

M • The abbot himself holds Balsham. There are 9 hides. [There is] land for 19 ploughs. In demesne [are] 5 hides, and there are 5 ploughs, and there can be 2 more. There are 12 villans and 12 bordars with 12 ploughs. There are 2 slaves, and 1 mill [rendering] 4*s.*, woodland for 200 pigs, and 12 acres of meadow, [and] 32*d.* from pasture. In all it is worth £17; when received, £10; TRE £12. This manor pertains and always pertained to the demesne of the Church of Ely.

• In the same vill Hardwin holds 80 acres from the abbot. There is land for 1 plough, and there is [1 plough]. It is and always was worth 13*s.* 4*d.* 3 sokemen, the men of the Abbot of Ely, held this land: they could neither give nor sell their land without his leave, yet they provided cartage-due, and escort-service.

In 'Staploe' Hundred

• In Soham the same abbot holds half a hide. There is land for 2 ploughs. In demesne is 1 [plough]; and 3 villans and 10 bordars with 1 plough. [There is] meadow for 2 ploughs, pasture for the livestock of the vill, and a boat which fishes in the mere by custom. It is worth 30*s.*; when received, 20*s.*; TRE 30*s.* This land always pertained to the church.

In 'Staine' Hundred

• In Swaffham Prior the same abbot holds 3 hides. There is land for 5 ploughs. In demesne [is] 1 hide and 3 virgates, and there are 2 ploughs; and 5 villans and 2 bordars with 3 ploughs. There are 2 slaves, and 6*s.* from a fishing-net toll, [and] 6*d.* from the fen. It is and always was worth 100*s.* This land pertains and always pertained to the church.

• In the same vill Hardwin holds 2 hides and 3 virgates under the abbot. There is land for 3 ploughs. In demesne [is] 1 plough; and 2 villans with 2 ploughs. [There is] meadow for 2 oxen. It is and always was worth 70*s.* 4 sokemen held this land, and could not depart without the leave of the abbot.

• In Stow cum Quy Picot holds 3 hides and 3 virgates under the abbot. There is land for 4 ploughs. In demesne [are] 2 ploughs; and 5 villans with 2 ploughs. There is 1 slave,

|[in margin]| and half a mill [rendering] 40*d*.|, [and] meadow for 4 ploughs. It is worth £6; when received and TRE, £4. 2 sokemen held this land under the abbot; they could not depart without his leave.

IN FLEAMDYKE HUNDRED

• In Fulbourn the same abbot holds 4½ hides. There is land for 6 ploughs. In demesne [are] 3 hides, where there can be 3 ploughs, but none is reckoned there. There are 8 villans and 6 bordars with 3 ploughs. [There is] meadow for the ploughs. It is and was worth 20*s*.; TRE £6. This land pertains and always pertained to the demesne of the Church of Ely at farm.

• In Teversham the same abbot holds 1 hide. There is land for 1½ ploughs. In demesne is 1 plough, and 2 villans and 2 bordars. It is and was worth 20*s*.; TRE 40*s*. This land always pertained to the church.

M • HORNINGSEA is assessed at 7 hides. There is land for 17 ploughs. In demesne [are] 3½ hides, and there are 8½ ploughs. There are 22 villans and 14 bordars with 9 ploughs. There are 15 slaves, and 1 mill rendering 10*s*. and 1,000 eels, [and] meadow for the ploughs. In all it is worth £18; when received, £14; and as much TRE. This land always pertained and pertains to the demesne of the Church of Ely.

IN CHILFORD HUNDRED

• In West Wickham the same abbot holds 1½ hides. There is land for 4 ploughs. In demesne [is] half a hide, and there are 2½ ploughs. There are 6 villans and 2 bordars with 2 ploughs. There are 2 slaves, and 4 acres of meadow, [and] woodland for 50 pigs. It is worth 65*s*.; when received, 60*s*.; TRE 40*s*. This land pertains and always pertained to the demesne of the Church of Ely.

• In Barham a sokeman holds half a virgate under the abbot. It is and was worth 40*d*. This man provided escort-service for the sheriff TRE.

• In Babraham Hardwin holds half a virgate of land under the abbot. It is and was worth 40*d*. 2 sokemen held it; they could not depart.

• In Pampisford the same abbot holds 2 hides and 3½ virgates. There is land for 6 ploughs. In demesne [is] 1 hide and 1½ virgates, and there are 2 ploughs. There are 12 villans and 5 bordars with 4 ploughs. There are 3 slaves, and 1 mill rendering 20*s*., [and] meadow for 1 plough. It is and always was worth £7. This land always pertained and pertains to the demesne of the Church of Ely.

In the same vill Hardwin holds 10 acres from the abbot. [There is] land for 1 ox. It is worth 12*d*. Snelling held this land from the abbot, but he could not depart.

IN THRIPLOW HUNDRED

• The abbot himself holds 6½ hides in Thriplow. There is land for 8 ploughs. In demesne [are] 3 hides, and there are 3 ploughs. There are 12 villans and 5 bordars with 5 ploughs. There are 5 slaves, and meadow for 1 plough, [and] pasture for the livestock of the vill. In all it is and was worth £11; TRE £12. This land pertains and always pertained to the demesne of the church.

• In the same vill Hardwin holds under the abbot as it were by the grace of the abbot himself 1 hide of the demesne for the sustenance of the monks till he confers with the king about it. There is land for 1 plough. It is and always was worth 20*s*. TRE this land always pertained to the demesne of the Church of Ely.

• In the same vill Hardwin held 2 acres of the abbot's land, for which he does not have a warrantor nor a livery officer, but seized them in defiance of the abbot, as the men of the hundred bear witness.

M • HAUXTON is assessed at 8½ hides. There is land for 12 ploughs. In demesne [are] 5 hides, and there are 4 ploughs; and 16 villans and 4 bordars with 8 ploughs. There are 3 slaves, and 2 mills rendering 50*s*., meadow for 4 ploughs, [and] pasture for the livestock of the vill. In all it is and was worth £13; TRE £14. This manor pertains and always pertained to the demesne of the Church of Ely.

• In Harston Picot holds 1½ hides from the abbot by the king's command, and they are valued in Harston. A certain sokeman held this land under the Abbot of Ely TRE. He could depart without his leave, but the soke remained with the abbot.

M • GREAT SHELFORD is assessed at 9 hides and 24 acres. There is land for 11 ploughs. In demesne [are] 5 hides, and there are 3 ploughs. There are 20 villans and 8 bordars with 8 ploughs. There are 7 slaves, and 2 mills at 45*s*. and rendering 2 pigs, [and] meadow for 4 ploughs. In all it is and was worth £12; TRE £14.

• In the same vill Hardwin holds 2½ hides and 9 acres and a minster of the demesne farm of the monks of Ely, and they were there TRE, as the hundred bears witness. Now the abbot does not have them.

• In the same vill 7 sokemen hold 1½ hides and 6 acres of the soke of the abbot. They could not depart with the land, but the soke remained with the Church of Ely. This manor always pertained and pertains to |the demesne of the Church of Ely.| |[in margin]|

M • STAPLEFORD is assessed at 10 hides. There is land for 11 ploughs. In demesne [are] 6½ hides, and there are 4 ploughs. There are 16 villans and 4 bordars with 7 ploughs. There are 7 slaves, and meadow for 5 ploughs, pasture for the livestock of the vill, [and] woodland to repair fences. In all it is and was worth £12; TRE £13. This manor pertains and always pertained to the demesne of the Church of Ely.

• In Whaddon Hardwin holds 2½ hides. There is land for 3 ploughs. In demesne [is] 1 hide, and 1 plough. There are 6 villans and 15 cottars with 1½ ploughs, and there can be another half [-plough]. [There is] meadow for 2 ploughs, [and] pasture for the livestock of the vill. This land is valued with the land of Hardwin. Thorbiorn held 1 hide of this land from the abbot: he could not alienate it from the church [or put it] outside the farm of the monks TRE nor on the day of his [King Edward's] death; and 12 sokemen had 1½ hides: they could sell them, but the soke remained with the abbot.

• In Meldreth Hardwin holds 1 virgate of the abbot's soke.

• In the same vill the abbot holds 2 hides and 3 virgates. There is land for 7 ploughs. In demesne [are] 1½ hides, and 1½ ploughs, and there can be [another] half [-plough]. There are [. . .] 10 bordars with 3 ploughs. There are 3 slaves, and 1 mill [rendering] 3*s*., [and] meadow for 5 ploughs. It is and was worth 100*s*.; TRE £6. This land pertains and always pertained to the demesne of the church.

In the same vill Hardwin holds 1½ hides and 1 minster

§ In the same vill Guy de Raimbeaucourt holds 10 sokeman. One of them could not sell [his land] in the time of King Edward; the others could; the hundred bears witness to this.

of the demesne farm of the monks, which they held both during the life and at the death of King Edward, as the men of the hundred bear witness. §

• In Melbourn the Abbot of Ely holds 2 hides and 1 virgate of land. There is land for 5 ploughs. In demesne [is] 1 hide and 1 virgate, and there are $1\frac{1}{2}$ ploughs, and there can be [another] half [-plough]. There are 6 villans and 9 bordars with 3 ploughs. There are 3 cottars, and 1 mill rendering 2*s*. 8*d*., meadow for 5 ploughs, [and] pasture for the livestock of the vill. It is and was worth 100*s*.; TRE £6. This land pertains and always pertained to the demesne of the Church of Ely.

• In Shepreth Hardwin holds half a virgate, which belonged to the Church of Ely on the day of King Edward's death.

In Longstowe Hundred

• In Hardwick the Abbot of Ely holds 3 hides and 1 virgate and 12 acres. There is land for 6 ploughs. In demesne [are] $1\frac{1}{2}$ hides and 12 acres, and there are 2 ploughs. There are 7 villans with 4 ploughs. There are 4 slaves, meadow for 4 ploughs, [and] a wood for fences. It is and was worth 100*s*.; TRE £6. This land pertains and always pertained to the demesne of the Church of Ely.

• In the same vill Ralph holds 10 acres from the abbot. [There is] land for 1 ox. It is and was worth 12*d*. Cabe held this land under the abbot; he could not depart from him.

M • Little Gransden is assessed at 5 hides. There is land for 9 ploughs. In demesne [are] $2\frac{1}{2}$ hides, and there is 1 plough, and there can be 2 [ploughs]. There are 8 villans and 3 bordars with 6 ploughs. There are 4 slaves, meadow for 3 ploughs, [and] pasture for the livestock of the vill. [There is] woodland for 60 pigs, and from the customary dues of the woodland, 2*s*. In all it is worth £8; when received, £9; TRE £15. This manor pertains and always pertained to the demesne of the Church of Ely.

In Papworth Hundred

M • Willingham is assessed at 7 hides. There is land for 7 ploughs. In demesne [are] 4 hides, and there are 2 ploughs. There are 12 villans with 5 ploughs. There are 8 cottars and 1 slave. [There is] meadow for 7 ploughs, [and] pasture for the livestock of the vill. From the fen, 6*s*. In all it is and was worth 100*s*.; TRE £8. This manor pertains and always pertained to the demesne of the Church of Ely.

In 'Northstowe' Hundred

• In Oakington Ælfgeat the priest holds 15 acres from the abbot. There is land for 1 ox. It is and always was worth 3*s*. The same man held it TRE and could give it, but the soke remained with the abbot.

M • Impington is assessed at $6\frac{1}{2}$ hides. There is land for 6 ploughs. In demesne [are] $3\frac{1}{2}$ hides, and there is half a plough, and there can be $1\frac{1}{2}$ ploughs. There is 1 villan and 8 bordars with 2 ploughs, and there can be 2 [. . .]. There are 7 cottars and 1 slave, [and] meadow for 2 ploughs. It is and was worth 40*s*.; TRE £8. This manor pertains and always pertained to the demesne of the Church of Ely.

In Chesterton Hundred

M • Cottenham is assessed at 10 hides. There is land for 8 ploughs. In demesne [are] 6 hides, and 1 plough. There are 16 villans and 10 cottars with 6 ploughs. There are 2 slaves, meadow for 8 ploughs, [and] pasture for the livestock of the vill. In all it is and was worth 100*s*.; TRE £8. This manor pertains and pertained to the demesne of the Church of Ely.

• In Histon the abbot holds 1 hide and 3 virgates. This land is valued with Impington.

In the Two Hundreds Of Ely Which Meet at Witchford

M • The Church of Ely holds Whittlesey for 2 hides. There is land for $4\frac{1}{2}$ ploughs. In demesne [is] 1 hide, and there are $1\frac{1}{2}$ ploughs. There are 8 villans and 4 cottars with 3 ploughs. There are 3 slaves, meadow for 1 plough, [and] pasture for the livestock of the vill. From the weir, 2*s*. It is worth £4; when received, £3; TRE 100*s*. This manor pertains and always pertained to the Church of Ely in demesne farm.

M • The Abbot of Ely holds Doddington for 5 hides. There is land for 8 ploughs. In demesne [are] $2\frac{1}{2}$ hides, and there are 3 ploughs. There are 24 villans with 5 ploughs. There are 8 sokemen with 1 hide, and 8 cottars and 1 slave. [There is] meadow for 8 ploughs, pasture for the livestock of the vill, [and] woodland for 250 pigs. From the fisheries, 27,150 eels, [and] from gifts [of fish], 24*s*. In all it is worth £16; when received, £10; TRE £12. This manor pertains and pertained to the demesne of the Church of Ely. To this manor pertains 1 Berewick, March, where there are 12 villans, each with 12 acres. This is valued with the manor.

• In Chatteris the same abbot holds 2 hides and half a virgate. There is land for 3 ploughs. In demesne [is] half a hide, and there are 6 oxen. There are 6 villans and 2 bordars and 2 cottars with 2 ploughs and 2 oxen. [There is] meadow for 3 ploughs, [and] woodland for 20 pigs. From the fisheries, 1,500 eels. It is worth 40*s*.; when received, 30*s*.; TRE 50*s*. This land pertained and pertains to the demesne of the Church of Ely.

M • The Abbot of Ely holds Littleport for $2\frac{1}{2}$ hides. There is land for 6 ploughs. In demesne [is] 1 hide, and there are 2 ploughs. There are 15 villans and 8 cottars with 4 ploughs. There are 8 slaves, and meadow for 6 ploughs, [and] pasture for the livestock of the vill. From the fisheries, 17,000 eels, [and] 12*s*. 9*d*. from gifts of fish. In all it is worth £10; when received, £7; TRE £6. This manor pertains and always pertained to the Church of Ely in demesne.

• In Stuntney the abbot holds $1\frac{1}{2}$ hides. There is land for 3 ploughs. In demesne [is] 1 hide, and 1 plough. There are 6 villans and 5 cottars and 3 slaves with 2 ploughs. [There is] meadow for 3 ploughs, [and] pasture for the livestock of the vill. From the fisheries, 24,000 eels, and from gifts [of fish], 18*s*. All together it is and was worth £10. 14*s*.; TRE £12. This land is a Berewick of the manor of Ely.

• The same abbot holds Little Thetford [for] 1 hide. There is land for 1 plough, and there is [1 plough] in demesne. There is 1 villan with 6 acres, and 4 cottars, meadow for 1 plough, [and] pasture for the livestock of the vill. From the fishery, 500 eels, [and] $4\frac{1}{2}$*d*. from gifts [of fish]. It is worth 40*s*.; when received, 20*s*.; TRE 30*s*. This land is a Berewick of Ely.

M • Stretham is assessed at 5 hides. There is land for 9 ploughs. In demesne [are] 3 hides, and there are 4 ploughs. There are 12 villans, each [having] 10 acres, and 11 villans with 1 hide; these have 5 ploughs. There are 10 cottars and 2 slaves. [There is] meadow for 9 ploughs, [and] pasture for the livestock of the vill. From the fisheries, 3,250 eels, [and] 7*s*. 7*d*. from gifts [of fish]. In all it is worth £9;

when received, £6; TRE £12. This manor pertains and always pertained to the demesne of the Church of Ely.

M • The Abbot of Ely holds WILBURTON. There are 5 hides. There is land for 7 ploughs. In demesne [are] 3 hides and 1 virgate, and there are 3 ploughs. There are 4 sokemen who neither could nor can depart, and 9 villans with 4 ploughs. There are 9 cottars and 8 slaves, meadow for 7 ploughs, [and] pasture for the livestock of the vill. From reeds, 16*d*. All together it is worth £7; when received, £4; TRE £10. This manor pertains and always pertained to the demesne of the Church of Ely.

M • The Abbot of Ely holds 'LINDEN' [in Haddenham]. There are 4 hides. There is land for 6 ploughs. In demesne [are] $2\frac{1}{2}$ hides, and there are 4 ploughs. There are 2 sokemen who neither could nor can depart, and 14 villans with 2 ploughs. There are 9 cottars and 1 bordar and 10 slaves. From the fisheries, 3,333 eels, [and] 4*s*. from gifts [of fish]. [There is] meadow for 6 ploughs, [and] pasture for the livestock of the vill. All together it is worth £8; when received, £4; TRE £9. This manor pertains and pertained to the demesne of the church.

• The Abbot of Ely holds HILL ROW. There are 2 hides. There is land for 5 ploughs. In demesne [is] 1 hide and 1 virgate and 10 acres, and there are 3 ploughs. There are 10 villans with 2 ploughs. There are 4 cottars and 5 slaves, meadow for 5 ploughs, pasture for the livestock of the vill, and from the port, 3 ploughshares. It is worth 100*s*.; when received, 40*s*.; TRE £6. This land is a Berewick of 'Linden' [in Haddenham].

• Under the abbot 7 sokemen, who neither could nor can depart, hold Haddenham. There are 3 hides. There is land for 5 ploughs, and there are [5 ploughs]. There are 8 villans, each [having] half a virgate, and 4 bordars, each [having] 5 acres. There are 6 cottars, meadow for 5 ploughs, [and] pasture for the livestock of the vill. It is and was worth £8; TRE £12.

SO FAR ONE HUNDRED. NOW THE OTHER

M • The Abbot of Ely holds WISBECH. There are 10 hides. There is land for 10 ploughs. In demesne [is] 1 hide and 1 virgate, and there are 2 ploughs. There are 15 villans, each [with] 10 acres, and 13 sokemen with $2\frac{1}{2}$ hides who neither could nor can depart. All these men [have] 8 ploughs. There are 17 cottars and 2 slaves. From the fisheries, 1,500 eels. [There is] meadow for 10 ploughs, [and] pasture for the livestock of the vill. All together it is and was worth 100*s*.; TRE £6. This manor pertains and pertained to the demesne of the church.

• In the same vill 2 fishermen render to the abbot 14,000 eels, and 13*s*. 4*d*. from gifts [of fish]. The abbot has soke over all the men of this vill.

M • ELY is assessed at 10 hides. There is land for 20 ploughs. In demesne [are] 5 hides, and there are 5 ploughs, and there can be a sixth. There are 40 villans, each [with] 15 acres, with 14 ploughs. There are 28 cottars and 20 slaves. From the fisheries, 3,750 eels, [and] from gifts [of fish], 2*s*. 3*d*. [There is] meadow for 20 ploughs, [and] pasture for the livestock of the vill. There are 3 arpents of vineyard. In all it is worth £30; when received, £20; TRE £33. All this manor always was and is demesne.

• Hainey is an island on which is half a hide of land. This does not pay geld nor did it ever pay it TRE.

M • The Abbot of Ely holds LITTLE DOWNHAM. There are 4 hides. There is land for 8 ploughs. In demesne [are] $2\frac{1}{2}$ hides, and there are 4 ploughs. There are 15 villans, each with 12 acres, with 4 ploughs. There are 8 cottars and 8 slaves. [There is] meadow for 8 ploughs, pasture for the livestock of the vill, 300 eels and 2*s*. from a fishery, [and] woodland for 100 pigs. In all it is worth £10; when received, 100*s*.; TRE £12. This manor pertains and always pertained to the demesne of the Church of Ely.

M • The Abbot of Ely holds WITCHFORD. There are 3 hides. There is land for 7 ploughs. In demesne [are] $1\frac{1}{2}$ hides, and there are 2 ploughs, and there can be a third. There are 5 sokemen with half a hide, who neither could nor can depart, and 17 villans, each with 7 acres. All these together [have] 4 ploughs. There are 7 cottars and 8 slaves, meadow for 7 ploughs, [and] pasture for the livestock of the vill. In all it is worth £10; when received, £8; TRE £12. This manor belonged and belongs to the demesne of the church.

M • The Abbot of Ely holds WENTWORTH. There are $3\frac{1}{2}$ hides. There is land for 7 ploughs. In demesne [is] 1 hide, and there is 1 plough, and there can be another. There are 9 villans, each with 10 acres, and 2 sokemen with 1 hide, who neither could nor can sell [their land] without the abbot's leave, and 1 sokeman with 1 virgate, [holding] in the same manner, and under these sokemen 9 villans, each with 10 acres. There are 17 cottars, and meadow for 7 ploughs, pasture for the livestock of the vill, [and] woodland for 20 pigs. In all it is worth £10. 10*s*.; and as much when received; TRE £12. This manor pertains and always pertained to the demesne of the church.

All these men [have] 5 ploughs

M • The Abbot of Ely holds WITCHAM. There are 4 hides and 1 virgate. There is land for 7 ploughs. In demesne [are] 2 hides, and there are 2 ploughs, and there can be a third. There are 12 sokemen with 2 hides less half a virgate, who neither could nor can give [their land] without the abbot's leave. There are 2 villans with 10 acres, and 2 bordars, each with 5 acres. All these men [have] 4 ploughs. There are 4 cottars and 5 slaves, meadow for 7 ploughs, [and] pasture for the livestock of the vill. It is and was worth 100*s*.; TRE £7. This manor belonged and belongs to the demesne of the Church of Ely.

M • The Abbot of Ely holds SUTTON. There are 5 hides. There is land for 10 ploughs. [. . .] In demesne [are] 2 hides, and there are 3 ploughs, and there can be a fourth. There are 9 sokemen with 2 hides, who neither could nor can depart without the abbot's leave, and 8 villans, each with $7\frac{1}{2}$ acres, and 15 cottars, all these men with 6 ploughs. There are 7 slaves, meadow for 10 ploughs, [and] pasture for the livestock of the vill. From the fisheries, 44*s*. [There is] woodland for 5 pigs. In all it is and was worth £12; TRE £16. This manor belonged and belongs to the demesne of the Church of Ely.

VI. THE LAND OF ST EDMUND

• THE ABBOT of St Edmundsbury holds in the 2 hundreds of Ely 16 acres in March. There is land for half a plough, and there is [half a plough], with 3 bordars. [There is] meadow for 4 ploughs or oxen, [and] woodland for 4 pigs. It is and always was worth 3*s*.; and pertains and always pertained to the demesne of the Church of St Edmundsbury.

• In Wisbech the same abbot has 1 fisherman rendering 5,000 eels.

• In Soham the abbot himself holds 6 acres of land. There is 1 fisherman having a seine in the mere of the same vill. It is and was worth 4*s*.; TRE 5*s*. This land pertains and always pertained to the Church of St Edmundsbury.

VII. THE LAND OF THE CHURCH OF RAMSEY

IN LONGSTOWE HUNDRED

• THE ABBOT of Ramsey holds 1 hide in Bourn, and 2 knights [hold] from him. There is land for 1 plough. There are 2 bordars, [and] meadow for 1 plough. It is and always was worth 10*s*., and pertains and always pertained to the Church of St Benedict of Ramsey, and is a Berewick of Longstowe.

M • In LONGSTOWE Guy holds 2 hides under the abbot himself. There is land for 5 ploughs. In demesne are 2 ploughs; and 5 villans and 6 bordars with 3 ploughs. There is 1 cottar, and meadow for 2 ploughs, pasture for the livestock of the vill, [and] a wood for fences and houses. All together it is worth 50*s*.; when received, £4; TRE £6. This manor pertains and pertained to the demesne of the Church of St Benedict of Ramsey.

IN PAPWORTH HUNDRED

M • The Abbot of Ramsey holds GRAVELEY. There are 5 hides. [There is] land for 7 ploughs. In demesne [are] 2½ hides, and there are 2 ploughs. There are 8 villans and 8 bordars with 5 ploughs. There are 4 slaves, [and] a wood for fences and houses. It is and was worth £6; TRE £8. This manor pertains and always pertained to the Church of St Benedict.

M • The Abbot of Ramsey holds ELSWORTH. There are 9 hides and 1 virgate and 5 acres. There is land for 22 ploughs. In demesne [are] 4 hides, and there are 3 ploughs, and there can be a fourth. There are 19 villans and 17 bordars, and 1 Frenchman having 3 virgates. These have together 18 ploughs. There are 5 cottars, meadow for 4 ploughs, and 4 slaves, pasture for the livestock of the vill, [and] a wood for the houses of the hall. In all it is worth £16; when received, £14; TRE £20. This manor always pertained and pertains to the demesne of the Church of St Benedict.

M • The Abbot of St Benedict holds KNAPWELL. There are 5 hides. There is land for 8 ploughs. In demesne [are] 1½ hides, and there are 2 ploughs. There are 8 villans and 4 sokemen having 1½ hides, and 4 bordars, each with 5 acres. There are 4 cottars and 4 slaves, a wood for fences, [and] meadow for 2 ploughs. In all it is and was worth £6; TRE £8. This manor pertains and always pertained to the demesne of the Church of St Benedict. The aforesaid 4 sokemen could give and sell their land TRE without the abbot's leave, but the soke remained with the abbot.

• In Boxworth the same abbot holds half a hide. There is land for half a plough, [and] meadow for half a plough. It is and was worth 4*s*. This land pertains and pertained to the demesne of the church.

• In Fen Drayton the same abbot holds 3 virgates. There is land for 4 oxen, and there are [4 oxen]. [There is] meadow for 4 oxen. There are 2 slaves. It is and always was worth 3*s*. This land pertains and always pertained to the demesne of the church.

M • The Abbot of Ramsey holds OVER. There are 10 hides and 3 virgates. There is land for 10½ ploughs. In demesne [are] 6 hides, and there is 1 plough and there can be another. There are 14 villans and 2 bordars and 3 cottars with 6 ploughs, and there can be 2½ ploughs more. There are 2 slaves, meadow for 10½ ploughs, [and] pasture for the livestock of the vill. From the fen, 6*s*. 4*d*. In all it is worth £8; when received, £6; TRE £10. This manor pertains and always pertained to the demesne of the Church of St Benedict.

IN 'STAPLOE' HUNDRED

M • The Abbot of Ramsey holds BURWELL. There are 10 hides and 1 virgate. There is land for 16 ploughs. In demesne [are] 3 hides and 40 acres, and there are 4 ploughs. There are 42½ villans with 12 ploughs. There are 8 slaves, meadow for 10 ploughs, pasture for the livestock of the vill, and 2 mills rendering 6*s*. 8*d*. In all it is and was worth £16; TRE £20. This manor pertains and always pertained to the demesne of the Church of St Benedict.

IN 'NORTHSTOWE' HUNDRED

• The Abbot of Ramsey holds GIRTON. There are 8 hides and 2½ virgates. There is land for 6 ploughs. In demesne [are] 3 hides, and there is 1 plough, and there can be another. There are 7 villans and 6 bordars with 4 ploughs. There are 2 slaves, [and] meadow for 6 ploughs. In all it is worth £4; when received, £6; TRE £8. This manor pertains and pertained to the Church of St Benedict.

• In the Two Hundreds of Ely the Abbot of Ramsey holds 3 hides, less half a virgate, in Chatteris. There is land for 4 ploughs. In demesne [are] 1½ hides, and there is 1 plough; and 10 villans and 5 bordars and 2 slaves with 3 ploughs. [There is] meadow for 4 ploughs, [and] woodland for 100 pigs. From the fisheries, 3,000 eels, [and] 27*d*. from gifts [of fish]. It is worth 60*s*.; when received, 20*s*.; TRE £4. This land pertains and pertained to the Church of St Benedict.

In Wisbech the Abbot of Ramsey has 8 fishermen rendering 5,260 eels.

VIII. THE LAND OF THE CHURCH OF THORNEY

IN THE TWO HUNDREDS OF ELY

• THE ABBOT of THORNEY holds in WHITTLESEY 4 hides. There is land for 6 ploughs. In demesne [are] 2 hides, and there are 2 ploughs; and 16 villans, each [having] 8 acres, and 6 cottars with 4 ploughs. There is 1 slave, meadow for 6 ploughs, [and] pasture for the livestock of the vill. From the weir, 4*s*., and from fish 20*s*. besides this. In all it is worth £6; when received, 20*s*.; TRE £7. This manor pertained and pertains to the demesne of the Church of Thorney, but the Abbot of Ely has the soke.

IX. THE LAND OF THE CHURCH OF CROWLAND

IN 'NORTHSTOWE' HUNDRED

• THE ABBOT of CROWLAND holds 7½ hides in OAKINGTON. There is land for 8 ploughs. In demesne [are] 4 hides, and there are 2 ploughs. There are 14 villans and 3 bordars with 6 ploughs. There are 4 cottars and 3 slaves, [and] meadow for 2 ploughs. In all it is and was worth £6; TRE £8. This manor was and is in the demesne of the Church of St|Guthlac.| |[in margin]|

IN CHESTERTON HUNDRED

• The Abbot of Crowland holds COTTENHAM. There are 11 hides. There is land for 8 ploughs. In demesne [are] 6 hides, and there is 1 plough, and there can be another. There are 12 villans and 8 bordars with 6 ploughs. There is 1 slave, meadow for 8 ploughs, [and] pasture for the livestock of the vill. From the fen, 500 eels, and 12*d*. from gifts [of fish]. In all it is and was worth £6; TRE £8. This manor always was and is in the demesne of the Church of St Guthlac.

• In Dry Drayton the Abbot of Crowland holds 7½ hides. There is land for 6 ploughs. In demesne [are] 4 hides and 3 virgates, and there is 1 plough, and there can be another. There are 11 villans and 5 bordars with 3 ploughs, and there can be a fourth. There are 4 cottars, [and] meadow for 2 ploughs. It is and was worth £3. 10*s*.; TRE 100*s*. This land pertains and pertained to the demesne of the Church of St Guthlac.

In the Hundred[s] of Ely

• In Wisbech the Abbot of Crowland has 3 fishermen rendering 4,000 eels.

X. THE LAND OF SAINT-WANDRILLE

In 'Radfield' Hundred

• The Abbot of Saint-Wandrille holds Dullingham from the king. There are 6 hides. There is land for 12 ploughs. In demesne [are] 3 hides, and there are 3 ploughs. There are 17 villans and 10 bordars with 9 ploughs. There are 2 slaves, and meadow for 1 plough, woodland for 100 pigs, [and] pasture for the livestock. In all it is worth £12; when received, £15; TRE £15. Earl Ælfgar held this land.

XI. THE LAND OF THE CHURCH OF CHATTERIS

In Thriplow Hundred

• The Abbess of Chatteris holds 5 hides and 40 acres in Foxton from the king. There is land for 8 ploughs. In demesne [is] 1 hide and 40 acres, and there are 2 ploughs. There are 16 villans and 11 bordars with 6 ploughs. There is half a mill rendering 10*s*. 8*d*., [and] meadow for all the ploughs. It is and was worth £6; TRE £7. This land always pertained and pertains to the demesne of the church.

In 'Staploe' Hundred

• In Burwell the nuns of the †Church† of Chatteris hold half a hide. [There is] land for half a plough, and there is [half a plough, and] meadow for 2 oxen. It is and was always worth 10*s*. This land belonged and belongs to the demesne of the church.

In 'Wetherley' Hundred

• In Barrington the Church of Chatteris holds 2 hides. There is land for 3 ploughs. In demesne [is] 1 hide, and there is 1 plough. There are 8 bordars and 5 cottars with 2 ploughs. There are 3 slaves, and 1 mill [rendering] 25*s*. 4*d*., [and] meadow for 3 ploughs. It is and was worth £3; TRE £4. This land pertained and pertains to the demesne of the Church of Chatteris.

• In Shepreth the same church holds 1 hide and 1½ virgates. There is land for 1½ ploughs. In demesne [is] half a hide, and there is half a plough. There is 1 villan and 3 bordars and 4 cottars with 1 plough. There is 1 slave, and 1 mill rendering 5*s*. 4*d*., [and] meadow for 1½ ploughs. It is and was worth 30*s*.; TRE 40*s*. This land pertains and always pertained to the demesne of the Church of Chatteris.

• In Orwell the same church holds the fourth part of a virgate. There is land for half an ox, and it is worth 12*d*. It always pertained to the church.

• In Over the same church holds 1 hide. There is land for 1 plough, and there is [1 plough], with 4 villans. [There is] meadow for 1 plough, [and] pasture for the livestock. It is and was worth 16*s*. This land always pertained and pertains to the demesne of the Church of Chatteris.

XII. THE LAND OF THE COUNT OF MORTAIN

In Whittlesford Hundred

• The Count of Mortain holds 2 hides in Sawston, and the Abbot of Grestain [holds] from him. There is land for 3 ploughs. In demesne is 1 [plough]; and 6 villans and 3 bordars have 2 ploughs. There is 1 mill [rendering] 26*s*. 2*d*., [and] meadow for 3 ploughs. It is and was always worth £6. Ordgar held this land under Earl Harold, and could give it to whom he would.

In 'Wetherley' Hundred

• In Barton Robert holds 1 hide from the count. There is land for 1 plough, and there is [1 plough], with 2 bordars and 1 slave. [There is] meadow for 1 plough. It is and was worth 40*s*.; TRE 50*s*. Iudichael, King Edward's huntsman, held this land and could give it to whom he would.

• In Grantchester the same Robert holds 1 virgate from the count. There is land for 4 oxen, and there are [4 oxen], with 1 villan. [There is] meadow for 2 oxen. It is and was worth 5*s*. Iudichael the huntsman held this land and could give it to whom he would.

In 'Northstowe' Hundred

• In Girton Morin holds 2½ hides and half a virgate from the count. There is land for 2½ ploughs. In demesne is 1 plough, and there can be [another] half[-plough]. There is 1 villan and 5 bordars and 3 cottars with 1 plough. [There is] meadow for 1 plough. It is and was worth 40*s*.; TRE £4. Iudichael held this land and could sell it to whom he would.

In Chesterton Hundred

• In Histon Morin holds 1 virgate and 10 acres from the count. This land is valued in Girton.

XIII. THE LAND OF EARL ROGER

In 'Arringford' Hundred

• Earl Roger holds 1 hide and the fourth part of 1 virgate in Steeple Morden. There is land for 2 ploughs. In demesne [is] half a hide and the fourth part of 1 virgate, and there is 1 plough; and 6 bordars with 1 plough. [There is] meadow for 2 ploughs, [and] pasture for the livestock of the vill. It is and was worth 40*s*.; TRE 50*s*. Goda held this land from Earl Ælfgar, and could give it to whom he would.

• In another Morden [Guilden Morden] Earl Roger holds half a hide and half a virgate. There is land for 1 plough and 2 oxen. In demesne [is] 1 virgate of land, and there are 2 oxen. There are 4 bordars with 1 plough. [There is] meadow for 1 plough. It is and always was worth 20*s*. Goda held this land under Earl Ælfgar, and it pertains to Shingay. Hardwin de Scales usurped 4 acres of this land in defiance of the earl, as the hundred bears witness.

• In Croydon Earl Roger holds 3 virgates of land. There is land for 6 oxen, and meadow for as many oxen. It is and was always worth 10*s*. Almær, the man of Earl Waltheof, held this land and could sell it.

• Earl Roger holds Shingay. It is assessed at 5 hides. There is land for 6 ploughs. In demesne [are] 3 hides, and there are 2 ploughs. There are 11 bordars and 7 cottars with 4 ploughs, and 1 mill rendering 10*s*., meadow for 6 ploughs and 2*s*. from the rent of the meadow, [and] pasture for the livestock of the vill. In all it is and was worth £7; TRE £14. Goda held this land under Earl Ælfgar.

• In Abington Pigotts Earl Roger holds 1 virgate of land which pertains to Shingay, his own manor. It is and always was worth 13*s*. 4*d*. Goda held this land under Earl Ælfgar.

• In Meldreth the Abbot of Saint-Evroul holds 2 hides from Earl Roger. There is land for 5 ploughs. In demesne [are] 2 ploughs; and 5 villans and 3 bordars with 3 ploughs. There are 2 slaves, and 2 mills rendering 15*s.* 4*d.*, [and] meadow for 2 ploughs. All together it is worth £6; when received, 40*s.*; TRE £8. Goda [held] this land under Earl Ælfgar [and] could sell it.

• In Melbourn the same abbot holds from Earl Roger half a hide less the fourth part of a virgate. There is land for half a plough, and there is [half a plough], with 1 villan. [There is] meadow for half a plough. It is and always was worth 5*s.* Goda held this land from Earl Ælfgar and could sell it.

• In Orwell Earl Roger holds 1 hide and 1 virgate and the third part of a virgate. There is land for 1½ ploughs. In demesne [is] half a hide, and there is half a plough; and 2 villans and 3 bordars with 1 plough. There is 1 slave, and meadow for 1 plough, and a wood to repair fences. It is worth 20*s.*; when received, 30*s.*; TRE 50*s.* 6 sokemen held this land and could give and sell their land. One of them was King Edward's man and provided escort-service for the sheriff. Picot lent 3 of these sokemen to Earl Roger to hold his pleas, but afterwards the earl's men seized them and kept them with their lands without a livery officer and the king neither had nor has their service, as the sheriff himself says.

• In 'Ratford' the earl holds 2 hides and 2 parts of a virgate. There is land for 3 ploughs. In demesne [is] 1 hide and 2 parts of 1 virgate, and there is half a plough, and there can be another half. There are 2 cottars and 15 bordars with 2 ploughs. There are 2 slaves, and meadow for 2 ploughs. It is and was worth 40*s.*; TRE 60*s.* 6 sokemen held this land, and could sell their land to whom they would.

• In 'Witewell' Earl Roger holds 1 virgate of land and the third part of a virgate. There is land for 4 oxen. It is and was worth 2*s.* 3 sokemen held this land and could sell it to whom they would.

M • In ARRINGTON Earl Roger holds 3½ hides. There is land for 8 ploughs. In demesne [are] 2 hides, and there are 3 ploughs and there can be a fourth. There are 6 villans and 6 cottars with 4 ploughs. There are 3 slaves, and meadow for 2 ploughs, and a wood for fences. All together it is worth £9; when received, £10; TRE £11. Ælfric, King Edward's thegn, held this manor, and there were 3 sokemen, one of them the man of Earl Waltheof, and another the man of the Abbot of Ely, and the third the man of Robert fitzWimarc, and they could depart whither they would.

IN LONGSTOWE HUNDRED

• In Kingston the earl holds 2 parts of a virgate. There is land for 2 oxen. It is and was worth 2*s.* Almær, the man of Earl Waltheof, held this land and could give it to whom he would.

XIIII. THE LAND OF COUNT ALAN

IN FLEAMDYKE HUNDRED

• COUNT ALAN holds 8 hides in Fulbourn. There is land for 13 ploughs. In demesne [are] 4 hides, and there are 3 ploughs, and there can be 2 more. There are 16 villans and 10 bordars with 8 ploughs. There are 4 slaves, and 1 mill rendering 20*s.*, [and] meadow for the ploughs. In all it is and always was worth £15. Godwine Cild, the man of Eadgifu the Fair, held this manor; he could not depart.

M • Count Alan holds CHERRY HINTON. There are 7 hides. There is land for 13 ploughs. In demesne [are] 3½ hides, and there are 4 ploughs. There are 19 villans and 22 bordars with 9 ploughs. There are 4 slaves, and meadow for 3 ploughs, and 4 mills rendering 25*s.*, pasture for the livestock of the vill, and 4 ploughshares. From the fen, 25*d.*, and 6*d.* from the carts. In all it is and was worth £18; TRE £12. Eadgifu the Fair held this manor, and there were 8 sokemen, who provided 2 cartage-dues and 4 watchmen for the sheriff.

• In Teversham Count Alan holds 1½ hides. There is land for 2 ploughs, but there are no [ploughs]. This land is valued with Cherry Hinton, the count's manor. 2 sokemen, the men of Eadgifu, held this; they could not depart from her, and they provided 1 cartage-due and 1 watchman for the sheriff.

• In the same vill Robert holds 1 hide from Count Alan. There is land for 1 plough, and there is [1 plough], and meadow for 1 plough. It is and was always worth 10*s.* 5 of Eadgifu's men held this land, and they could not depart from her, and they provided 3 watchmen for the sheriff.

IN CHILFORD HUNDRED

• In Horseheath Count Alan holds 2 hides and 2½ virgates. There is land for 5 ploughs, and there are [5 ploughs], with 8 villans and 5 bordars. It is worth 100*s.*; when received, £4; TRE 100*s.* Eadgifu held this land, and [there were] 2 sokemen, her men; one provided cartage-due, the other escort-service.

• In the same vill Alwine holds from Count Alan 1 virgate of land. There is land for 6 oxen. There are 2 bordars, and woodland for 20 pigs. It is and was worth 5*s.* Godwine, the man of Eadgifu, held this land; he could not depart.

• In West Wickham Count Alan holds 2 hides. There is land for 5 ploughs. In demesne [are] 1½ hides, and there are 2 ploughs; and 4 villans and 4 bordars with 3 ploughs. There are 4 slaves, and meadow for 2 ploughs, [and] woodland for 100 pigs. All together it is and was worth £10; TRE £8. Eadgifu held this land, and 2 sokemen, her men, provided 1 cartage-due and 1 watchman. In the same place 1 sokeman holds the fourth part of a virgate under the count. It is worth 12*d.*

• In Barham Ansketil holds 3 hides less half a virgate from Count Alan. There is land for 5 ploughs. In demesne are 3 ploughs; and 6 villans and 4 bordars with 2 ploughs. There are 6 slaves, meadow for 2 ploughs, and 1 mill rendering 5*s.* All together it is and was worth £9.

• In the same vill Morin holds 1½ hides under the count. There is land for 3½ ploughs. In demesne are 2 [ploughs]; and 6 villans and 2 bordars with 1½ ploughs. [There is] meadow for 1 plough, and 1 mill rendering 2*s.*

It is and was worth 60*s*. Eadgifu held these 2 estates. In the same vill 1 sokeman holds 1 virgate under the count. There is land for 4 oxen, and there are [4 oxen]. This land is and was worth 4*s*. This man held it under Eadgifu, and provided escort-service.

M • Count Alan holds LINTON. There are 3 hides and 3 virgates. There is land for 8 ploughs. In demesne [are] 2 hides, and there are 3 ploughs. There are 16 villans and 5 bordars with 5 ploughs. There are 6 slaves, and 2 mills rendering 16*s*., meadow for 2 ploughs, [and] woodland for 30 pigs. All together it is worth £12; when received and TRE, £15. In the same place 1 sokeman holds 1 virgate under the count, and it is valued with Linton. Eadgifu held this land, and there was 1 sokeman who provided cartage-due for the sheriff.

• In Cambridge Count Alan has 10 burgesses.

M • Count Alan holds another LINTON [Little Linton]. There are $2\frac{1}{2}$ hides. There is land for 5 ploughs. In demesne [are] $1\frac{1}{2}$ hides, and there are 2 ploughs. There ...rtly in margin]| are 8 villans and 2 bordars| with 3 ploughs|. There are 4 slaves, and 1 mill rendering 8*s*., meadow for 1 plough, [and] woodland for 20 pigs. All together it is worth £7; when received and TRE, 100*s*. Eadgifu the Fair held this manor.

M • The count himself holds Little Abington. There are 5 hides. There is land for 8 ploughs. In demesne [are] $2\frac{1}{2}$ hides, and there are 3 ploughs. There are 11 villans and 5 bordars with 5 ploughs. There are 4 slaves, and 1 mill rendering 6*s*. 8*d*., meadow for 2 ploughs, [and] woodland for 20 pigs. All together it is and was worth £10. Eadgifu held this manor.

• In Babraham Brian holds $2\frac{1}{2}$ hides and 24 acres under Count Alan. There is land for 4 ploughs. In demesne is 1 [plough]; and 17 villans and 3 bordars with 3 ploughs. There is 1 slave, and meadow for 4 oxen. It is and was worth 50*s*. 6 sokemen held this land under Eadgifu; they could not depart without her leave. These provided 4 cartage-dues and 2 watchmen.

• In the same vill Ralph holds 1 hide, less half a virgate, under the count. There is land for 1 plough, and there is [1 plough. There is] meadow for 1 plough, and 3 villans and 3 bordars, and 1 mill rendering 5*s*. 4*d*. It is and was worth 20*s*. Alric the priest held this land under Eadgifu; he could not depart from her.

• In Pampisford 2 knights hold 1 hide and 22 acres under the count. There is land for 2 ploughs and 2 oxen. In demesne [is] 1 plough; and 2 villans and 5 bordars with 1 plough. [There are] $2\frac{1}{2}$ acres of meadow. It is worth 30*s*.; when received, 10*s*.; TRE 30*s*. Almær held this land under Eadgifu, and could depart, but the soke remained with Eadgifu.

IN WHITTLESFORD HUNDRED

• In Whittlesford Gerard holds half a virgate of land from the count. It is and was worth 2*s*. He himself holds sake and soke of $1\frac{1}{2}$ virgates from the count, which $1\frac{1}{2}$ virgates a man of the count holds. Eadgifu held it.

• In Duxford Gerard holds from the count 6 hides from the count. There is land for 6 ploughs. In demesne are 2 [ploughs]; and 4 villans and 5 bordars with 4 ploughs. There is 1 slave, and meadow for 2 ploughs. All together it is and was worth 100*s*.; TRE £7. Eadgifu held this land.

IN THRIPLOW HUNDRED

• In Fowlmere 2 knights hold 1 hide from Count Alan. There is land for 1 plough and 2 oxen, [and] meadow for 1 plough. It is and was worth 20*s*.; TRE 25*s*. Eadgifu held this land, and this land provided 2 watchmen for the sheriff.

• In Harston Odo holds $5\frac{1}{2}$ virgates of land from the count. There is land for $1\frac{1}{2}$ ploughs, and there are $1\frac{1}{2}$ ploughs, with 1 villan and 3 bordars. It is worth 20*s*.; when received, 15[*s*.]; TRE 30*s*. 4 sokemen held $4\frac{1}{2}$ virgates of this land under Eadgifu and provided 2 watchmen for the sheriff, and yet they could depart; and a priest held 1 virgate under Ordgar, provided 1 watchman, and could depart.

• In Little Shelford Hardwin holds $1\frac{1}{2}$ hides and 6 acres from the count. There is land for 2 ploughs, and there are [2 ploughs], with 6 villans and 2 bordars. [There is] meadow for 2 ploughs. It is worth 30*s*.; when received, 20[*s*.]; TRE 40*s*. 6 sokemen held this land under Eadgifu, provided 4 watchmen, and could depart.

IN 'ARRINGFORD' HUNDRED

• In East Hatley Almær holds 1 hide and 3 virgates from the count. There is land for 3 ploughs. In demesne is 1 plough; and 2 villans and 5 bordars with 3 ploughs. There are 3 slaves, meadow for 1 plough, [and] woodland for fences. It is and was worth 40*s*.; TRE 60*s*. This man held it under Eadgifu TRE, and provided 1 watchman, and could depart.

• In Croydon Almær holds $2\frac{1}{2}$ virgates under the count. There is land for 6 oxen, and there are [6 oxen], with 1 bordar and 1 cottar. It is and was worth 10*s*.; TRE 15*s*. Godgifu held this land under Eadgifu, and could depart.

• In the same vill Fulchei holds 1 virgate of land from the count. It is and was worth 5*s*. Leofgifu held this under Eadgifu, and could depart.

• In Wendy Odo holds 4 hides and 3 virgates from Count Alan. There is land for 6 ploughs. In demesne are 2 [ploughs]; and 6 villans and 5 bordars with 4 ploughs. There are 4 slaves, and 2 mills rendering 45*s*., meadow for 6 ploughs, [and] a wood for fences. All together it is worth £8; when received, £6; TRE £10. 6 sokemen held 1 hide of this land under Eadgifu, and could depart.

M • Count Alan himself holds 7 hides and $1\frac{1}{2}$ virgates in BASSINGBOURN. There is land for 18 ploughs. In demesne [are] 4 hides, and there are 5 ploughs, and there can be 2 more. There are 8 villans and 11 bordars and 10 cottars with 11 ploughs. There are 3 slaves, and 2 mills rendering 20*s*., [and] meadow for 5 ploughs. In all it is worth £30; when received, £26; and as much TRE. Eadgifu held this manor, and there were 10 sokemen; and 8 of them, men of Eadgifu, could sell their land, but the soke remained with her; and the other 2, the men of Earl Ælfgar, provided 4 watchmen for the sheriff, and they themselves could sell their land.

• In Whaddon Kolsveinn holds half a hide from Count Alan. There is land for 1½ ploughs. In demesne [is] 1 plough; and 1 villan has half a plough. It is and was worth 20*s*.; TRE 40*s*. This man held it from Eadgifu TRE and could sell it.

• In the same vill Ralph holds 2 hides and 1 virgate of land from the count. There is land for 4 ploughs. In demesne are 2 [ploughs]; and 2 villans and 1 bordar with 2 ploughs. There are 4 slaves, and 1 mill rendering 12*d*., meadow for 1 plough, [and] pasture for the livestock of the vill. All together it is and was worth £6; TRE £8. Leofwig, the man of Esger the staller, held this land, and could give and sell it to whom he would.

• In the same [vill] 2 men hold 1 virgate from the count. There is land for half a plough. It is and was worth 4*s*.; TRE 6*s*. 2 sokemen held this land; one was the man of Kolsveinn, the other of the soke of St Æthelthryth and he could sell, but the soke remained with the church.

• In the same [vill] Odo holds 2 hides and 1 virgate from the count. There is land for 3 ploughs. In demesne are 1½ ploughs; and 2½ villans with 4 bordars have 1½ ploughs. There are 2 slaves, [and] meadow for 1 plough. It is worth 100*s*.; when received, 30*s*.; TRE £6. Eadgifu held this land. On this land was and is 1 sokeman holding half a virgate. There is land for 2 oxen. It is and was worth 2*s*. A man of Eadgifu held it.

• In Meldreth Kolsveinn holds 1 virgate from the count. There is land for 1 plough, and there is [1 plough], with 2 cottars, and there are 2 mills rendering 18*s*., [and] meadow for 2 ploughs. It is worth 30*s*.; when received, 20*s*.; TRE 40*s*. This man held it under Eadgifu and could give it.

• In Melbourn Kolsveinn holds 3 virgates of land from the count. There is land for 1½ ploughs, and there are [1½ ploughs], with 3 bordars and 1 slave. [There is] meadow for 4 oxen. It is worth 20*s*.; when received, 15*s*.; TRE 40*s*. This man held it under Eadgifu, and could depart from her.

In 'Wetherley' Hundred

• In Grantchester Gollan holds 1½ virgates under the count. There is land for 1 plough, and there is [1 plough], with 1 villan and 3 cottars and 1 slave. [There is] meadow for 4 oxen. It is and was worth 20*s*. Godmann, the man of Eadgifu, held this land; he could not depart without her leave.

• In this same hundred Count Alan holds 2 mills rendering 100*s*., which he received at £8; TRE they were worth £6. Eadgifu held them.

• In Haslingfield Robert holds 1 hide and half a virgate from the count. There is land for 1½ ploughs. In demesne is 1 plough; and 4 villans with 1 bordar have half a plough. [There is] meadow for 4 oxen. It is worth 20*s*.; when received, 22*s*.; and as much TRE. Ealdræd held this land under Eadgifu; he could not depart without her leave.

• In the same vill the count himself holds half a hide in demesne which pertains to Swavesey, his manor. There is land for half a plough. It is and was worth 8*s*. Eadgifu the Fair held it.

• In the same vill Robert holds 12 acres of land from the count. It is and was worth 2*s*. Merewine held it from Eadgifu and could give it.

• In Barrington Picot holds half a virgate from the count. There is land for 2 oxen, and there are [2 oxen], with 2 bordars. [There is] meadow for 2 oxen. It is and was worth 2*s*.; TRE 32*d*. A man of King Edward held this land; he provided 1 watchman for the sheriff, and could give it to whom he would.

• In Shepreth Reginald holds 1½ virgates from the count. There is land for half a plough, and there is [half a plough], with 1 villan, and the sixth part of 1 mill rendering 14*d*. [There is] meadow for 4 oxen. It is worth 8*s*.; when received, 5*s*.; TRE 8*s*. Hemming, the man of King Edward, held this land. He provided escort-service and could sell his land.

• In Orwell Picot holds 3 virgates and the fourth part of a virgate and 5 acres from the count. There is land for 1½ ploughs, and there are [1½ ploughs], with 6 bordars. [There is] meadow for 1 plough. It is and was worth 20*s*.; TRE 30*s*. Thorbiorn held this land under Eadgifu, and could depart from her.

• In 'Ratford' the count himself holds 1 virgate and the third part of 1 virgate. There is land for half a plough, [and] meadow for 4 oxen, with 1 villan. It is and was worth 8*s*.; TRE 10*s*. 1 sokeman held this land under Eadgifu, and could give and sell it.

• In 'Witewell' Fulcui holds half a hide from the count. There is land for 1 plough, and there is [1 plough], with 3 cottars. [There is] meadow for half a plough, and a wood for fences. It is and was worth 10*s*.; TRE 20*s*. Godwig held this land under Eadgifu, and could depart from her.

• In Wimpole the count himself holds 2 hides and 2½ virgates. There is land for 3 ploughs. In demesne [are] 2 hides, and there is 1 plough, and there can be half [a plough] more. There 2 villans with 1 bordar have 1½ ploughs. There are 6 cottars and 2 slaves, [and] meadow for half a plough. All together it is worth £7; when received, £6; TRE £8. Eadgifu the Fair held this land.

• In Arrington Fulcui holds half a hide from the count. There is land for half a plough, and there is [half a plough], with 2 villans. [There is] meadow for 4 oxen, [and] woodland for fences. It is and was worth 10*s*.; TRE 20*s*. Leofgifu held this land under Eadgifu and could depart from her.

In Longstowe Hundred

• In [Great and Little] Eversden Robert and 2 Englishmen hold 1 hide from the count. There is land for 2 ploughs, and there are [2 ploughs], with 2 villans and 3 bordars and 1 cottar. [There is] meadow for 2 ploughs, and a wood for fences. It is worth 25*s*.; when received, 10*s*.; TRE 20*s*. 2 sokemen, the men of Eadgifu, held this land and could give and sell it.

• In Kingston Almær holds 1 virgate from the count. There is land for 2 oxen, and there are [2 oxen. There is] meadow for 2 oxen. It is and was worth 2*s*. Ælfgeat, the man of Earl Ælfgar, held this land and could sell it.

• In Toft the count holds 2 hides and 1 virgate and 8 acres. There is land for 4 ploughs. In demesne [is] 1 hide and 8 acres, and there is 1 plough. There 5 villans with 2 cottars have 4 ploughs. There are 2 slaves, meadow for 2 ploughs, and a wood for fences. All together it is worth £4; when received, £3; TRE 40*s*. This land is a Berewick of Swavesey. Eadgifu held it.

• In Bourn Almær holds 4 hides and 1 virgate from the count. There is land for 5½ ploughs. In demesne is 1 plough, and there can be half [a plough] more. There 9 villans with 13 bordars have 3 ploughs, and there can be a fourth. There are 2 slaves, meadow for 5½ ploughs, pasture for their livestock, [and] a wood for houses and fences. It is and was worth £4; TRE 100*s*. Almær, who now holds them, held this land and the other 3 which follow. He was the man of Eadgifu and provided 1 watchman, and could depart without leave, and give and sell his land to whom he would.

• In Caldecote Almær holds half a hide from the count. There is land for 1½ ploughs. In demesne is 1 plough; and 3 bordars with half a plough. There are 2 slaves, and meadow for 1½ ploughs, [and] a wood for houses and fences. It is and was always worth 30*s*.

• In Longstowe Almær holds 1½ virgates of land from the count. There is land for 6 oxen, and there are [6 oxen]. There are 2 slaves, and meadow for 6 oxen, pasture for the livestock of the vill, [and] a wood for fences and houses. It is worth 30*s*.; when received, 10*s*.; TRE 30*s*.

• In Hatley St George Almær holds 1 virgate from the count. There is land for 2 oxen. It is and always was worth 2*s*. 4*d*.

IN PAPWORTH HUNDRED

M • The count himself holds PAPWORTH EVERARD. There are 5 hides. There is land for 7 ploughs. In demesne [are] 2½ hides, and there are 2 ploughs. There are 10 villans and 5 bordars with 5 ploughs. There are 4 slaves, meadow for 2 ploughs, [and] a wood for fences and houses. In all it is worth £8; when received, £9; and as much TRE. Goda held this manor under Eadgifu, and could sell it.

• In Boxworth 2 sokemen hold 1 hide under the count. There is land for 1 plough, and there is [1 plough, and] meadow for 1 plough. It is and was worth 18*s*. 8*d*.; TRE 26*s*. These men held it under Eadgifu and could sell.

M • The count himself holds SWAVESEY. There are 13 hides. There is land for 14 ploughs. In demesne [are] 6 hides, and there are 3 ploughs, and there can be a fourth. There are 10 villans with 19 bordars, and 8 sokemen holding 3 hides of this land. These together have 10 ploughs. There are 17 cottars and 2 slaves, and 1 mill rendering 40*s*. From the fisheries, 4,000 eels, less 250. [There is] meadow for 14 ploughs, [and] pasture for the livestock of the vill. In all it is worth £16; when received, £8; TRE £18. Eadgifu held this manor, and the 8 sokemen themselves could sell their land without her leave.

• In Fen Drayton 5 sokemen hold 4½ hides from the count. There is land for 2 ploughs, and there are [2 ploughs], with 1 villan and 5 bordars and 3 cottars. [There is] meadow for 2 ploughs, [and] pasture for the livestock of the vill. It is and was worth 20*s*.; TRE 27*s*. The sokemen themselves held under Eadgifu, and could sell to whom they would.

• In Willingham 1 sokeman holds 1 virgate of land from the count. There is land for 2 oxen, [and] meadow for 2 oxen. It is and always was worth 3*s*. Oswulf, the man of Eadgifu, held this land: he could sell it but the soke remained with the Abbey of Ely.

IN 'NORTHSTOWE' HUNDRED

• In Longstanton Picot holds 4 hides and 1½ virgates from the count. There is land for 5 ploughs. In demesne [are] 2 ploughs; and 4 villans and 12 bordars and 6 cottars have 6 ploughs. There is 1 slave, and meadow for 2 ploughs. It is and was worth 100*s*.; TRE £8. 13 sokemen held this land. Of these, one was the man of Bishop Wulfwig, the rest were the men of Eadgifu. All of them could give and sell their land.

• In Landbeach Walter holds 4½ hides, less 12 acres, from the count. There is land for 4 ploughs. In demesne [are] 1½ hides and 18 acres, and there is 1 plough. There 3 villans with 13 bordars have 3 ploughs. There are 17 cottars, meadow for 6 ploughs, [and] pasture for the livestock of the vill. [From] the fen, 450 eels. In all it is worth £6. 10*s*.; when received, £6; TRE £3. Eadgifu held this manor, and 1 sokeman held 2 hides and 1 virgate there under her. He could give [his land] to whom he would, but the Abbot of Ely had sake and soke of the virgate.

• In Dry Drayton the monks of Swavesey hold 3 hides under Count Alan. There is land for 3 ploughs. In demesne is 1 plough; and 5 villans with 2 cottars have 2 ploughs. [There is] meadow for 1 plough. It is and was worth 40*s*.; TRE 60*s*. Eadgifu held this land.

IN CHEVELEY HUNDRED

• Wighen holds WOODDITTON from Count Alan. It was assessed at 5 hides TRE, and now at 3 hides. There is land for 10 ploughs. In demesne [are] 4 ploughs. There 10 villans with 8 bordars have 6 ploughs. There are 4 slaves, pasture for the livestock of the vill, [and] woodland for 150 pigs. In all it is worth £10; when received, £14; TRE £7. Eadgifu held this manor.

• In Cheveley Enisant holds 1½ hides and 20 acres from the count. There is land for 3 ploughs, and there are 2 [ploughs] in demesne; and 4 bordars with 1 plough. There is 1 slave, woodland for 12 pigs, [and] pasture for the livestock of the vill. It is and always was worth 40*s*. Heoruwulf, the man of Eadgifu, held this land; he could give and sell it.

IN 'STAINE' HUNDRED

• In Swaffham Bulbeck Geoffrey holds 1 hide and 3 virgates from the count. There is land for 4 ploughs. In demesne is 1 [plough]; and 3 villans have 3 ploughs. There are 2 slaves, and 1 mill rendering 4*s*. 4*d*. and 100 eels, meadow for 1 plough, [and] pasture for their livestock. It is worth 40*s*.; when received, 20*s*.; TRE the same. 6 sokemen held this land under Eadgifu; they could not depart without her leave, but they provided 3 watchmen and 1 cartage-due a year for the sheriff.

In the same vill 3 knights hold 3 hides and 1 virgate from the count. There is land for 4 ploughs, and there are [4 ploughs], with 3 villans and 2 slaves. [There is] meadow for 2 ploughs. It is worth 100*s*.; when received, 55*s*.; TRE the same. Huscarl, the man of King Edward, held 3 virgates of this land and provided cartage-due. He could give and sell his land, but the soke remained with the king.

Eadgifu held 1 hide and 1 virgate of the same land, and Wulfwig, her man, 1 hide and 1 virgate. Eadgifu had its soke.

• Odo holds 4 hides from Count Alan [Great Wilbraham]. There is land for 9 ploughs. In demesne are 2 [ploughs]; and 8 villans with 7 bordars have 7 ploughs. There are 6 slaves, and 1 mill [rendering] 5*s.* 4*d.*, meadow for 9 ploughs, [and] pasture for the livestock of the vill. In all it is and was worth £12; TRE £10. Ordmær, the man of Eadgifu, held this land, and could give it to whom he would.

• Odo holds 1 hide from the count [Stow cum Quy]. There is land for 2 ploughs, and there is [*sic*] [2 ploughs], with 3 bordars. [There is] meadow for 1 plough, and 1 mill [rendering] 18*s.* It is worth 40*s.*; when received, 20*s.*; TRE 40*s.* Grimbald, the man of Eadgifu, held this land; he could neither give nor sell it.

In 'Staploe' Hundred

• Ordmær holds Badlingham from the count. It was assessed at 3½ hides TRE, and now at 2½ hides. There is land for 6 ploughs. In demesne are 2 [ploughs]; and 9 villans with 6 bordars have 4 ploughs. There are 6 slaves, and 2 mills, one rendering 6*s.* and the other the milling for the demesne, meadow for 2 ploughs, [and] pasture for the livestock of the vill. In all it is and was worth 60*s.*; TRE 100*s.* Ordmær held this manor under Eadgifu, and could give it to whom he would.

• In Exning [Suffolk] Wihomarc holds 1½ hides from the count. There is land for 3 ploughs. In demesne are 2 ploughs; and 4 villans have 1 plough. There are 8 slaves, and 1 mill [rendering] 5*s.* 4*d.*, fisheries [rendering] 1,200 eels, meadow for 2 ploughs, [and] pasture for the livestock of the vill. It is and was worth 50*s.*; TRE 60*s.* Alsige, the man of Eadgifu, held this land, and could depart without her leave.

• In Burwell Alan holds 2½ hides from Count Alan. There is land for 5 ploughs. In demesne are 2 [ploughs]; and 4 villans have 3 ploughs. There are 4 slaves, and 2 mills rendering 6*s.* 8*d.*, meadow for 3 ploughs, [and] pasture for the livestock of the vill. It is worth £4; when received, £3; TRE £6. 2 sokemen held this land under Eadgifu; they could depart without her leave. One of them provided escort-service or 4*d.* for the king's service.

• In the same vill Geoffrey holds 1 hide and 1 virgate from Count Alan. There is land for 2 ploughs, and there are [2 ploughs] in demesne, with 3 villans and 2 slaves. [There is] meadow for 1 plough, [and] pasture for the livestock of the vill. It is worth 40*s.*; when received, 30*s.*; TRE 40*s.* 1 sokeman held this land under Eadgifu; he could depart without her leave.

• In Fordham Wihomarc holds 3½ hides from the count. There is land for 4 ploughs. In demesne [is] 1 hide, and 1 plough; and the sokemen have 3 ploughs. [There is] meadow for 1 plough, [and] pasture for the livestock of the vill. It is worth £4; when received, £3; TRE 70*s.* 3 sokemen held this land, of whom 2 [were] the men of Eadgifu, the third [was] the man of Earl Ælfgar; they could depart without their leave. They provided escort-service and cartage-due for the sheriff.

• In Isleham Geoffrey holds 40 acres of land from the count. There is land for 4 oxen, meadow for these oxen, and 2 villans. It is worth 10*s.*; when received, 5*s.*; TRE 10*s.* 2 sokemen held this land. They were the men of King Edward; they could depart. They provided cartage-due or escort-service for the sheriff.

• In Soham Adestan holds 1 hide from the count. There is land for 4 ploughs. In demesne [is] 1 plough; and 6 villans with 8 bordars have 2 ploughs, and there can be a third. [There is] meadow for 3 ploughs, pasture for the livestock of the vill, and 1,500 eels, and 1 seine in Soham mere [. . .] by custom. It is worth 60*s.*; when received, £6; and as much TRE. Alsige held this land under Eadgifu, and could depart without her leave.

• The count himself holds Wicken. It was assessed at 7 hides TRE, and now at 5 hides. [There is] land for 12 ploughs. In demesne [are] 3 hides, and 3 ploughs, and there can be a fourth. There 11 villans with 8 bordars have 8 ploughs. There are 5 slaves, and 3 mills rendering 28*s.* and 4,250 eels, meadow for 12 ploughs, pasture for the livestock of the vill, and by custom 3 seines in Soham mere. In all it is and was worth £14; TRE £6. Eadgifu the Fair held this manor.

In 'Radfield' Hundred

• In Dullingham 2 knights hold 2 hides and 10 acres from the count. There is land for 2 ploughs, and there are [2 ploughs], with 2 villans and 9 bordars and 2 slaves. [There is] meadow for 2 oxen. It is and always was worth 44*s.* 3 sokemen held this land; they could not depart.

• In Stetchworth Count Alan holds half a hide. There is land for half a plough, and there is [half a plough]. It is and always was worth 10*s.* Grim, the man of Eadgifu, held this; he could not depart.

• In Westley Waterless 2 knights hold 1 hide from the count. There is land for 2 ploughs, and there are [2 ploughs], with 4 bordars. It is and always was worth 20*s.* 7 sokemen held this land under Eadgifu. 4 provided cartage-dues in the king's service; they could not depart without the leave of their lady.

M • The count himself holds Burrough Green. There are 5 hides. There is land for 8 ploughs. In demesne [are] 3 hides, and there are 4 ploughs. There 7 villans with 10 bordars have 4 ploughs. There are 2 slaves, and 4 acres of meadow, [and] a park for wild beasts. In all it is worth £9; when received, £8; TRE £10. Eadgifu held this land.

• In Carlton Wihomarc holds 1 virgate of land from the count. A certain sokeman held it, and provided cartage-due.

• The same Wihomarc holds 1½ hides from the count [Weston Colville]. There is land for 3 ploughs. In demesne are 2 [ploughs]; and 3 villans with 3 bordars have 1 plough. There are 3 slaves, meadow for 2 oxen, [and] woodland for 10 pigs. It is and was worth £3. Godwine Cild held this land under Eadgifu; he could not depart.

• In West Wratting Almær holds 1½ hides from the count. There is land for 4 ploughs. In demesne are 2 [ploughs]; and 3 villans with 1 bordar have 2 ploughs. There is 1 slave, and woodland for 8 pigs. It is worth 60*s.*; when received, 20*s.*; TRE the same. 2 sokemen held this land under Eadgifu; they could not depart from her. One of them provided cartage-due for the sheriff.

In Balsham Almær holds 40 acres of land from the count. This is valued with the other land. Leofflæd held it under Eadgifu; she could not depart from her.

XXV. THE LAND OF COUNT EUSTACE

In Whittlesford Hundred

• Count Eustace holds Ickleton. It is assessed at 19½ hides. There is land for 24 ploughs. In demesne [are] 9 hides, and there are 3 ploughs, and there can be a fourth. There 30 villans with 10 bordars have 16 ploughs, and there can be 4 more. There are 3 slaves, and 2 mills [rendering] 30*s*., [and] meadow for 3 ploughs. All together it is worth £20; when received, £24; and TRE the same. Alsige, King Edward's thegn, held this manor.

• In Duxford the count himself holds 5 hides and 3 virgates. There is land for 6 ploughs. In demesne is 1 plough, and there can be 2 more. There 2 villans with 6 bordars have 2 ploughs, and there can be a third. There was 1 mill rendering 12*s*.; [it is] now broken, but can be repaired. [There is] meadow for 2 ploughs. All together it is worth 100*s*.; when received, £7; and as much TRE. Ernulf holds this land from Count Eustace. Heoruwulf held 7 virgates from King Edward, and Archbishop Stigand 3½ hides. Guy holds half a hide of this land and 1 mill at farm from Count Eustace. All together it is worth 28*s*. 8*d*. Ingvar held this land from King Edward, and could sell it.

In Thriplow Hundred

• In Trumpington Ernulf d'Ardres holds 2 hides and 1½ virgates under the count. There is land for 2½ ploughs. In demesne are 1½ [ploughs]; and 3 villans have 1 plough. There is 1 slave, and meadow for the ploughs. All together it is and was worth £4; TRE 100*s*. Heoruwulf, King Edward's thegn, held this land; he could give it to whom he would.

In 'Wetherley' Hundred

• In Grantchester 2 knights hold 2 hides and 3 virgates from the count. There is land for 6 ploughs. In demesne are 3 [ploughs]; and 3½ villans with 13 bordars and 16 cottars have 3 ploughs. There is 1 mill rendering 40*s*.; [and] meadow for 4 ploughs. All together it is worth £8; when received, £10; and as much TRE. 3 sokemen held this land, of whom 2, the men of King Edward, could sell, and the third, the man of Esger the staller, had half a hide and provided cartage-due, yet he could sell his land.

XXVI. THE LAND OF THE CANONS OF BAYEUX

In Longstowe Hundred

• The canons of Bayeux hold 3 hides in Eltisley. There is land for 9 ploughs. In demesne [are] 1½ hides, and there are 3 ploughs; and 6 villans with 10 bordars have 6 ploughs. There are 5 cottars and 6 slaves, meadow for 3 ploughs, [and] woodland for 20 pigs. In all it is and always was worth £13. Earl Ælfgar held this manor.

XXVII. THE LAND OF WALTER GIFFARD

In 'Staine' Hundred

• Walter Giffard holds Bottisham. It is assessed at 10 hides. There is land for 20 ploughs. In demesne [are] 5 hides, and there are 6 ploughs. There 25 villans with 12 bordars have 14 ploughs. There are 14 slaves, and 4 mills rendering 14*s*., [and] meadow for 6 ploughs. From the fen, 3 ploughshares and 400 eels. In all it is and was worth £20; TRE £16. Earl Harold held 8 hides of this manor, and Alric the monk had 2 hides which he could not give or sell without the leave of the Abbot of Ramsey, whose man he was.

• In Swaffham Bulbeck Hugh holds 7½ hides and 10 acres from Walter. There is land for 11 ploughs. In demesne are 3 [ploughs]; and 12 villans with 4 bordars have 8 ploughs. There are 3 slaves, and 3 mills rendering 30*s*., less 4*d*., and 300 eels, meadow for 3 ploughs, [and] pasture for the livestock of the vill. In all it is worth £12; when received, £10; and as much TRE. Alwig the harper held 3 hides and 1 mill of the demesne farm of the monks of Ely [in] this manor; and they themselves [*sic*] had them both during the life and at the death of King Edward: he could not depart without the leave of the abbot; and 3 sokemen, men of the abbot, held 2½ hides and 10 acres, nor could these men depart without the leave of the abbot; and 19 sokemen, the men of King Edward, held 2 hides: they could not depart without the leave of their lord, but they always provided cartage-due and escort-service for the king's sheriff.

• In the same vill Hugh holds 3 virgates from Walter. There is land for 1 plough, and there is [1 plough], with 4 bordars. [There is] meadow for 1 plough. It is and was worth 10*s*.; TRE 20*s*. Wulfwine, the man of the Abbot of Ely, held this land; he could not depart from the church without his leave.

In 'Wetherley' Hundred

• In Harlton Walter fitzAubrey holds 4 hides from Walter Giffard. There is land for 6 ploughs. In demesne are 2 [ploughs]; and 7 villans with 9 bordars have 4 ploughs. There are 2 slaves, and half a mill rendering 13*s*. 4*d*. and 100 eels, [and] meadow for 3 ploughs. All together it renders £7; when received, £6; TRE £8. Aki, the thegn of King Edward, held this land, and there were 5 sokemen, and they provided 5 watchmen and could sell their land.

• In Barrington the same Walter holds 40 acres from Walter Giffard. There is land for 6 oxen, and there are [6 oxen], with 2 cottars. [There is] meadow for 6 oxen. It is and always was worth 10*s*. Aki, Earl Harold's man, held this land and could give and sell it.

• In Orwell Walter holds 1 virgate from Walter Giffard. There is land for 2 oxen. There are 3 bordars. It is and always was worth 2*s*. Aki, Earl Harold's man, held this land. This pertains to Harlton.

XXVIII. THE LAND OF WILLIAM DE WARENNE

In 'Radfield' Hundred

• William de Warenne holds 2 hides and 7½ acres in Carlton. Walter de Grandcourt holds of him. There is land for 4 ploughs. In demesne are 3 [ploughs]; and 1½ villans with 3 bordars have 1 plough. There are 3 slaves, meadow for 2 oxen, [and] woodland for 12 pigs. It is and always was worth £4. Toki, King Edward's thegn, held this manor.

• In the same vill the Abbot of Cluny holds 4 hides and 2 acres from William. There is land for 7 ploughs. In demesne are 3 [ploughs]; and 4 villans with 14 bordars have 3 ploughs. There are 3 slaves, [and] woodland for 100 pigs. It is and always was worth £8. Earl Ælfgar held this land.

M • William himself holds Weston Colville. It is assessed at 7 hides. There is land for 15 ploughs. In demesne [are] 4 hides, and there are 2 ploughs, and there can be a third. There 19 villans with 7 bordars have 12 ploughs. There are 5 slaves, and 4 acres of meadow, [and] woodland for 300 pigs. All together it is worth £16 and 1 ounce of gold; when received, £10; and as much TRE. Toki held this land from the Abbot of Ely on the day on which King Edward was alive and dead, in such a way that he could not alienate it from the church because it was [of] the demesne farm of the abbey, as the men of the hundred bear witness. There were 2 sokemen on this land; one provided cartage-due and the other escort-service. They were the men of Godwine Cild and could not depart from him. Walter holds 1 virgate from William in the same vill.

• In West Wratting Lambert holds 3 virgates from William. There is land for half a plough, and there is [half a plough], with 1 villan, and half an acre of meadow. It is and always was worth 5*s*. Toki held this land from King Edward and provided 1 cartage-due.

In Chilford Hundred

☒ • In West Wickham Lambert holds 1 hide from William. There is land for 3½ ploughs. In demesne are 2 [ploughs]; and 10 bordars have 1½ ploughs. There are 3 slaves, and meadow for 1 plough, [and] woodland for 12 pigs. It is and always was worth 100*s*. Toki held this land, and there was 1 sokeman who provided cartage-due.

In Thriplow Hundred

• In Trumpington William holds 4½ hides. There is land for 5 ploughs. In demesne are 2 [ploughs]; and 9 villans with 4 bordars have 3 ploughs. There is 1 mill rendering 20*s*., meadow for 5 ploughs, pasture for the livestock of the vill, and 4 ploughshares. It is and was worth £6; TRE £7. Toki held this land from the Church of Ely on the day on which King Edward was alive and dead; he could neither give nor sell it nor alienate it from the church. Afterwards Frederick, William's brother, had this land.

In 'Staploe' Hundred

M • Kennett was assessed at 3½ hides TRE, and now at 2½ hides. There is land for 10 ploughs. Nicol holds it from William. In demesne are 5 ploughs; and 7 villans with 5 bordars have 5 ploughs. There are 12 slaves, and 1 mill rendering nothing, meadow for 2 ploughs, [and] pasture for the livestock of the vill. In all it is worth £12; when received, £9; TRE £12. Toki, King Edward's thegn, held this manor, and in the same place 1 sokeman had 1 virgate under him; he provided cartage-due or 8*d*., yet could give and sell his land.

In the Hundred[s] of Ely

• In Wisbech William has 6 fishermen rendering 3,500 eels and 5*s*.

XXV. THE LAND OF RICHARD SON OF COUNT GILBERT

In Papworth Hundred

• Richard, son of Count Gilbert, holds 1 virgate of land in Papworth [?St Agnes], and William [holds] from him. There is land for 4 oxen, and meadow for as many oxen. It is worth 4*s*.; when received, 5*s*.; TRE 8*s*. Ælfric, a priest, held this land from the Abbot of Ely, and could not depart from him. The soke also always pertained to the church. Richard seized this land in defiance of the king, and took from it 20*s*. worth of livestock.

In Chilford Hundred

• In Horseheath Wulfgifu holds half a virgate from Richard. There is land for 4 oxen. It is and was worth 5*s*.

• In West Wickham Wulfgifu holds half a virgate from Richard, and it is worth 5*s*.; and 1 sokeman [holds] the fourth part of 1 virgate, and it is worth 12*d*.

In 'Arringford' Hundred

• In Whaddon Hardwin holds 1 virgate of land from Richard. There is land for 4 oxen. It is and was worth 5*s*.; TRE 15*s*. Sægifu held this land under Eadgifu the Fair, and could give it to whom she would. This did not pertain to the predecessor of Richard, nor was he ever seised of it, but Ralph Guader held it on the day on which he offended against the king.

THE LAND OF ROBERT DE TOSNY

In Whittlesford Hundred

• Robert de Tosny holds 4½ hides in Duxford. Gilbert holds from him. There is land for 5 ploughs. In demesne is 1 [plough], and there can be 2 more; and 4 villans with 5 bordars have 2 ploughs. There are 2 slaves, and 2 mills rendering 50*s*., [and] meadow for 2 ploughs. It is worth £7. 10*s*.; when received, 110*s*.; TRE £8. Ulf, King Edward's thegn, held this land.

THE LAND OF ROBERT GERNON

In Chilford Hundred

• Robert Gernon holds 2 hides in Shudy Camps, and Turstin [holds] of him. There is land for 6 ploughs. In demesne are 2 [ploughs]; and 8 villans with 8 bordars have 4 ploughs. There are 6 slaves, meadow for 2 ploughs, [and] woodland for 12 pigs. It is worth £4; when received, 30*s*.; TRE 40*s*. Leofsige held this land under Earl Harold, and could depart without his leave.

• In Duxford Robert holds half a hide. It is and was worth 5*s*.; TRE 6*s*. Ælfric held this from King Edward and could depart.

In Thriplow Hundred

M • Robert himself holds Fowlmere. It is assessed at 10 hides. There is land for 11 ploughs. In demesne [are] 5 hides, and there are 2½ ploughs. There 22 villans with 10 bordars have 8½ ploughs. There are 4 slaves, and 1 mill rendering 10*s*. 8*d*., meadow for all the ploughs, [and] pasture for the livestock of the vill, and 10*d*. In all it is and always was worth £12. Ælfric Cap held this manor from King Edward.

• In Harston Ranulph holds 1 hide and 1 virgate from Robert. There is land for 1 plough and 2 oxen, and they are there, with 3 bordars and 1 cottar. [There is] meadow for 1 plough. It is worth 30*s*.; when received, 20*s*.; TRE 30*s*. 1 sokeman held this land under King Edward [. . .] and provided 1 watchman, and he could sell his land, but the soke remained with the king.

In 'Wetherley' Hundred

• In Barrington Robert holds 7 hides and 2½ virgates. There is land for 11 ploughs. In demesne [are] 3½ hides and 2 parts of a virgate, and there is 1 plough, and there can be another. There 20 villans with 7 bordars and 3 cottars have 9 ploughs. There are 2 slaves, and 1½ mills rendering 32*s*., [and] meadow for 6 ploughs. In all it is worth £12; when received, £8; TRE £16. On this land there were 15 sokemen holding 4 hides and 1½ virgates from King Edward and providing for the sheriff 12½ cartage-dues and 4 watchmen; and 4 others, the men of Earl Ælfgar, held 2 hides and half a virgate; and 3 others, the men of Esger the staller, held 1 hide. All these men could give and sell their land. Of this land also Eadric Pur held

3 virgates under King Edward and could sell them, and the same Eadric held half a virgate which on the day of King Edward's death pertained to the Church of Chatteris. Robert Gernon usurped this in defiance of the abbess, as the men of the hundred bear witness.

• In Orwell Robert holds 1 virgate. There is land for 3 oxen, and there are [3 oxen], with 2 bordars. [There is] meadow for 2 oxen, and 1 mill rendering 12*s.* It is and always was worth 18*s.* 8*d.* 1 sokeman of King Edward held this land, and he provided 1 cartage-due, and yet he could sell his land.

IN PAPWORTH HUNDRED

• In Conington Picot holds 1 hide and 1 virgate from Robert. There is land for 1 plough, and there is [1 plough], with 3 bordars. [There is] meadow for 1½ ploughs. It is worth 16*s.*; when received, 20*s.*; and as much TRE. 1 man of Earl Waltheof held this land. Its soke pertained to Longstanton.

• In Boxworth Picot holds 3½ hides from Robert. There is land for 3 ploughs. In demesne are 2 [ploughs]; and 3 villans with 3 cottars have 1 plough. There are 2 slaves, [and] meadow for 3 ploughs. It is worth 30*s.*; when received, 10*s.*; TRE 60*s.* Leofsige, Earl Waltheof's man, held this land and could sell it.

• In Swavesey Picot holds 1 hide from Robert. There is land for 1 plough, and there are 2 bordars, [and] meadow for 1 plough. It is and was worth 5*s.*; TRE 20*s.* Leofsige, Earl Waltheof's man, held this land and could give and sell it. Picot the sheriff holds these lands [. . .] from Robert Gernon as his wife's dowry.

XX. THE LAND OF GEOFFREY DE MANDEVILLE

IN FLEAMDYKE HUNDRED

• GEOFFREY de Mandeville holds 2½ hides in Fulbourn. There is land for 3 ploughs. William holds them from him. There are 3 ploughs, [and] meadow for 1 plough. It is worth 50*s.*; when received, 60*s.*; and as much TRE. Alsige held this land from Esger and could give it without his leave.

IN WHITTLESFORD HUNDRED

• In Sawston Roger holds 2 hides from Geoffrey. There is land for 2 ploughs, and there are [2 ploughs], with 6 villans and 4 bordars. There is 1 slave, and meadow for 2 ploughs, and 1 mill rendering 26*s.* 8*d.* It is and always was worth 100*s.* Sigar held this land from Esger the staller, and could give and sell it without his leave.

IN THRIPLOW HUNDRED

• In Thriplow Sigar holds 1½ hides from Geoffrey. There is land for 2 ploughs. In demesne [is] 1 [plough]; and 4 villans have the other. There is 1 slave, [and] pasture for the livestock. It is and always was worth 40*s.* This Sigar held it under Esger and could give or sell it without his leave, but the soke remained with the lord.

• In Foxton Sigar holds 3½ hides and 20 acres from Geoffrey. There is land for 5 ploughs. In demesne are 2 [ploughs]; and 5 villans with 10 bordars have 3 ploughs. There is 1 slave, and meadow for 5 ploughs. It is and always was worth £4. This Sigar held it under Esger; he could sell and give it, but the soke remained with the lord.

• In the same vill is half a mill rendering 10*s.* 8*d.* which Robert Gernon usurped in defiance of Geoffrey, as the men of the hundred bear witness.

IN 'STAPLOE' HUNDRED

M • CHIPPENHAM was assessed at 10 hides TRE, but a certain sheriff reduced them to 5 hides by permission of the same king because its farm was a burden on him, and now it is assessed at 5 hides. There is land for 17 ploughs. Geoffrey holds it from the king. In demesne are 3 hides, and there are 3 ploughs. There 19 villans with 13 bordars have 14 ploughs. There are 6 slaves, meadow for 3 ploughs, [and] pasture for the livestock of the vill. From the fishery, 1,500 eels. In all it is worth £20; when received, £16; TRE £12. Ordgar, King Edward's sheriff, who was afterwards the man of Esger the staller, held this manor. 5 hides of this land were in King Edward's farm, and 2 sokemen had 2 hides from the king and could give their land to whom they would, and yet each one provided 8*d.* or 1 horse in the king's service, and paid their forfeitures in Fordham.

• Ordgar the sheriff himself had 3 hides of this land, and could give them to whom he would. Ordgar put this land in pledge for 7 marks of gold and 2 ounces, as Geoffrey's men say, but the men of the hundred have seen neither any writ nor any messenger of King Edward concerning it, nor do they produce any testimony.

IN 'ARRINGFORD' HUNDRED

• In Guilden Morden Richard holds 3 virgates of land from Geoffrey. There is land for 2 ploughs. In demesne [is] 1 plough; and 1 villan with 5 cottars have 1 plough. There are 3 other cottars, and meadow for 4 oxen, [and] pasture for the livestock. It is worth 20*s.*; when received, 15*s.*; TRE 40*s.* Godwine held this land from Esger the staller and could sell it.

IN 'WETHERLEY' HUNDRED

• In Haslingfield Roger holds 5 hides from Geoffrey. There is land for 6 ploughs. In demesne are 2 [ploughs]; and 8 villans with 18 cottars have 4 ploughs. [There is] meadow for 2 ploughs. All together it is worth £7; when received and TRE, £6. Sigar, the man of Esger the staller, held this land and could give or sell it, but the soke remained with the lord.

• In Shepreth Sigar holds 1 hide from Geoffrey. There is land for 1 plough, and there is [1 plough], with 1 villan and 2 bordars, and 2 mills rendering 10*s.* 8*d.*, [and] meadow for 1 plough. It is and was worth 20*s.*; TRE 23*s.* This man held it from Esger and could give or sell it.

In Orwell Sigar holds 1 virgate and the third part of a virgate from Geoffrey. There is land for 4 oxen, and there are [4 oxen. There is] meadow for 2 oxen, with 1 villan. It is and was worth 8*s.*; TRE 10*s.* This man held it under Esger and could sell.

XXI. THE LAND OF GILBERT DE GHENT

IN PAPWORTH HUNDRED

• GILBERT de Ghent holds 1½ virgates in Papworth [?St Agnes]. Alweald holds from him. There is land for 4 oxen, and there are [4 oxen], with 1 villan. [There is] meadow for 4 oxen. It is and was worth 5*s.*; TRE 10*s.* Ulf, King Edward's thegn, held this land, and it pertains to Fenstanton [Hunts.].

• In Elsworth 2 sokemen hold half a hide less 5 acres from Gilbert. There is land for 6 oxen, and there are [6 oxen], and meadow for 6 oxen. It is and always was worth 6*s.* 8*d.* 2 sokemen, the men of Ulf, held this land;

one of them provided escort-service for the sheriff, yet both could depart with their land.

• In Conington 8 sokemen hold 2 hides and 3 virgates from Gilbert. There is land for 2½ ploughs, and there are [2½ ploughs], with 8 cottars. [There is] meadow for 2½ ploughs. It is and was worth 25*s*.; TRE 30*s*. These men held from Ulf and could give and sell [their land].

• In Boxworth 6 sokemen hold 1 hide and 1 virgate from Gilbert. There is land for 1 plough, and there is [1 plough, and] meadow for 1 plough. It is worth 10*s*.; when received, 16*s*.; TRE 20*s*. These men held from Ulf and could sell [their land]. Their soke pertained to Fenstanton [Hunts.].

• In Swavesey Gilbert holds 1 hide. There is land for 1 plough, and there is [1 plough], with 2 villans and 3 bordars and 2 cottars. From the fen, 225 eels. It is and was worth 10*s*.; TRE 20*s*. Ulf, King Edward's thegn, held this land.

• In Fen Drayton Gilbert holds 3 hides and 1 virgate. There is land for 1½ ploughs. In demesne [is] 1 hide, and 1 sokeman having 1 hide and 1 virgate, and there are 4 villans, meadow for 1½ ploughs, [and] pasture for the livestock of the vill. It is and was worth 10*s*.; TRE 20*s*. Ulf, King Edward's thegn, held this land, and this 1 sokeman was his man, yet he could give and sell his land without his leave.

XXII. THE LAND OF GILBERT FITZTUROLD

In 'Northstowe' Hundred

• Gilbert fitzTurold holds 4½ hides in Longstanton. There is land for 6 ploughs. Hugh holds of him. In demesne are 2 ploughs; and 7 villans with 9 bordars and 13 cottars have 4 ploughs. There are 3 slaves, [and] meadow for 2 ploughs. From the fen, 3,200 eels and 2*s*. 8*d*. It is and was worth £6; TRE £8. Saxi, King Edward's thegn, held this land and could give or sell it.

XXIII. THE LAND OF EUDO FITZHUBERT

In Chilford Hundred

• Eudo the steward holds 1½ virgates of land in Babraham, and Pirot holds from him. There is land for half a plough. There are 2 villans. It is and was worth 2 orae. Ælfric held this land and could give and sell it.

• In Pampisford Pirot holds 5 acres from Eudo. It is and was worth 6*d*. Burro held it from Ælfric Campe and could depart.

In Whittlesford Hundred

• In Sawston Pirot holds 4 hides from Eudo. There is land for 5 ploughs. In demesne are 2 [ploughs]; and 11 villans with 6 bordars have 3 ploughs. There is 1 slave, and 2 mills rendering 30*s*. 8*d*., [and] meadow for 5 ploughs. It is and always was worth £8. Ælfric held this land from the king, and there were 3 sokemen under him, and they could not depart.

In 'Arringford' Hundred

• In 'Clopton' [in Croydon] Humphrey holds 1½ hides from Eudo. There is land for 2 ploughs, and there are [2 ploughs], with 7 bordars. [There is] meadow for 2 ploughs, and woodland for repairing fences. It is worth £4; when received, 40*s*.; and as much TRE. Earl Gyrth held this land.

• In East Hatley Humphrey holds 1 hide and 1 virgate from Eudo. There is land for 1 plough, and there are 2 bordars. [There is] meadow for 1 plough. It is and was worth 20*s*.; TRE 30*s*. Almær, the man of Robert fitzWimarc, held this land and could give and sell his land.

• In Croydon Humphrey holds 2 hides from Eudo. There is land for 2 ploughs, and there are [2 ploughs], with 6½ villans. [There is] meadow for 2 ploughs. It is and always was worth 40*s*. Earl Gyrth held this land.

In 'Wetherley' Hundred

• In Wimpole Humphrey holds 1 hide and 1½ virgates from Eudo. There is land for 2 ploughs, and there are [2 ploughs] in demesne, and 1 villan and 1 slave, meadow for 1 plough, [and] woodland for fences. It is and always was worth 100*s*. Earl Gyrth held this land.

In Longstowe Hundred

• In Kingston Humphrey holds 10 acres of land from Eudo. There is land for 1 ox. It is and always was worth 8*d*. Almær, the man of Earl Waltheof, held this land and could depart.

• In Gamlingay Eudo holds 18 hides. There is land for 18 ploughs. In demesne [are] 9 hides, and there are 3 ploughs. There 30 villans with 12 bordars have 15 ploughs. There 1 Frenchman has half a hide, and 12 cottars and [there are] 4 slaves. [There is] meadow for 12 ploughs, woodland for 10 pigs, [and] pasture for the livestock of the vill. In all it is worth £18; when received, £10; and as much TRE. Wulfmær of Eaton Socon held this manor, and there were 9 sokemen who held 4 hides and could give and sell [their land], and besides these hides they held 1 virgate which pertains to Little Gransden, a manor of the Abbot of Ely, [and] which Lisois de Moutiers seized in defiance of the abbot, so the hundred bears witness.

• In Hatley St George Eudo holds 1 hide. There is land for 1 plough, but there is no [plough] recorded there. In demesne are 3 virgates and 10 acres, with 3 bordars with 20 acres. [There is] a wood for fences. It is worth 5*s*.; when received, 10*s*.; TRE 20*s*. 2 sokemen of Robert fitzWimarc held this land and could sell it.

XXIIII. THE LAND OF HARDWIN DE SCALES

In 'Staine' Hundred

• Hardwin de Scales holds 1 virgate of land in Swaffham Prior. There is land for 2 oxen. It is and always was worth 5*s*. 6 sokemen held this land, of whom 3 provided cartage-due and the other 3 escort-service.

• In 'Staploe' Hundred Hardwin holds half a hide from the king [Burwell]. There is land for 4 oxen, and there are [4 oxen, and] meadow for these oxen. It is worth 20*s*.; when received, 16*s*.; TRE 20*s*. Turch, the man of the Abbot of Ramsey, held this land. He could not depart without his leave, and yet provided either escort-service or 4*d*. in the king's service.

In 'Radfield' Hundred

• In Dullingham Hardwin holds 2 hides, less 20 acres. There is land for 2 ploughs, and there are [2 ploughs], with 7 villans and 1 bordar. [There is] woodland for 4 pigs. It is and always was worth 40*s*. 16 sokemen held this land, and they could give and sell their land, and yet they provided cartage-dues.

• In Westley Waterless Hardwin holds 15 acres of land. It is and always was worth 16*d*. 2 sokemen of Earl Harold held them and could not depart.

• In Carlton 2 knights hold half a hide, less 3 acres, from Hardwin. There is land for half a plough, and there is [half a plough]. It is and always was worth 10*s*. 2 sokemen held 38 acres of this land under Harold, and provided 1 watchman for the sheriff. The third held 8 acres from Earl Ælfgar, and provided cartage-due, but he could not depart.

• In Weston Colville Durand holds 1 hide from Hardwin. There is land for 1 plough, and there is [1 plough], and meadow for the plough, [and] woodland for 12 pigs. It is worth 20*s*.; when received, 10*s*.; and as much TRE. Thorger, the man of Earl Ælfgar, held this land. He could not depart without his leave.

• In the same vill Hardwin holds 1 virgate of land in demesne. There is land for 2 oxen. It is and always was worth 5*s*. This land provided cartage-due and escort-service; 2 sokemen held this under Earl Harold and could not depart.

• In West Wratting Hardwin holds 1 virgate of land. There is land for 2 oxen. There are 2 bordars. It is and was worth 3*s*. Toki and Wihtgar held this; one provided cartage-due and the other provided escort-service.

In Chilford Hundred

• In Horseheath 5 villans hold half a hide from Hardwin. There is land for 1 plough, and there is [1 plough], and meadow. [There is] woodland for 24 pigs. It is and always was worth 25*s*. 4 men held 1½ virgates of this land from the king, and yet provided 1 cartage-due and 2 watchmen, and Leodmær held half a virgate under the predecessor of Aubrey de Vere; he could not depart without his leave.

• In West Wickham Hardwin holds 1 virgate from the king. There is land for half a plough, and there is [half a plough], with 3 bordars, and half an acre of meadow. It is and was worth 40*d*.; TRE 5*s*. 4*d*. 3 sokemen held it and provided 1 cartage-due.

• In Babraham Durand holds half a hide under Hardwin. There is land for half a plough, and there is [half a plough], with 4 bordars. It is and was worth 18*s*. 8*d*. 4 sokemen held this land; they provided 4 cartage-dues and could not depart. This land is [part] of the king's fief.

• In Pampisford Hardwin holds 1 virgate. It is and always was worth 65*d*. 2 sokemen held it from the king and could not depart.

In Whittlesford Hundred

• In Whittlesford Hardwin holds 1 virgate. There is land for 2 oxen. It is and was worth 32*d*. A man of Earl Gyrth held this; he could not sell it.

• In Hinxton Durand holds 1 hide from Hardwin. There is land for 1 plough, and there is [1 plough], with 2 slaves, and meadow for 1 plough. It is worth 20*s*.; when received, 10*s*.; and as much TRE. Eastræd held this land under Earl Ælfgar; he could give and sell it to whom he would.

• In Ickleton Durand holds half a hide from Hardwin. There is land for 4 oxen. It is worth 32*d*.; when received, 12*d*.; TRE 5*s*. Eastræd held this under Earl Ælfgar and he could sell it.

• In Duxford Payne holds 3 hides and 1 virgate from Hardwin. There is land for 3 ploughs and 2 oxen. In demesne are 2 ploughs; and 1 villan with 4 bordars have 1 plough and 2 oxen. There are 3 slaves, [and] meadow for 1 plough. From the pasture, 1 ploughshare. It is worth 50*s*.; when received, 60*s*.; TRE 100*s*. 13 sokemen held this land, 11 of whom were the men of King Edward and provided 2 cartage-dues and 9 watchmen for the sheriff, yet they could sell their lands; and the remaining 2 held 1½ hides: one [was] the man of Earl Ælfgar, the other the man of Eadgifu, but they could not sell their land.

In Thriplow Hundred

• In Hauxton Hardwin holds 1½ hides. There is land for 2 ploughs, and there are [2 ploughs], with 4 bordars. In demesne are 1½ hides, and 1 mill rendering 20*s*., meadow for 2 ploughs, [and] pasture for the livestock of the vill. It is and was worth 60*s*.; TRE £4.

Bondi held 3 virgates of this land from the Abbot of Ely, and could sell them, but the soke remained with the abbot; and another sokeman of Earl Ælfgar held 3 virgates and could depart with his land.

• In Little Shelford Hardwin holds 6 hides and 1 virgate and 7 acres. There is land for 6 ploughs and 2 oxen, and there are 8 ploughs. In demesne [is] 1 hide, and there is 1 plough; and 13 villans with 4 bordars have 7 ploughs. [There is] meadow for 4 ploughs, [and] pasture for the livestock. It is and was worth £6; TRE £8. 2½ hides and 9 acres of this land and a minster were in the demesne of the Church of Ely, TRE and on the day on which the same king [Edward] died, and now belong to the demesne farm, as the hundred bears witness. Moreover, 7 sokemen held 1½ hides and 6 acres of this land of the soke of the Abbot of Ely: they could not depart with the land, but the soke remained with the Church of Ely. 3 sokemen held half a hide of the same land under Earl Gyrth: they could not depart without his leave; their soke pertained to Whittlesford. Alsige held half a hide from Earl Ælfgar: he could give or sell it, but the soke remained with the earl, and he provided 1 watchman. 2 sokemen held 1 virgate and 7 acres from Earl Harold: they could not depart without leave; and 5 sokemen held 3½ virgates under King Edward and provided 1 cartage-due and 2 watchmen for the sheriff: they could sell their land, but their soke remained with the king.

In 'Arringford' Hundred

• In Steeple Morden Hardwin holds 1 hide less the fourth part of 1 virgate. There is land for 2 ploughs, and there are [2 ploughs]. There are 2 mills rendering 2 orae, meadow for 2 ploughs, [and] pasture for the livestock of the vill. It is and was worth 30*s*.; TRE 40*s*. 7 sokemen now hold this land from Hardwin, and the men themselves held it TRE; they could give and sell their land but the soke remained in Steeple Morden.

• In Guilden Morden Alverad holds half a virgate from Hardwin. There is land for half a plough. There is 1 cottar, and 1 acre of meadow. It is and was worth 5*s*.; TRE 10*s*. Vetrlithr held this land from Earl Ælfgar; he could not sell it. This land pertains to Litlington.

• In Croydon 2 knights hold 3 hides and 1 virgate from Hardwin. There is land for 4 ploughs. There are 3 ploughs, and there can be a fourth. There are 8 bordars, and meadow for 1 plough. It is and always was worth 65*s*. Alflæd, commended to Archbishop Stigand, held 1 hide of this land, and could give and sell it. 4 sokemen held 1 hide from King Edward and provided 4 watchmen for the sheriff, but could give or sell their land; and a man of Esger the staller held 5 virgates and could give and sell [his land].

• In Wendy Alvred holds 1 virgate from Hardwin. There is land for 3 oxen. It is and always was worth 5*s*. Goda, commended to Earl Ælfgar, held this land; he could give and sell it to whom he would.

• In Litlington Adelulf holds 2½ virgates from Hardwin at farm. There is land for 1 plough. There is half a plough, and there can be [another] half [-plough]. There is 1 bordar. It is and was worth 15*s*.; TRE 40*s*. Algar, the man of Archbishop Stigand, held half a hide of this land, and Alwig, the man of Earl Ælfgar, half a virgate, [and] he could not alienate it from Ickleton.

• In Abington Pigotts 2 knights hold 1 hide and 1½ virgates from Hardwin. There is land for 2 ploughs, and there are [2 ploughs], with 5 bordars. [There is] meadow for 4 oxen. It is worth 55*s*.; when received, 25*s*.; TRE 60*s*. A man of King Edward held 1 virgate of this land and provided 1 cartage-due for the sheriff;

and 2 other sokemen, the men of Earl Ælfgar, could give and sell their land to whom they would.

• In Bassingbourn Lyfing holds 1 hide from Hardwin. There is land for 1 plough, and there is [1 plough], with 2 bordars. [There is] meadow for 2 oxen. It is and was worth 30*s*.; TRE 40*s*. 2 sokemen of Earl Ælfgar held this land; they could give and sell it to whom they would.

• In Whaddon Hardwin holds 1 hide and 3 virgates. There is land for 2 ploughs. In demesne [is] 1 hide, and there is 1 plough; and 3 villans with 5 cottars have 1 plough. [There is] pasture for the livestock of the vill, [and] meadow for 1 plough. It is worth £4. 15*s*.; when received, 60*s*.; TRE £4. 15*s*. 2 sokemen held this land. One [was] the man of Archbishop Stigand, the other the man of Earl Ælfgar, and they could depart.

• In Whaddon Hardwin holds 2½ hides. There is land for 3 ploughs. In demesne [is] 1 hide, and there is 1 plough. There 6 villans and 15 cottars have 1½ ploughs, and there can be half [a plough] more. [There is] meadow for 2 ploughs, [and] pasture for the livestock of the vill. It is and was worth 70*s*.; TRE £4. Thorbiorn held 1 hide of this land under the Abbot of Ely in such a way that he could neither give nor alienate it from the church outside the demesne farm of the monks in the time of King Edward and on the day of his death; and 12 sokemen, the men of the Abbot of Ely, held 1½ hides [and] they could give and sell [their land] to whom they would, but the soke remained with the church.

• In the same vill Hardwin holds half a virgate. There is land for 2 oxen. It is and always was worth 2*s*. Denemund, the man of Esger the staller, held this, and could sell it.

• In Meldreth Hardwin holds 1 virgate. There is land for half a plough. It is and always was worth 2*s*. Almær held this under the Abbot of Ely and could sell it, but the soke remained with the church.

• In the same vill Hugh holds 1½ hides from Hardwin. There is land for 2 ploughs, and there are [2 ploughs], with 3 cottars and 1 slave. There is 1 minster, and 1 mill rendering 5*s*. 4*d*., meadow for 2 ploughs, [and] pasture for the livestock of the vill. It is and was worth 40*s*.; TRE £4. This land pertained to the Church of Ely in the demesne of the monks both during the life and at the death of King Edward, as the men of the hundred bear witness.

• In Melbourn Durand holds 1 hide and 1 virgate from Hardwin. There is land for 1½ ploughs. There is 1 [plough], and there can be [another] half [-plough]. There is 1 villan with 2 bordars and 3 cottars, meadow for 1 plough, [and] pasture for the livestock. It is worth 25*s*.; when received, 30*s*.; TRE 40*s*. Sigeræd, the man of Earl Ælfgar, held this land and could give and sell it.

• In Shepreth Hardwin holds 2 hides and half a virgate. There is land for 2 ploughs and 2 oxen, and they are there, with 2 villans and 9 cottars and 1 slave. [There is] meadow for all the ploughs. 1 knight holds this land, and 2 Englishmen under him. There is 1 mill rendering 7*s*., less 2*d*. It is and was worth 42*s*.; TRE 50*s*. 5 sokemen held this land. One of them [was] the man of Earl Ælfgar and the others were the men of King Edward, and they provided 2 cartage-dues and 2 watchmen and yet they could sell their land.

• In Shepreth Hugh holds half a virgate from Hardwin. There is land for 2 oxen, and meadow for 2 oxen. It is and always was worth 2*s*. This land pertained to the demesne of the Church of Ely both during the life and at the death of King Edward, as the men of the hundred bear witness.

• In Orwell Durand holds 3 virgates and the third part of a virgate from Hardwin. There is land for 1 plough, and there are 6 oxen, with 4 cottars, and 1 mill rendering 8*s*., [and] pasture for 6 oxen. [There is] a wood to close up [the gaps in] fences. It is and was worth 20*s*.; TRE 40*s*. 2 sokemen held this land. One, the man of Waltheof, held 3 virgates, the other, the king's man, held the third part of 1 virgate. They provided 2 watchmen and could depart.

• In 'Ratford' 2 knights hold 3 virgates from Hardwin. There is land for 1 plough. There are 6 cottars, and meadow for 1 plough. It is and was worth 25*s*.; TRE 50*s*. 2 sokemen held this land, one the man of Waltheof and the other the man of Robert fitzWimarc, and they could give and sell [their land].

• In 'Witewell' Robert the Bald holds 2 hides from Hardwin. There is land for 2 ploughs. In demesne is 1 plough; and 1 bordar with 4 cottars have 1 plough. [There is] meadow for 1 plough, [and] a wood to close up [the gaps in] fences. It is worth 30*s*.; when received, 20*s*.; TRE 40*s*. 8 sokemen held this land. 6 of them were the king's men and held 5 virgates and provided 3 cartage-dues and 3 watchmen, and the seventh, the man of Robert fitzWimarc, had half a hide, and the eighth, the man of Earl Ælfgar, held 1 virgate. All these men could depart.

IN LONGSTOWE HUNDRED

• In [Great and Little] Eversden Durand holds 1 virgate from Hardwin. There is land for 3 oxen, and there are [3 oxen], with 1 villan. [There is] meadow for 3 oxen. It is and always was worth 8*s*. 1 sokeman of Earl Ælfgar held this land and could depart.

• In Kingston 2 knights hold 1 virgate from Hardwin. There is land for 3 oxen, and meadow. It is and always was worth 2*s*. Goding Thorbert, the man of Eadgifu the Fair, held this land and could depart.

• In the same vill Robert the Bald holds 9 acres from Hardwin. There is land for half an ox. It is and always was worth 6*d*. Wulfmær, the man of Robert fitzWimarc, held this land and could give it.

• In Caldecote 2 knights hold 3 virgates and 10 acres from Hardwin. There is land for 2 ploughs, and there are [2 ploughs], with 6 bordars. [There is] meadow for 2 ploughs. It is and was worth 52*s*. 2 sokemen held this land under Eadgifu, and could depart.

• In Longstowe 1 knight and 2 Englishmen hold 3½ virgates. There is land for 1½ ploughs, and there are [1½ ploughs], with 4 bordars. [There is] meadow for 1½ ploughs, [and] a wood for fences. It is worth 42*s*.; when received, 30*s*.; TRE 42*s*. 4 sokemen held this land. One of these [was] the man of Archbishop Stigand, and the other 3 [were] the men of the Abbot of Ramsey. They could give and sell [their land].

M • Hardwin himself holds Caxton. It was assessed at 10 hides TRE, and now at 6 hides. There is land for 12 ploughs. In demesne [are] 5 hides, and there are 4 ploughs. There are 17 villans with 8 bordars and 10 cottars having 8 ploughs. [There is] meadow for 12 ploughs, [and] a wood for fences and houses. All together it is worth £11; when received, £6; TRE £14. Thorger, King Edward's thegn, held this manor, and there were 22 sokemen; 4 of these were King Edward's men: they held 1 hide and half a virgate.

This half-virgate provided 3 watchmen. These [sokemen] could give and sell their lands. The other 18 were the men of Earl Ælfgar and had 6 hides, less half a virgate, of this land.

• In Croxton Adelulf holds 1 hide from Hardwin. There is land for 1½ ploughs, and there are [1½ ploughs]. In demesne [is] 1 plough; and 5 bordars with 2 cottars have half a plough. [There is] meadow for 1½ ploughs, [and] pasture for the livestock. It is worth 20*s.*; when received, 13*s.*; TRE 40*s.* 2 sokemen, the men of King Edward, held this land and provided 2 cartage-dues for the sheriff.

In Papworth Hundred

• In Papworth St Agnes Payne holds 1½ virgates from Hardwin. There is land for 4 oxen, and there are [4 oxen], with 4 bordars, [and] meadow for 4 oxen. It is and always was worth 5*s.* 2 sokemen, the men of King Edward, held this land, and they provided 2 watchmen and could sell [their land].

• In Elsworth Payne holds 1 virgate from Hardwin. There is land for half a plough, and there is [half a plough], with 1 villan, [and] meadow for half a plough. It is and was worth 4*s.*; TRE 5*s.* 2 sokemen of King Edward held this land, and they provided 1 watchman and could sell [their land].

• In Conington Payne holds 2 hides from Hardwin. There is land for 2 ploughs. In demesne [is] 1 plough; and 1 villan with 4 bordars has 1 plough. There are 2 slaves, [and] meadow for 2 ploughs. It is worth 20*s.*; when received, 16*s.*; and as much TRE. 3 sokemen of King Edward held this land, and they provided 2 cartage-dues and 1 watchman and could depart.

• In Boxworth Payne holds 4½ hides from Hardwin. There is land for 4 ploughs. In demesne [is] 1 plough; and 8 villans with 6 bordars and 3 cottars have 3 ploughs. There are 2 slaves, and meadow for 4 ploughs. It is and always was worth 60*s.* 1 thegn of King Edward held 3½ hides [of] this land and could sell them to whom he would; and 7 sokemen of King Edward had 1 hide and provided 3 cartage-dues and 3 watchmen for the sheriff, and could sell their land.

• In Over Ralph holds 2 hides and 1 virgate from Hardwin. There is land for 2½ ploughs, and there are [2½ ploughs], with 3 villans and 1 bordar and 3 cottars. [There is] meadow for 2½ ploughs, [and] pasture for the livestock. It is and was worth 30*s.*; TRE 50*s.* They held this land [*sic*]. 1 sokeman held half a hide of this land under the Abbot of Ely: he could not give or sell it outside the church without the abbot's leave; and 2 other sokemen had 3 virgates, [and] could sell [their land, but] the soke remained with the Abbot of Ely; [. . .] and another 7 had 1 hide: they were the men of the Abbot of Ramsey, [and] could sell without the soke.

In Chesterton Hundred

• In Dry Drayton Payne holds 5 hides and 3 virgates from Hardwin. There is land for 5 ploughs. In demesne [are] 2 ploughs; and 9 villans with 3 bordars have 2 ploughs, and there can be a third. There are 7 cottars, and meadow for 2 ploughs. This land is worth £4; when received, 100*s.*; TRE £6. 19 sokemen held this land. 6 of these, the men of King Edward, had 2 hides, less half a virgate, and provided 6 watchmen for the sheriff, and could give their land; and 4 others, the men of Eadgifu, had 1½ hides and could depart without the soke; and 5 others were the men of the Abbot of Ely, 4 of whom held 1 hide [. . .] and could sell it without the soke, the fifth had half a virgate under the abbot but could not sell it; and the other 4 were the men of St Guthlac, [and] held 1 hide and 1 virgate of the demesne farm of the church.

In 'Radfield' Hundred

• In Stetchworth Hardwin holds 1 virgate. There is land for 2 oxen. It is and always was worth 5*s.* Godwine, the man of the Abbot of Ely, held this land; he could not sell it.

In Westley Hundred 8

[Drawing of a hand: Arthur Agarde 1570–1615, or earlier]

• In West Wratting Hardwin holds 3 hides. There is land for 4 ploughs. In demesne are 2 [ploughs]; and 5 villans with 4 bordars have 2 ploughs. There are 4 slaves, and 4 acres of meadow, [and] woodland for 12 pigs. It is worth £6; when received, 20*s.*; TRE 40*s.* 10 sokemen, the men of the Abbot of Ely, held this land; they could not sell it.

• In Balsham Hardwin [. . .] holds 80 acres of the abbot's land. There is land for 1 plough, and there is [1 plough]. It is and was worth 13*s.* 4*d.* 3 sokemen held this land; they could not sell it.

In 'Staine' Hundred

• In Swaffham Prior Hardwin holds 2 hides and 3 virgates. There is land for 3 ploughs. In demesne is 1 [plough]; and 2 villans have 2 ploughs. [There is] meadow for 2 oxen. It is and always was worth 70*s.* 4 sokemen of the Abbot of Ely held this land; they could not sell it.

In Fleamdyke Hundred

• In Babraham Hardwin holds half a virgate of the abbot's land from the king. It is and was worth 40*d.* 2 sokemen held it from the Abbot of Ely. They could not depart.

• In Pampisford Hardwin holds 10 acres. There is land for 1 ox. It is and was worth 12*d.* Snelling held this land from the Abbot of Ely; he could not depart.

In Thriplow Hundred

• In Thriplow Hardwin holds from the king 1 hide of the demesne for the sustenance of the monks. There is land for 1 plough, and there is [1 plough]. It is and always was worth 20*s.* This land belonged to the demesne of the Church of Ely.

• In the same vill Hardwin held 2 acres of the abbot's land, for which he does not have a warrantor or a livery officer, but which he has usurped in defiance of the abbot, as the men of the hundred bear witness.

XXV. THE LAND OF HUGH DE BERNIERES

In Longstowe Hundred

• Hugh de Bernieres holds 1 hide in [Great and Little] Eversden from the king. There is land for 1 plough, and there is [1 plough], with 1 villan and 1 slave. [There is] meadow for 1 plough, [and] a wood for fences. It is worth 13*s.*; when received, 10*s.*; TRE 20*s.* Eadwig, the man of the Abbot of Ely, held this land: he could give or sell it without his leave but Earl Ælfgar had the soke.

XXVI. THE LAND OF HUGH DE PORT

In 'Staploe' Hundred

• Hugh de Port holds 1½ hides and 20 acres in Isleham. There is land for 3 ploughs. In demesne is 1 [plough]; and 2 villans with 3 bordars have 2 ploughs. There are 2 slaves, meadow for 1 plough, [and] pasture for the livestock of the vill. It is and was worth 40*s.*; TRE 60*s.* Ordgar, King Edward's sheriff, held this manor; he could depart without the leave of his lord.

• Hugh himself holds Snailwell of the fief of the Bishop of Bayeux. It was always assessed at 5 hides. There is land for 10 ploughs. In demesne are 2 [ploughs], and there can be a third. There are 6 sokemen and 8 villans and 3 bordars and 3 slaves.

There are 4 mills rendering 14*s.* 4*d.*, meadow for 2 ploughs, [and] woodland for fencing, with 2 carts from the king's woodland of Cheveley. In all it is worth £14; when received, £12; TRE £15. Archbishop Stigand held this manor on the day King Edward was alive and dead; and there were 6 sokemen, the men of the same archbishop, who could depart without his leave and give or sell their land, but the soke remained with the archbishop. TRE this manor pertained to the demesne of the Church of Ely as demesne farm, but the abbot of that time leased it to the archbishop, as the hundred bears witness. Now Abbot Simeon reclaims it by right of his predecessors.

XXVII. THE LAND OF AUBREY DE VERE

In Cheveley Hundred

M • Aubrey de Vere holds Ashley from the king. Everard holds it from him. It was assessed at 3½ hides TRE, and now at 2 hides. There is land for 4 ploughs. In demesne [are] 2 [ploughs]; and the villans have 2 ploughs. [There is] 1 acre of meadow, woodland for 12 pigs, [and] pasture for the livestock. All together it is worth 100*s.*; when received, 40*s.*; and as much TRE. Wulfwine, King Edward's thegn, held this manor.

M [X] • Aubrey himself holds Saxon Street, and Everard [holds] of him. It was assessed at 5 hides TRE, and now at 3 hides. There is land for 7 ploughs. In demesne are 3 ploughs; and 10 villans with 4 bordars have 4 ploughs. [There is] meadow for 1 plough, pasture for the livestock of the vill, [and] woodland for 40 pigs. All together it is worth £8; when received, £7; and as much TRE. Wulfwine, King Edward's thegn, held this manor.

M • Aubrey himself holds Silverley. It was assessed at ||[partly in margin]|| 6½ hides | in the time of King Edward |, and now at 4 hides. There is land for 8 ploughs. In demesne [are] 2 hides, and there are 4 ploughs; and 12 villans with 2 bordars have 4 ploughs. There are 8 slaves, and 1 acre of meadow, woodland for 20 pigs, [and] pasture for the livestock of the vill. In all it is worth £16; when received, £20; and as much TRE. Wulfwine, King Edward's thegn, held this manor.

In 'Staine' Hundred • In Swaffham Prior Aubrey holds half a hide and 20 acres from the king. There is land for 1 plough, and there is [1 plough], with 1 villan, and 1 mill [rendering] 7*s.* It is and always was worth 10*s.* 1 sokeman of King Edward held this land. He could not depart without leave and provided cartage-due for the king's sheriff. Aubrey's predecessor did not have this land, as the men of the hundred bear witness, but Aubrey himself usurped it in defiance of the king.

M • Aubrey himself holds Little Wilbraham from the king. [. . .] There is land for 8 ploughs. In demesne [are] 2 hides, and there are 4 ploughs; and 8 villans with 5 bordars have 7 ploughs. There are 7 slaves, meadow for 3 ploughs, and 1 mill [rendering] 22*s.* In all it is worth £12; when received, £10; and as much TRE. Wulfwine, King Edward's thegn, held this manor.

• In the same vill Reginald holds half a hide and 30 acres from Aubrey. There is land for 1 plough, and there is [1 plough], with 1 bordar. It is and always was worth 10*s.* Godric, King Edward's man, held this land: he did not hold it of Aubrey's predecessor, to this the men of the hundred bear witness, but Aubrey usurped it in defiance of the king.

In Chilford Hundred

M • In Castle Camps Aubrey de Vere holds 2½ hides. There is land for 11 ploughs. In demesne [is] 1 hide and 1 virgate, and there are 4 ploughs. There 17 villans with 4 bordars have 7 ploughs. There are 6 slaves, meadow for 3 ploughs, [and] woodland for 500 pigs. From the herbage of the vill, 8*s.* In all it is worth £15; when received, £12; and as much TRE. Wulfwine, King Edward's thegn, held this manor.

Norman holds half a hide of this land from Aubrey. There is land for 1 plough, and there is [1 plough]. It is and always was worth 40*s.*

• In Horseheath Norman holds 1½ hides from Aubrey. There is land for 3 ploughs. In demesne is 1 [plough]; and 2½ villans with 3 bordars have 2 ploughs. There are 3 slaves, and 4 acres of meadow, [and] woodland for 40 pigs. It is and always was worth 60*s.* Wulfwine, King Edward's thegn, held this land and had sake and soke, and rendered cartage-due and escort-service.

M • Aubrey himself holds Hildersham. It is assessed at 5 hides. There is land for 11 ploughs. In demesne [are] 2½ hides, and there are 4 ploughs. There 16 villans have 7 ploughs. There are 4 slaves, and 1 mill rendering 10*s.*, meadow for 3 ploughs, [and] woodland for 20 pigs. All together it is worth £10; when received, £8; TRE £8. Wulfwine, King Edward's thegn, held this land.

M • Aubrey himself holds Great Abington, and Firmat [holds] from him. It is assessed at 6 hides. There is land for 8 ploughs. In demesne [are] 2 ploughs, and there can be a third. There 9 villans with 5 bordars have 4 ploughs, and there can be a fifth. [There is] meadow for 2 ploughs, woodland for 10 pigs, and 1 mill rendering 9*s.* From the pasture, 6 ploughshares. It is and was worth £8; TRE £6. The aforesaid Wulfwine, King Edward's thegn, held this manor. A certain priest held 1 hide of this land from Eadgifu the Fair; he could not depart without her leave; and now Count Alan claims it back from Aubrey's men, as the hundred bears witness.

• In Babraham Firmat holds half a virgate from Aubrey. It is worth 20*d.* Godwine held this land under Wulfwine, Aubrey's predecessor; he could not depart.

• In [?Little] Abington 1 sokeman has from the king half a hide, which is in the custody of Picot the sheriff, and is worth 12*d.* a year. Almær, King Edward's sokeman, held this and could give or sell it to whom he would TRE, and Aubrey de Vere seized this land from the king's soke, but Picot the sheriff proved his right to it against him, and he still retains 1 plough and 380 sheep which Aubrey has from that land, as the men of the hundred bear witness.

XXVIII. THE LAND OF EUSTACE OF HUNTINGDON

In Papworth Hundred

• Eustace of Huntingdon holds 1 hide and 3 virgates in Papworth St Agnes. There is land for 3 ploughs. In demesne is 1 [plough]; and 4 villans have 2 ploughs. There is 1 slave, and meadow for 1 plough. It is worth 40*s.*; when received, £4; TRE 50*s.* Ordnoth, the man of Robert fitzWimarc, held this land; he could give it to whom he would. Now Walter holds it from Eustace.

• In the same vill Ordnoth holds 1 hide and 3 virgates from Eustace by the king's command. There is land for 2 ploughs. There are 1½ ploughs, and there can be half [a plough more. There is] meadow for 1 plough. It is and was worth 20*s.*; TRE 50*s.* This man held [this land] from Robert fitzWimarc, and could sell it.

• In the same vill Walter holds 1½ virgates from Eustace. There is land for 4 oxen, and meadow for as many oxen. It is and was worth 5*s.*; TRE 10*s.* Godwine, the man of the Abbot of Ely, held this land and could not sell it.

XXIX. THE LAND OF GUY DE RAIMBEAUCOURT

• Guy de Raimbeaucourt holds 3 hides and 1 virgate from the king in Meldreth. There is land for 5 ploughs, and there are [5 ploughs]. In demesne [is] half a hide, and there is 1 plough; and 15 bordars with 3 cottars have 4 ploughs. There is 1 slave, and 2 mills rendering 10*s.* 8*d.*, meadow for 5 ploughs, [and] pasture for the livestock. All together it is worth 70*s.*; and as much when received; TRE 100*s.* This land

16 sokemen held. Of these, 10 had 2 hides and half a virgate of the soke of St Æthelthryth of Ely, of whom 1 could neither give nor sell his land, the other 9 could, to whom they would, but the soke of all remained with the church; and 5 other sokemen held 1 hide and half a virgate from Earl Ælfgar [and] could give or sell [their land].

• In the same vill Guy holds 5 hides and 1½ virgates and the fourth part of a virgate. There is land for 11 ploughs. In demesne [are] 2½ hides, and there are 2 ploughs, and there can be 2 more. There 6 villans with 18 bordars and 10 cottars have 7 ploughs. There is half a mill rendering 2*s.* 8*d.*, meadow for 6 ploughs, [and] pasture for the livestock of the vill. All together it is worth £10. 10*s.*; when received, £6; TRE £14. Eadric Spur, King Edward's thegn, held 2½ hides of this land [and] could give or sell them; and 8 sokemen, the men of the Abbot of Ely, held 2 hides and half a virgate; and 2 other sokemen, the men of King Edward, held 2 parts of 1 virgate and provided 2 watchmen. All these men could sell their lands, [but] the soke of the 8 sokemen remained with the Abbot of Ely.

IN 'WETHERLEY' HUNDRED

• In Barton Humphrey holds 3½ hides from Guy. There is land for 6 ploughs. In demesne [are] 3 ploughs; and 3 villans with 13 bordars have 3 ploughs. There is 1 slave, [and] meadow for 4 ploughs. All together it is worth £6; when received, £10; and as much TRE. There are 3 French knights on this land. 24 sokemen held this land One of these held half a hide under Eadgifu the Fair and could sell it; and all the others were King Edward's sokemen. They held 3 hides, and they could give and sell them, and provided 6 cartage-dues and 17 watchmen for the sheriff.

• In Grantchester 2 knights hold 3 virgates from Guy. There is land for 1 plough, but no [plough] is there. [There is] meadow for 4 oxen, and 3 bordars. It is worth 55*s.*; when received, 40*s.*; TRE £4. 5 sokemen, the men of King Edward, held this land and could sell it, and they provided 4 watchmen for the king's sheriff.

• In Orwell Ralph holds the third part of 1 virgate from Guy, and there is an ox. It is and was worth 2*s.*, and he could sell it, and provided the fourth part of a cartage-due for the sheriff.

• In 'Ratford' Ralph holds half a hide from Guy. There is land for half a plough, and there is [half a plough], with 2 villans and 2 bordars. [There is] meadow for half a plough, [and] a wood to repair fences. It is worth 20*s.*; when received, 10*s.*; TRE 20*s.* 2 sokemen of King Edward held this land; and they provided 2 cartage-dues, and could sell it.

IN LONGSTOWE HUNDRED

• In [Great and Little] Eversden Guy holds 6 hides and 10 acres of land. There is land for 10 ploughs. In demesne are 4 [ploughs], and there can be a fifth. There 5 villans with 2 bordars and 9 cottars have 5 ploughs. There is 1 slave, meadow for 2 ploughs and 2 oxen, [and] a wood for fences. All together it is worth £9; when received, £6. 5*s.*; TR[E] £16. Picot holds half a hide of this land, and Humphrey holds all the other land from Guy. 23 sokemen held this land. 2 of these, the men of Archbishop Stigand, held 1 hide and 3 virgates; and 7, the men of Earl Ælfgar, had 3 virgates; and 1, the man of Eadgifu, had 1 hide; and 14 others, King Edward's men, held 1½ hides and 10 acres, and they provided 9 cartage-dues and 5 watchmen for the sheriff. But all these men could give or sell their lands.

XXX. THE LAND OF PICOT OF CAMBRIDGE

IN 'STAINE' HUNDRED

M • PICOT of Cambridge holds 4½ hides and 10 acres in STOW CUM QUY. There is land for 5 ploughs. In demesne is 1 [plough]; and 8 villans have 4 ploughs. There are 2½ mills rendering 22*s.*, [and] meadow for the ploughs. All together it is and was worth £8. [. . .] Æthelric the monk and Godric, the men of the Abbot of Ramsey, held 3½ hides of this land, [and] could not depart without his leave; and 4 sokemen, the men of King Edward, held 1 hide and 10 acres [and] could neither give nor sell them without the king's leave. §

IN CHILFORD HUNDRED

• In Pampisford Ralph holds 3 virgates from Picot. There is land for 1 plough, and there is [1 plough], and 2 acres of meadow. It is and always was worth 10*s.* Eadric, the man of Ælfric Cild, held this and could depart with the land.

IN WHITTLESFORD HUNDRED

• PICOT himself [. . .] holds HINXTON. It is assessed at 15½ hides. There is land for 13 ploughs. In demesne [are] 7 hides and 3 virgates, and there is 1 plough, and there can be 3 more. There 20 villans with 12 bordars have 9 ploughs. There are 2 mills rendering 21*s.* 4*d.*, [and] meadow for 3 ploughs. In all it is worth £10; when received, £16; and as much TRE. Picot received this land as 2 manors, so he says. 20 sokemen held it. One of these, the man of Earl Ælfgar, had half a hide; he could not depart. But the others were the men of King Edward and could depart, and they provided 8 cartage-dues and 8 watchmen and 3 guards for the sheriff.

Picot himself holds 1½ hides from the king, and they are valued in this vill. A certain sokeman held under the Abbot of Ely and he could sell, but the soke remained with the abbot.

IN THRIPLOW HUNDRED

• In Harston Picot holds 7½ hides. There is land for 9 ploughs. In demesne [are] 3 hides, and there are 2 ploughs, and there can be a third. There 6 villans and 15 cottars have 4 ploughs, and there can be a fifth. There is 1 mill rendering 30*s.*, meadow for 5 ploughs, [and] pasture for the livestock. In all it is worth £8; when received, £4. 10*s.*; TRE £10. Ordgar held 4 hides of this land from Earl Harold and could depart; and 6 sokemen, the men of King Edward, held 2 hides and provided 1 cartage-due and 5 watchmen, and could depart with their land.

Fridebert held 1½ hides from the Abbot of Ely and could depart with his land, but the soke remained with the church. Picot serves the abbot for these 1½ hides, and holds them by the king's command.

• In Trumpington Hervey holds 2 hides and 1½ virgates from Picot. There is land for 2½ ploughs. In demesne [are] 1½ ploughs; and 3 villans with 1 bordar have 1 plough. There are 3 cottars and 1 slave, [and] meadow for the ploughs. From the weir, 450 eels. It is worth £4; when received, 30*s.*; TRE 100*s.* Heoruwulf held this land under King Edward and could sell it and depart to whom he would.

IN 'ARRINGFORD' HUNDRED

• In Tadlow Picot holds 2 hides and 1½ virgates. There is land for 6 ploughs. In demesne [is] 1 hide and half a virgate, and there is 1 plough, and there can be another; and 2½ virgates which the villans hold, and 13 bordars have 3 ploughs and there can be a fourth. There is 1 mill rendering 10*s.*, meadow for 6 ploughs, [and] pasture for the livestock of the vill. It is worth 70*s.*; when received, £4; TRE £6. 3 sokemen held this land and provided 1 cartage-due and 1 guard, and could give and sell their land.

[1] how many villans

• In Guilden Morden Picot holds 3½ hides. There is land for 7 ploughs. In demesne is 1 hide, and there is 1 plough, and there can be another. There 8 villans with 11 bordars and 18 cottars have 3½ ploughs, and there can be 1½ [ploughs more]. There is 1 mill rendering 4*s.*, meadow for 7 ploughs, [and] pasture for the livestock of the vill.

§ • In the same place Picot holds 3 hides 3 virgates. There is land for 4 ploughs. In demesne are 2 [ploughs]; and 5 villans have 2 ploughs. There is 1 slave, and meadow for 4 ploughs. It is worth £6; when received it was worth £4; and as much TRE. 2 sokemen of the Abbot of Ely held this land; they could not sell it without his leave. In this vill [there is] half a mill rendering 40*d.*

All together it is worth £6. 10*s.*; when received, £8; TRE £10. 8 sokemen held this land. 3 of these, the men of Archbishop Stigand, had 1 hide and 3 virgates and could give and sell [their land], but the soke remained in Guilden Morden; and 2 others, the men of Earl Ælfgar, had 3 virgates and could sell [their land, but] the soke remained with the earl; and 2 others, the men of King Edward, held 3 virgates and provided 2 watchmen, and could give and sell [their land]; and 1, the man of Eadgifu, had half a virgate and could sell it.

• In 'Clopton' [in Croydon] Picot holds a garden of the soke of King Edward which rendered 1 watchman to the king's sheriff.

• In East Hatley Picot holds 2 hides. There is land for 3 ploughs. There are 1½ ploughs, and there can be as many [more. There is] meadow for 2 ploughs, and 2 bordars, [and] woodland to repair fences. It is and was worth 40*s.*; TRE 60*s.* 8 sokemen held this land and could give and sell it. Of these, 2 were the men of King Edward and provided 2 watchmen; and 3 were the men of Archbishop Stigand, [and] their soke pertained to Guilden Morden; and 1 [was] the man of Earl Gyrth; and 1 the man of Robert fitzWimarc; and 1 the man of Wulfmær of Eaton Socon. Picot says he has 1 hide of this land in exchange for Eynesbury [Hunts.] and the other in exchange for Rushden [Herts.] because Ilbert of Hertford delivered it to him.

• In Croydon Ansketil holds 2 hides less half a virgate from Picot. There is land for 2 ploughs, but there are only oxen [*sic*], with 1 villan and 2 bordars. It is worth 30*s.*; when received, 40*s.*; and as much TRE. 1 man of Esger the staller held this land; he could give and sell it.

• In the same vill Alvred holds 1 hide and 1 virgate from Picot. There is land for 2 ploughs, and there are [2 ploughs]. In demesne [is] 1 [plough]; and 5 bordars with another plough, and 2 cottars. [There is] meadow for 2 ploughs, [and] a wood to repair fences only. It is worth £4; when received, 40*s.*; and as much TRE. 1 man of Robert fitzWimarc held this land. He could give and sell it but the soke remained with Robert.

• In Abington Pigotts Picot holds half a virgate. There is land for 2 oxen. It is and always was worth 2*s.* Asgot, the man of Archbishop Stigand, held this land; it pertains and pertained to Guilden Morden.

In 'Wetherley' Hundred

• In Comberton 2 men hold 2 hides and 2 acres from Picot. There is land for 4 ploughs. In demesne [are] 2 [ploughs]; and 7 villans with 11 bordars have 2 ploughs. [There is] meadow for 1 plough. It is and was worth 60*s.*; TRE £4. 7 sokemen of King Edward held 1 hide and 1 virgate of this land, and provided 5 cartage-dues and 3 watchmen; and 2 other sokemen had 3 virgates and could depart: of these, one was the man of Archbishop Stigand, and the other the man of Earl Waltheof.

• In Grantchester Robert holds half a virgate from Picot. There is land for 3 oxen, and there is 1 villan. It is and was worth 5*s.* Wulfric held this land of the king's soke.

• In Haslingfield Seifrid holds 4 hides and 3 virgates from Picot. There is land for 4 ploughs. In demesne [are] 2 ploughs; and 4 villans with 22 bordars have 2 ploughs, and [there is] 1 mill rendering 2*s.*, [and] meadow for 2 ploughs. It is worth £4; when received, 40*s.*; TRE £4. 6 sokemen held this land. Of these, one, the man of Esger, held 1 hide and 3 virgates and could sell [his land]; and the other 5, the men of King Edward, held 3 hides and provided 2 cartage-dues and 3 watchmen. They could give and sell their land.

• In Harlton Seifrid holds 1 hide from Picot. There is land for 1 plough, but there is no [plough. There is] meadow for 4 oxen, and 2 bordars. It is and always was worth 20*s.* Godmann held this land under Esger the staller, and could depart.

• In Barrington Ralph holds 20 acres from Picot. There is land for 3 oxen, and there are [3 oxen], with 1 sokeman and 1 bordar. [There is] meadow for 3 oxen. It is and always was worth 5*s.* Eadsige held this land under Robert fitzWimarc and could give it.

• In 'Ratford' Ralph holds 3 virgates from Picot. There is land for 3 oxen, and there are [3 oxen], with 2 cottars. [There is] meadow for 3 oxen. It is and was worth 3*s.*; TRE 5*s.* A sokeman of King Edward held this land, and he provided 1 watchman for the sheriff, and could sell his land.

• In 'Witewell' Ralph holds 1 hide and 2 parts of 1 virgate from Picot. There is land for 1½ ploughs. In demesne is 1 plough; and 1 villan with 2 cottars have half a plough. [There is] meadow for 2 ploughs, [and] a wood to close up [the gaps in] fences. It is worth 30*s.*; when received, 20*s.*; TRE £4. 3 sokemen held this land. One of these [was] the man of Ælfgar, and another the man of Robert fitzWimarc, and the third the man of King Edward. The last provided cartage-due and could sell [his land].

In Longstowe Hundred

• In Kingston Ralph holds 5½ hides and 16 acres from Picot. There is land for 7½ ploughs. In demesne [are] 2 ploughs; and 9 villans with 2 bordars and 5 cottars have 5½ ploughs. [There is] meadow for 3 ploughs, [and] a wood for fences. There are 4 slaves. All together it is worth £6; when received, £8; TRE £12. 14 sokemen held this land. Of these, 10 had 2 hides and 1½ virgates of the king's soke and provided 7 cartage-dues and 3 watchmen; and 2 others, the men of Earl Ælfgar, had 1 virgate; and 1, the man of Archbishop Stigand, held 3 virgates; and another of them, the man of the Abbot of Ely, had 1 virgate of the abbot's soke; and 2 others, the men of Earl Ælfgar, had 2 hides. They could all depart.

• In Toft 2 knights hold 1½ hides and 10 acres from Picot. There is land for 4 ploughs. In demesne are 2 [ploughs], and there can be a third; and 2 villans with 6 cottars have 1 plough. [There is] meadow for 1½ ploughs, [and] a wood for fences. It is worth £4; when received, 20*s.*; TRE £6. 1 of King Edward's men held 1 hide and 4 acres of this land and could give them; and a man of the Abbot of Ely held half a hide and 6 acres and could depart with the land, but the soke remained with the abbot.

M • Picot himself holds Bourn. It is assessed at 13 hides. There is land for 15 ploughs. In demesne [are] 5 hides, and there are 2 ploughs, and there can be 2 others. There are 8 villans with 4 bordars and 7 sokemen who hold 4 hides. They have 4 ploughs, and there can be 7 more. There are 13 cottars and 6 slaves, meadow for 15 ploughs, pasture for the livestock of the vill, [and] a wood to repair fences and houses. In all it is worth £13; when received, £18; TRE £22. 2 knights hold 2 hides of this land under Picot. There is land for 2 ploughs, and there are [2 ploughs], with 4 cottars. [There is] meadow for 2 ploughs, a wood for fences and houses, [and] pasture for the livestock of the vill. It always was and is worth 40*s.* A thegn held 3 hides of the land of this manor under King Edward TRE; and 2 priests, the men of this |[in margin]| thegn, had 1 hide. |They could not withdraw from the church.| And 3 sokemen of Archbishop Stigand [had] 4 hides; and a man of Esger the staller had 1 hide; and 2 men of the Abbot of Ramsey had 1½ hides; and 1 man of Earl Ælfgar had half a hide; and 13 men of King Edward had 2 hides and they themselves provided 6 cartage-dues and 7 watchmen for the sheriff. All 22 could give and sell their lands. Picot says he received this land as 2 manors.

• In Hatley St George Roger holds 2 hides from Picot. There is land for 2 ploughs. In demesne is 1 [plough]; and 4 bordars with 6 cottars and 1 villan have half a plough, and there can be half [a plough more. There is] a wood for fences and houses. It is worth 20*s.*; when received, 60*s.*; TRE 100*s.* Alweard, the man of Robert fitzWimarc, held this land and could sell it.

• In the same vill Picot holds 1 hide. There is land for 1 plough. There is half a plough, and there can be half [a plough more. There is] a wood for fences and houses. There are 3 villans. It is worth 10*s.*; when received, 20*s.*; TRE 40*s.* 3 sokemen of King Edward held this land, and provided 1 cartage-due and 2 watchmen for the sheriff. Picot says he has this [land] in exchange for Rushden [Herts.] which Sigar holds.

In Papworth Hundred

• In Papworth [?St Agnes] Picot holds half a virgate. There is land for 2 oxen. It is and was worth 2*s.* A sokeman of King Edward held this land, and provided 1 watchman for the sheriff.

• In Fen Drayton Roger holds 1 hide from Picot. There is land for half a plough, and there are 2 oxen, [and] meadow for 4 oxen. It is and was worth 3*s.*; TRE 5*s.* 2 sokemen held this land. One of these, the man of the Abbot of Ely, could sell his land without the soke. The other, the man of King Edward, provided 1 watchman for the sheriff and could give his land.

• In Over Sæwine holds half a hide from Picot. There is land for half a plough, and there is [half a plough. There is] meadow for half a plough, [and] pasture for the livestock. It is and was worth 5*s.*; TRE 10*s.* A man of the Abbot of Ramsey held this land, and could sell it without the soke.

• In Willingham Roger holds 1 virgate of Picot. There is land for 2 oxen, with meadow, [and] pasture for the livestock. It is and was worth 3*s.* Golda held this land under the Abbot of Ely; he could not give or sell it.

In 'Northstowe' Hundred

• In Longstanton Guy holds 3 hides from Picot. There is land for 4 ploughs. In demesne are 2 [ploughs]; and 6 bordars with 5 cottars can have 2 ploughs. [There is] meadow for 2 ploughs. It is worth £4; when received, £8; TRE £10. 15 sokemen held this land. Of these, 11, the men of King Edward, had 1½ hides, and provided 2 cartage-dues and 5 watchmen for the sheriff, and could give and sell their land; and 3 others had 1 hide under the Abbot of Ely and could sell, but the soke remained with the abbot; and 1, the man of Saxi, had half a hide and could not give it.

• Roger holds Rampton from Picot. It was assessed at 6 hides TRE, and now at 4½ hides. There is land for 6 ploughs. In demesne is 1 plough, and there can be 2 more. There 12 villans with 7 cottars have 3 ploughs. There is 1 slave, and meadow for 6 ploughs, [and] pasture for the livestock. In all it is worth 100*s.*; when received, £8; and as much TRE. 6 sokemen held this manor. One of these, the man of Eadgifu, had 1½ virgates and could depart; and the others were the men of the Abbot of Ely, and 4 could sell their land but the soke remained with the abbot, and the fifth had 1½ virgates and could not depart.

• In Lolworth Robert holds from Picot 9 hides as 1 manor. [It is] now [assessed] at 5 hides. There is land for 5 ploughs. In demesne are 2 [ploughs]; and 4 villans with 9 bordars and 3 cottars have 3 ploughs. There 1 Frenchman has 1½ hides, and [there is] 1 slave. [There is] meadow for 1 plough, and 1 mill rendering nothing, [and] a wood for fences. In all it is worth 100*s.*; when received, 40*s.*; TRE £6. An almswoman of King Edward held this manor. She had 3½ hides, and there were 10 sokemen. Of these, 7, the men of King Edward, held 1½ hides and 4 gardens, and provided 2 cartage-dues and 4 watchmen; and 2 others, the men of Eadgifu, had 1 hide; the tenth, however, the man of the Abbot of Ely, held 1½ hides. All these could sell their lands. Only the soke of the Abbot of Ely's man remained with the church.

• In Madingley Picot holds 11 hides and 2½ virgates. There is land for 8 ploughs. In demesne [are] 4 hides and 3 virgates, and there are 2 ploughs, and there can be a third. There 7 villans with 4 bordars and 6 cottars have 4 ploughs, and there can be a fifth. There are 3 slaves, meadow for 4 ploughs, [and] a wood for fences. 2 knights hold 3 hides and 3 virgates of this land. In all it is worth £6. 5*s.*; when received, £9. 10*s.*; and as much TRE. 12 sokemen held this manor. Of these, 7, the men of King Edward, held 8 hides and 1 virgate and provided 5 cartage-dues and 5 watchmen; and the other 5, the men of the Abbot of Ely, had 3 hides and 1½ virgates, and 4 of these could depart, and the fifth held half a hide but could not depart.

• In Girton William holds 3 hides and 3 virgates from Picot. There is land for 3 ploughs. In demesne [is] 1 plough, [and] there can be half [a plough more]; and 2 villans with 8 bordars have 1½ ploughs. [There is] meadow for half a plough. It is worth £3; when received, £4; TRE £5. Blæcwine, King Edward's sheriff, held this land and could depart.

• In Oakington 2 knights hold 3 hides and 1 virgate and 10 acres from Picot, and in the same place a third knight holds half a hide and 9 acres and 3 gardens. There is land for 3½ ploughs. There are 2 [ploughs], and there can be 1½ [more]. There are 12 villans with 3 bordars and 8 cottars. All together it is worth £4. 10*s.*; when received, 100*s.*; TRE £8. Blæcwine the sheriff held half a hide and 9 acres of this land from the king; and 2 other men of the king held 1 hide and 3 virgates, and provided 1 cartage-due and 1 watchman; and a man of the Abbot of Ely had 1½ hides and 10 acres: he could sell [his land] but the soke remained with the abbot.

• In Impington Walter holds 3½ hides from Picot. There is land for 3 ploughs, and there are [3 ploughs], with 4 bordars and 4 cottars. [There is] meadow for 1 plough. All together it is worth 60*s.*; when received, 50*s.*; TRE £4. 3 sokemen of the Abbot of Ely held this land. 2 of these had 1 hide and 1 virgate [and] could sell, but the soke remained with the abbot; the third had 2 hides and 1 virgate, but he could not sell.

• In Milton Ralph holds 12 hides from Picot. There is land for 7 ploughs. In demesne are 2 [ploughs], and there can be 2 others. There 10 villans with 12 bordars and 9 cottars have 3 ploughs. There are 5 slaves, meadow for 4 ploughs, [and] pasture for the livestock. From the fen, 650 eels and 12*d*. In all it is worth £7; when received, £8; TRE £12. Æthelbeorht, the abbot's steward, held 6 hides and 3 virgates of this manor in such a way that he could not sell them nor alienate them from the Church, but after his death it was to be restored to the Church of Ely; and 4 sokemen held 4 hides and 2½ virgates under the abbot and could sell them without the soke; and a man of King Edward had 2½ virgates and could sell them where he would.

• In Landbeach Osmund holds 1½ hides and 10 acres from Picot. There is land for 1½ ploughs. In demesne is 1 plough, and there can be half [a plough more]. There are 8 bordars and 6 cottars, meadow for 1½ ploughs, [and] pasture for the livestock. From the fen, 1,000 eels and 12*d*. from the gift [of fish]. It is worth 20*s*.; when received, 30*s*.; and as much TRE. Blæcwine the sheriff held 3 virgates and 12 acres of this land and could give them where he would; and 4 sokemen of King Edward held 3 virgates [and] provided 1 cartage-due and 1 watchman for the sheriff.

• In Waterbeach Muceull holds 6 hides from Picot. There is land for 3 ploughs. In demesne is 1 [plough]; and 6 villans with 4 bordars and 9 cottars have 2 ploughs. [There is] meadow for 3 ploughs, [and] pasture for the livestock of the vill. It is worth £4. 6*s*.; when received, £3; TRE £4. 10*s*. Blæcwine held 2 hides and 3 virgates of this land from the king; and 4 men of King Edward had 2 hides and provided 3 cartage-dues and 1 watchman for the sheriff; and Albert, the man of the Abbot of Ely, had 1 hide which he could neither sell nor alienate from the church; and another man of the abbot had 1 virgate and could sell it but the soke remained with the abbot.

In Chesterton Hundred

• In Cottenham Roger holds 5 hides from Picot. There is land for 3 ploughs. In demesne is 1 [plough], and there can be another. There 6 villans with 8 cottars have 1 plough. [There is] meadow for 3 ploughs, [and] pasture for the livestock of the vill. From the fen, 150 eels. It is worth 40*s*.; when received, 50*s*.; TRE 60*s*. 3 sokemen held this land. 1 of these, the man of St Æthelthryth, held 3½ hides, less 14 acres, [and] could not give [his land] because it belonged to the demesne of the church; and another, the man of the abbot, had 1½ hides and could give them without the soke; and the third, the man of Earl Waltheof, had 14 acres and could give and sell them.

• In Cottenham Picot holds 40 acres and 1 garden of the demesne of the Church of Ely.

• In the same Cottenham Picot himself holds 40 acres of land and 5 acres of meadow of the demesne of the Church of St Guthlac.

• In Westwick Odo holds 3 hides from Picot. There is land for 2 ploughs. In demesne are 1½ [ploughs]; and 2 villans with 1 bordar have half a plough. [There is] meadow for 2 ploughs. It is worth 60*s*.; when received, 70*s*.; TRE 100*s*. Blæcwine the sheriff, the man of King Edward, held this land and could sell it; and a sokeman of the Abbot of Ely had 40 acres of this land and could depart, but the soke remained with the abbot.

• In Childerley Robert holds 2 hides from Picot. There is land for 1 plough. This [land] is valued in Lolworth but is assessed in Childerley. 4 sokemen held this land. 3 of these were the men of King Edward and the fourth the man of Eadgifu the Fair and they could sell.

XXXI. THE LAND OF PETER DE VALOGNES

In Longstowe Hundred

• Peter de Valognes holds 1 hide and 3 virgates in Bourn. There is land for 2 ploughs, but there are no [ploughs]. There are 2 bordars and 3 cottars, [and] a wood for fences. It is worth 30*s*.; when received, [. . .]*s*.; TRE 50*s*. Almær, King Edward's thegn, held this land and could sell it. Now Picot holds it from Peter, the sheriff of Essex.

XXXII.

In Longstowe Hundred

• Ranulph the brother of Ilger holds 1 hide of the king in Gamlingay. There is land for 1 plough. It is and always was worth 10*s*. Ingvar, King Edward's thegn, held this land and could sell it.

XXXIII. THE LAND OF JOHN FITZWALERAN

In Fleamdyke Hundred

• John fitzWaleran holds 6 hides in Fulbourn. There is land for 7 ploughs. In demesne [are] 3 hides, and there are 3 ploughs. There 8 villans with 10 bordars and 4 cottars have 3 ploughs. [There is] meadow for 7 ploughs, [and] pasture for the livestock of the vill. It is and always was worth £12. Sigar held 3 hides of this land from King Edward and could sell; and a man of Earl Ælfgar held 2 hides and could give and sell them; and 3 men of Eadgifu had 1 hide from which they provided 2 cartage-dues, and they could not depart from her. Count Alan claims this hide; the men of the hundred bear witness for him.

• In Teversham John holds 3½ hides. There is land for 4½ ploughs. In demesne [are] 2 hides, and there are 2 ploughs. There 5 villans with 17 bordars have 2½ ploughs. There is 1 slave, [and] meadow for 2 ploughs. It is and was worth £3; TRE £4. 2 sokemen held 1½ hides and 20 acres of this land from Earl Ælfgar [and] could not depart from him. The predecessor of Abbot Simeon of Ely bought the third hide of this vill from Earl Ælfgar; and at that time this land provided cartage-due, [but] after it pertained to the church it did not provide it. With this hide belongs a church of that vill, as the men of the hundred bear witness, and 2 men of Godwine Cild provided 1 cartage-due and 2 watchmen.

XXXIIII. THE LAND OF WILLIAM FITZANSCULF

In 'Northstowe' Hundred

• William fitzAnsculf holds half a virgate from the king in Longstanton. There is land for 2 oxen, [and] meadow for 2 oxen. It is and was worth 2*s*.; TRE 5*s*. Hoc held this land under Earl Waltheof; he could not give it. Now Picot holds it from William.

XXXV. THE LAND OF WILLIAM DE KEYNES

In 'Wetherley' Hundred

• William de Keynes holds 1½ virgates in Comberton. There is land for 1 plough, but there is no plough. [There is] meadow for 1 plough, and 1 villan. It is and always was worth 10*s*. 1 man of Earl Waltheof held this land and could give and sell it. The Bishop of Bayeux delivered this to William, but the men of the hundred do not know on what grounds.

• In Barton William himself holds 2½ hides in the same manner. There is land for 5 ploughs. In demesne are 4 [ploughs]; and 1 villan with 8 bordars have 2 ploughs. There are 2 slaves, [and] meadow for 2 ploughs. It is worth £8; when received, £10; and as much TRE. 4 sokemen, the men of Earl Waltheof, held this land. 2 of these held 1 hide and 2½ virgates but could not depart without his leave. But the other 2 could give and sell their land.

XXXVI. THE LAND OF ROBERT FAFITON

In Chilford Hundred

• Robert Fafiton holds 1 hide and 1 virgate from the king in Babraham. There is land for 2½ ploughs. In demesne are 3 virgates, and there is 1 plough, and there can be another; and 4 villans have half a plough. It is worth 21*s*.; when received, 10*s*.; TRE 26*s*. 8*d*.

Godgifu held this land under Earl Ælfgar. She provided escort-service, and yet could depart and give her land.

IN THRIPLOW HUNDRED

• In Trumpington Robert holds 2 hides. There is land for †3† ploughs. In demesne [is] 1 hide, and 1 plough; and 4 villans with 1 bordar †and† 5 cottars with 2 ploughs. [There is] meadow for 1 plough, [and] pasture for the livestock †of the vill†. It is and was worth 100*s.*; TRE £6. Northmann held 1 hide and 3 virgates of this land from Earl Tosti and could sell them and depart where he would; and a man of King Edward held 1 virgate and provided cartage-due for the sheriff, and yet he could depart with the land. Robert usurped this virgate in defiance of the king, as the hundred bears witness.

IN 'WETHERLEY' HUNDRED

• In Grantchester Robert holds 2 hides and 3 virgates. There is land for 4 ploughs. In demesne [is] 1 hide, and there are 2 ploughs. There 4 villans with 7 bordars have 2 ploughs. There are 22 cottars, and 1 mill rendering 40*s.* From half a weir, half a thousand eels. All together it is and was worth £7; TRE £10. 4 sokemen held this land. One of these, the man of Earl Ælfgar, held 3 virgates; and the others, men of Earl Waltheof, held 2 hides and could give and sell their lands.

IN LONGSTOWE HUNDRED

• In Gamlingay 2 men hold 1 hide from Robert. There is land for 1 plough, and there is [1 plough], with 3 cottars. [There is] meadow for 1 plough, [and] a wood for fences. It is and was worth 20*s.*; TRE 40*s.* 1 man of Earl Ælfgar held this land and could sell it.

IN CHESTERTON HUNDRED

• In Dry Drayton Avesgot holds 3 hides from Robert. There is land for 3 ploughs. In demesne is 1 [plough]; and 4 villans with 1 bordar have 2 ploughs. [There is] meadow for 3 ploughs. It is worth 40*s.*; when received, 13*s.* 4*d.*; TRE 60*s.* Sægar, the man of Earl Waltheof, held this land and could depart where he would with the sake [*sic*].

XXXVII. THE LAND OF DAVID D'ARGENTAN

IN LONGSTOWE HUNDRED

• DAVID d'Argentan holds 1 virgate and 20 acres in Caldecote. There is land for 1 plough, and there is [1 plough], with 3 bordars and 1 cottar. [There is] meadow for 1 plough. It is and was worth 20*s.*; TRE 30*s.* Sigar, the man of Earl Waltheof, held this land and could depart.

• In Croxton David holds 6 hides. There is land for 9½ ploughs. In demesne [are] 3 hides, and there are 2 ploughs, and there can be a third. There 7 villans with 7 bordars and 2 cottars have 3 ploughs, and there can be 3½ more. [There is] meadow for 9½ ploughs, pasture for the livestock, and from the herbage 16*d.* From the fen, 500 eels a year. Eustace of Huntingdon usurped this in defiance of David, as the whole hundred bears witness. In all it is and was worth £8; TRE £10. 3 men of Earl Ælfgar and a fourth, the man of Earl Waltheof, held this manor and could sell it.

IN CHESTERTON HUNDRED

• In Westwick Robert holds 1 hide from David. There is land for 1 plough, and there is [1 plough, and] meadow for 1 plough. It is worth 20*s.*; when received, 10*s.*; TRE 20*s.* Guthmund, the man of Earl Waltheof, held this land; the soke remained with the Abbot of Ely.

XXXVIII. THE LAND OF TWO OF THE KING'S CARPENTERS

IN 'NORTHSTOWE' HUNDRED

• In Waterbeach 2 carpenters hold 5 hides from the king. There is land for 2½ ploughs. In demesne [are] 4 hides and 1 virgate, and there are 2 ploughs. There 3 villans with 10 cottars have half a plough. It is worth 110*s.*; when received, £4. 10*s.*; TRE £7. 10*s.* 1 man of Waltheof held 1½ hides of this land, and provided 1 cartage-due, and could sell [his land]; and Oswig, the man of the Abbot of Ely, held 3½ hides, [and] could not sell [his land] nor alienate it from the church, as the men of the hundred bear witness.

XXXIX. THE LAND OF COUNTESS JUDITH

IN CHEVELEY HUNDRED

M • Countess JUDITH holds KIRTLING. It was assessed at 10 hides TRE; and now at 6 hides. There is land for 21 ploughs. In demesne are 4 hides, and there are 4 ploughs. There 28 villans with 17 bordars have 16 ploughs. There are 7 slaves, meadow for 21 ploughs, woodland for 60 pigs, pasture for the livestock of the vill, [and] a park for wild beasts. From the fisheries, 5,500 eels. In all it is and always was worth £18. Earl Harold held this manor.

IN 'RADFIELD' HUNDRED

• In Dullingham the countess holds 10 acres, with 1 bordar. It is worth 12*d.*

• In Westley Waterless the countess holds 3 virgates and 10 acres. There is land for 2 ploughs. There is 1 [plough], and there can be another. There is 1 villan with 1 bordar, and 2 acres of meadow. It is and always was worth 20*s.* 2 men of Earl Harold held this land; they could not depart, and provided cartage-due in the king's service.

• In Carlton the countess holds 3 hides. There is land for 8 ploughs. In demesne [are] 1½ hides, and there are 2 ploughs; and 12 villans with 2 bordars have 6 ploughs. There are 2 slaves, and 2 acres of meadow, [and] woodland for 12 pigs. It is and always was worth £6. Earl Harold held this land. 3 sokemen hold 4½ acres of the same land from the countess, and they themselves held them TRE and provided escort-service; and a man of Earl Ælfgar held 2 acres and provided escort-service.

IN CHILFORD HUNDRED

• In Babraham the countess holds 1½ virgates. There is land for 4 oxen. It is and was worth 4*s.* A man of Earl Gyrth held this land and could not depart.

• In Pampisford a priest holds half a virgate from the countess. It is and was worth 64*d.* A certain sokeman of Earl Gyrth held this; he could neither depart nor sell it.

IN WHITTLESFORD HUNDRED

M • In Whittlesford the countess holds 11 hides and 1 virgate. There is land for 11 ploughs. In demesne [are] 5 hides, and there are 2 ploughs; and 13 villans with 15 bordars have 9 ploughs. There are 5 slaves, and 3 mills rendering 60*s.*, [and] meadow for the ploughs. In all it is worth £16; when received, £15; and as much TRE. Earl Gyrth held this manor.

IN THRIPLOW HUNDRED

• In Trumpington Gollam holds half a hide from the countess. There is land for half a plough, and there is [half a plough]. It is and always was worth 10*s.* A certain sokeman of Earl Waltheof held this land; he could not depart.

IN 'ARRINGFORD' HUNDRED

• In Tadlow Picot holds 1 hide and 1½ virgates from the countess. There is land for 2½ ploughs. In demesne there can be 1 plough. There a half-villan with 7 bordars have 1½ ploughs. [There is] woodland to repair fences. It is and was worth 30*s.*; TRE 40*s.* Thorkil, Earl Tosti's priest, held this land and could sell it.

IN LONGSTOWE HUNDRED

• The same Picot holds 3 virgates from the countess. There is land for 1 plough, but there is no [plough], only 1 bordar. [There is] a wood for fences. It is worth 5*s.*; when received, 10*s.*; TRE 20*s.* 2 sokemen of King Edward held this land and could sell it.

IN PAPWORTH HUNDRED

• The same Picot holds 1 hide from the countess. There is land for 1 plough, but there is no [plough. There is] meadow for 1 plough. It is and was worth 7*s.*; TRE 20*s.* 1 housecarl of Earl Waltheof held this land and could sell it.

IN 'NORTHSTOWE' HUNDRED

• The same Picot holds 3 hides from the countess. There is land for 2 ploughs. There is 1 [plough], and there can be another. There are 4 villans and 4 bordars. It is worth 30*s.*; when received, 40*s.*; and as much TRE. 4 men of Earl Waltheof held this land and could sell it.

• In Oakington Roger holds 1½ hides and 10 acres from the countess. There is land for 1½ ploughs. There is half [a plough], and there can be a plough. There is 1 villan and 6 cottars. It is worth 30*s*.; when received, 20*s*.; TRE £4. Godwine, the man of Earl Waltheof, held this land, and could sell it.

IN PAPWORTH HUNDRED

• In Over Roger holds half a hide from the countess. There is land for 4 oxen, and there are [4 oxen], and meadow for the oxen themselves, and 3 cottars, [and] pasture for the livestock of the vill. It is and always was worth 20*s*. Godwine, the man of Earl Waltheof, held this land and could give it, but the soke remained with the Abbot of Ramsey.

IN CHESTERTON HUNDRED

• In Dry Drayton Roger holds 3 virgates from the countess. There is land for 4 oxen, and there are [4 oxen], and meadow for the oxen themselves. There is 1 villan. It is worth 16*s*.; when received, 30*s*.; TRE 20*s*. 1 man of Earl Waltheof held this land and could sell it.

• In Childerley Picot holds 5 hides from the countess. There is land for 5 ploughs. In demesne is 1 [plough]; and 5 villans with 6 bordars and 3 cottars have 4 ploughs. There is 1 slave, [and] a wood for fences. It is worth £4; when received, 70*s*.; TRE £8. 1 man of Earl Waltheof held this land and could sell it.

XL. THE LAND OF THE WIFE OF RALPH TAILLEBOIS

IN 'ARRINGFORD' HUNDRED

• AZELINA, the wife of Ralph Taillebois, holds 1 hide and 1 virgate in Tadlow from the king. There is land for 2 ploughs, and there are [2 ploughs], with 5 bordars. [There is] meadow for 2 ploughs, [and] pasture for the livestock of the vill. It is worth 40*s*.; when received, 10*s*.; TRE 40*s*. Wulfmær of Eaton Socon, King Edward's thegn, held this land; now Walter the monk holds it from the aforesaid Azelina.

XLI. THE WIFE OF BOSELIN DE DIVES

IN 'NORTHSTOWE' HUNDRED

• In Oakington the wife of Boselin de Dives holds 1½ hides which the Bishop of Bayeux delivered to her, but the men of the hundred do not know on what grounds. There is land for 1½ ploughs. There are 6 oxen, and there can be 1 plough. There are 3 villans and 2 cottars. It is and was worth 30*s*.; TRE 60*s*. Siward, the man of Earl Waltheof, held this land and could sell it, but the soke remained with the Abbot of Ely.

XLII. THE LAND OF ERCHENGER

IN 'WETHERLEY' HUNDRED

• ERCHENGER the baker holds 1 hide, less 20 acres, in Comberton from the king. There is land for 2 ploughs. In demesne [is] 1 plough, [and] half a hide less 20 acres. There 4 villans with 8 bordars have 1 plough. There is 1 slave, and meadow for 4 oxen. It is worth 30*s*.; when received, 20*s*.; TRE 40*s*. 3 sokemen held this land. One of these, the king's man, had 1 virgate and provided half a cartage-due; and another, the man of Archbishop Stigand, 1½ virgates; and the third, the man of Waltheof, 1½ virgates; and they could sell [their land] and depart.

IN LONGSTOWE HUNDRED

• In Toft Erchenger holds 1 hide from the king. There is land for 2 ploughs. In demesne there can be 1 plough; and 1 villan with 5 cottars have 1 plough. [There is] meadow for 4 oxen, [and] a wood for fences and for fuel. It is worth 40*s*.; when received, 10*s*.; TRE 60*s*. 5 sokemen of the Abbot of Ely held this land: they could neither give nor sell it outside the Church of St Æthelthryth TRE and at the death of the king [Edward] himself.